THE DAWN OF THE DRONE

From the Back-Room Boys of World War One

STEVE MILLS

CASEMATE

Oxford & Philadelphia

Published in Great Britain and the United States of America in 2019 by
CASEMATE PUBLISHERS
The Old Music Hall, 106–108 Cowley Road, Oxford OX4 1JE, UK
and
1950 Lawrence Road, Havertown, PA 19083, USA

Hardcover Edition: ISBN 978-1-61200-789-2
Digital Edition: ISBN 978-1-61200-790-8 (ePub)

A CIP record for this book is available from the British Library

Printed and bound in the United Kingdom by TJ International

Typeset in India for Casemate Publishing Services. www.casematepublishingservices.com

For a complete list of Casemate titles, please contact:

CASEMATE PUBLISHERS (UK)
Telephone (01865) 241249
Email: casemate-uk@casematepublishers.co.uk
www.casematepublishers.co.uk

CASEMATE PUBLISHERS (US)
Telephone (610) 853-9131
Fax (610) 853-9146
Email: casemate@casematepublishers.com
www.casematepublishers.com

Front cover: The successor of the RFC's first drone, a 1930s Queen Bee aerial target guided by a Royal Air Force ground controller 'pilot'. (RAF)
Back cover: Royal Aircraft Factory drawing of the 1917 Aerial Target. (FAST archive)

Contents

Acknowledgements

One person, by her support and patience has bought this book to you. Her name is Gillian, my wife. Without her I would not have overcome the doubts that accompany such a daunting undertaking. So thank you Gill.

It was at Brooklands Museum working with the small Vickers' Guided Weapons team of volunteers that I first heard of the WWI Aerial Target (AT) project and I thank that team, the museum and the museum's library volunteers for their assistance in assembling the strands of this amazing story.

When the Imperial War Museum confirmed that they had the control equipment used on this 'first drone' and made it available for a quick viewing at their storage facility in Duxford, the need to document this 'little known' history became a necessity; a responsibility to unravel the story. Thanks to the IWM, we have been able to include their images of this equipment in this volume.

I would like to thank Dr Graham Rood and FAST (Farnborough Air Sciences Trust) for their assistance and for adding even more weight to the project by providing the earliest drawing of the AT.

Robert and Terry Morley deserve their place in this story having saved and renovated the only remaining Distance Control Boat (DCB) and I am grateful for their work in preserving such an important boat and researching its history.

I am grateful for the assistance provided by the New Mexico Museum of Space History and their International Space Hall of Fame, the College Archivist and Corporate Records Manager at Imperial College London and for the enthusiastic support of Nadine Gilbert of Old Barn Farm Estates. My thanks also go to the University College London Legacies of British Slave-ownership project and the Secretary of The Magic Circle. Many others have assisted including those at Flight Global and Royal Aero Club Trust.

My thanks to family and friends are of a somewhat different variety – more in the form of gratitude for their forbearance and for the delicate and gentle enquiries they have made from time to time concerning progress.

Casemate Publishers have provided me with much-needed guidance and support for which I am most grateful.

Every effort has been made to obtain the necessary permissions with reference to copyright material, both illustrative and quoted. We apologise for any ommisions in this respect and will be pleased to make the appropriate acknowledgements in any future editions.

Once again my thanks to one and all, and most especially Gillian.

Steve Mills,
Guildford, 2019

CHAPTER 1

Introduction

The World's First Drone

Britain's armed forces operated a large fleet of purpose-built, remotely piloted aircraft for years before any other country developed one. These British unmanned aerial vehicles entered service in 1935 and were in use by the British forces at home and overseas up to the end of the 1940s. These full-sized biplanes were a variant of the world-famous Tiger Moths that were controlled by operators on the ground and were used mainly as targets to train anti-aircraft gunners. Called 'Queen Bees', they were the culmination of a long trail of development that was initiated by the Royal Flying Corps (RFC) during World War I.

This story of the drone is intimately associated with the development of military aviation in Britain as the war loomed and progressed. It is also part of the story of Britain's famous aviation sites at Farnborough and Brooklands.

There were many other developments in the era that heralded the Dawn of the Drone. It was still only daybreak for the use of motor cars, domestic electricity and telecommunications. The age of plastics had hardly begun and revolutionary social changes from controls on dangerous goods and the development of the entertainment industries to the emancipation of women were yet to gather momentum. Despite the immaturity of aircraft, or maybe because of this, the concept of remotely controlling an aircraft was an irresistible lure to the hard-pressed, ambitious British Army's RFC and it was considered to be a real objective, attainable within a useful timescale.

On Wednesday 21st March 1917, the RFC launched their first unmanned aircraft that responded to commands transmitted by radio from the ground. A fantastic, irrefutable and sizeable but fragmented body of evidence still exists from the dark days of World War I of these, the world's first military drones. They were full-sized, unmanned aircraft manoeuvred under radio control by an operator. They were officially misrepresented by the title 'Aerial Target' (AT) due to security considerations but they were developed with the intention of delivering an explosive charge onto their target, initially envisioned to be the marauding Zeppelins.

Amazingly parts of this aircraft have been carefully preserved in wooden crates and are stored away in the Imperial War Museum's (IWM) repository. They were presented to the museum in trust for the British Nation and the wider world when they were being displayed in a long-running exhibition at the IWM in the 1950s. The illustration section shows some of these and pictures of the engineers associated with their development. The exhibition's explanatory labels declare that these are 'the original control gear which made the first radio-guided flight under selective control on the 21st March 1917.' This same radio control technology was then applied to some of the Royal Navy's WWI Motor Torpedo Boats, more properly called Coastal Motor Boats (CMBs), and one of these that was converted still exists.

The provenance of this body of evidence resides principally with the UK National Archives, Farnborough Air Sciences Trust (FAST) and the IWM although the content of other museums, institutions, patents and publications support this history.

The story of how this development occurred and the intricacies of this astounding weapon are far from simple. Drone development started shortly after the world witnessed the blossoming of the aviation industry, which took place in France. Some will tell you that man started to fly aircraft in 1903 but many historians contend that the real 'start date' was 1908 when the pioneers began to fly regularly and in public. Even these flimsy early aircraft that the pilot sat 'on' rather than 'in' were not around in any significant numbers just seven years before the start of the World War I and the initial development of the first drone. The dawn of the drone and that of aircraft were almost contemporary events.

In 1919, two men flew across the Atlantic Ocean. It had taken a multitude of brave pilots of manned aircraft, with all the dangers to life and limb that flying involved, and less than 20 years, to progress from the short hops achieved by the Wilbur and Orville Wright in 1903 to a machine that could span one of the world's oceans. Comparing this with the development of unmanned aircraft indicates the huge difference in the complexity of the task when the man is 'remote' from the machine. Unmanned flight does not pose a mortal threat and trials are therefore more readily conducted, yet transatlantic flight by a drone was not achieved until August 1998. Indeed, man got automated vehicles into orbit, to the moon, into the ocean chasms and into the depths of space with probes to the planets more easily than accomplishing routine, reliable, long-duration, long-range unmanned flight in our turbulent atmosphere.

When we acknowledge the complexities of achieving manned flight at this time, we have to admire the RFC ambition to develop an unmanned aircraft. But who were these back-room boys of World War I and how did they create the first drone?

There are a chorus of characters that we will find associated in one way or another with inventions such as the first drone. Of course the physical artefacts of the AT are fascinating but so are the experiences of the 'back-room boys and girls' involved in such novel projects through the traumas of the war. The war was a catalyst and accelerator for technological, social and even legal changes which were influenced by others in the back rooms and we will encounter many of them. They were all service personnel and other professionals living and working in Britain and Northern France as it experienced its first 'Total War', the war of 1914 to 1918. Principal among these in the context of this AT development was Archibald Montgomery Low and the engineers at his secret 'Experimental Works' in Feltham, Middlesex; designers and innovators unknown to virtually all aeronautical commentators, radio enthusiasts and military historians.

On 24th January 1921, a White Paper was issued as the first report of the Royal Commission on Awards to Inventors, our back-room boys. Up to 31st July 1920 this Commission had considered 1,128 claims. After a lengthy preamble of over eight foolscap pages, only 84 awards are listed but amongst these a fair proportion are directly concerned with aviation.

The British Aerial Target programme would not have occurred without Archie's extraordinary early form of television that so impressed Harry Gordon Selfridge Sr. that he arranged for it to be included in one of his famous Selfridge Store Exhibitions just prior to the war and many years before demonstrations at the store of John Logie Baird's equipment. Named 'Televista', Low's invention was revolutionary enough for an American diplomat to research and write about it in some detail.

The AT artefacts in the storerooms of the IWM are not simple and they are not small dusty components. They are technically complex units; parts of the aircraft receiver and actuation system and items of the ground encoding and transmission system that were used during World War I. They are carefully preserved objects with a beguiling beauty; intriguing assemblies of brass and copper mounted on their wooden bases. We know an amazing amount about their purpose and use from the details in the secret patents written at the time but not published until they were declassified in the mid-1920s. They represent important developments in the history of both the 'aerospace' and 'wireless' disciplines and it is a great pity that they have not been on public display for over 60 years.

This development continued and eventually resulted in the naming of Remote Piloted Vehicles and Unmanned Aerial Vehicles (RPVs and UAVs) as 'drones'. The descendants of the consortium working on the 1917 AT project produced the fleet of Queen Bees. These were the Royal Aircraft Establishment, the de Havilland Aircraft Company and the British air and sea forces. The complexity of producing an RPV is such that it took 18 years of further development after 1917 to produce the Queen Bees and the first 'remote' guided offensive weapons, the German Henschel Hs293 and Fritz X, were not deployed until 1943.

Because of the success of the RFC's AT, the Royal Navy converted some of their 40-foot Coastal Motor Boats (CMBs) to be remotely controlled from the air by the RFC's system and carried out successful trials in 1918 before the war ended. These radio-controlled CMBs were redesignated as Distance Control Boats (DCBs) and the Royal Navy continued their work in this technology throughout the inter-war years.

The RFC's AT weapon was intended to be guided onto a target by the operator on the ground or in a 'mother aircraft'. It was a sizeable RPV designed to manoeuvre just like a manned aircraft and therefore, in today's terminology, it was a drone. However, as a security measure the weapon's true purpose was disguised by naming it an Aerial Target; in a similar manner to the naming of the 'Tank' (instead of calling that a 'Land Ship') and the Flakzielgerät (anti-aircraft target device) or Vergeltungswaffe (retribution weapon) more commonly known as the German V-1 flying bomb or the FZG76.

We have failed to commemorate the achievement of the RFC's AT. This should all be common knowledge in Britain but by the 1950s press articles about guided weapons implied that they were 'new' and developed elsewhere. Goaded by this, in 1952 Archie Low wrote in an article for *Flight* magazine: 'it rouses me to fury to hear and read so often that the first guided missiles were German, American, Russian, Czechoslovakian, Italian or French. I think perhaps I have mentioned it before … but I would like to repeat it. They were British.'

However, even the British Army seem to have forgotten and there has not been a detailed account of the development of the RFC drones, the background to their creation or even colour photographs of the World War I exhibits – until now.

Low's new Experimental Works were part of the Royal Flying Corps which was itself a very new but rapidly growing establishment within the British Army. The term 'back-room boys' wasn't coined until later decades but it is the most applicable characterisation of these World War I innovators like Archie. During World War I 'invention' was identified as a potential war winner and became more organised and managed. The Munitions Inventions Department (MID) applied an official hand of control over Archie Low's unit and involved him and others working in the back room in some remarkable investigations.

After years of development the AT control equipment produced by Low's Experimental Works was ready. The successful monoplanes and their engines used in these first trials were the products of those well-known designers Geoffrey de Havilland and Granville Eastwood Bradshaw. The control systems were installed into the de Havilland secret drones and the ground control equipment was housed in a customised lorry for the journey to the RFC base at Upavon near the world heritage site of Stonehenge on Salisbury Plain in Wiltshire in that wintery wet March.

Other unmanned aircraft were produced by a number of different design groups that were to use the same control system but these were not flown successfully. These were the product of other famous aircraft designers; Thomas Octave Murdoch Sopwith, Henry Phillip Folland and the like.

The importance placed upon this highly secret, venturous project is remarkable. In addition to the time devoted to AT development by these overworked prestigious aircraft designer teams, the project employed other highly competent officers and the Upavon trials were witnessed by an assembly of high-ranking officers from the

Allied forces. Why these very senior officers of various nationalities were present in such large numbers on the remote and windswept exposed flying field on Salisbury Plain in mid-March when such momentous events were occurring elsewhere is a question that needed to be addressed.

These drones were of an unheard of order of complexity, sophistication and vision; even for those heady days of innovation. They could lay very credible claims to a number of 'world's first'. The world's first drones of course, but also, as the drones were launched by a compressed air catapult mechanism this would qualify as another 'world's first'. What we would now call 'electronic countermeasures' were incorporated in the design and are perhaps another 'world's first'. And provision was made for recording the transmitted flight data, potentially another 'world's first'.

The AT trials at Upavon took place two and a half years into World War I. When the war started, for the second time in fifty years, Paris had been threatened by invading Prussian-German armies. To honour its alliances, Britain was fighting in a bloody ground war for the survival of France and fighting in the Middle East to protect its interests against the Ottoman Empire. In this spring of 1917 the outcome of the war hung in the balance and would do so until its climactic conclusion.

1917 was indeed a trying time for Britain, the RFC and the AT project. The aerial advantage was always with the latest new successful development. For this reason, at one point the RFC were purchasing French Nieuport aircraft as these were superior to their own available aircraft. At the time of the March trials, the Sopwith Camel, which was to become one of the most successful British fighter aircraft, was still being developed and was not introduced until the middle of 1917. Controlling all of the innovative endeavours and interdepartmental wrangling in the air services during the war proved problematic. Research and development works do not run without some significant problems and the odd scandal. Accounts of such events at Low's Works have survived in the archives and they add to our understanding of these times.

One question arises immediately. Were others developing similar drone aircraft at this time? The answer is 'No', or we should say it is highly unlikely that many others thought it possible. Some did work on the remote control of ships and airships, but there is scant evidence that many worked on the problems involved in getting an aircraft into the air and under remote control.

There were attempts to produce unmanned aircraft that would fly for a predefined distance after launch – classed as 'unguided cruise missiles'. Some of the earliest of these endeavours were undertaken at the Royal Aircraft Factory at Farnborough in 1914. In the US, Charles Franklin 'Boss' Kettering co-foundered the Dayton Engineering Laboratories Co. which became 'Delco' which enabled him to develop interests in his 'Kettering Bug'. The team of Elmer Ambrose Sperry, his son Lawrence Burst Sperry and Dr. Peter Cooper Hewitt were working on another aircraft. Both Kettering and Sperry were attempting to develop aircraft that would continue to fly in their launch direction. These were UAVs but not RPVs.

A host of queries arise. Why have they become known as drones? What came after this first drone was developed by the RFC? Should we class the AT a success? What was its legacy? Why has this story not been told in any detail until now and why has all the evidence of it been ignored? What did the British establishment learn from managing inventions and weapons development in the Great War? Is it possible that their experience of managing and encouraging innovation may just have been enough to influence the outcome of the subsequent war in the 1940s?

This AT national project was remarkable; occurring so soon in the development of both the heavier-than-air powered flight and of radio communications. This was the time when most of the population had grown up under the reign of Queen Victoria and could remember when they had first seen an electric light! The AT contained many innovations, breaking ground in so many new technologies. A number of different prototype aircraft were built and with the conclusion of the war, work on drones continued.

The nuts and bolts of the AT design are fascinating, revealing the meticulous detail and sheer scale of the work that was completed in those trying circumstances. It is also notable that those involved recognised the historical significance of their work and ensured that this record and the artefacts survived. We even know such mundane facts as the dimensions of the Experimental Works' laboratory and that the courtyard had York paving.

In the 1950s, although his health was failing, Professor A. M. Low assisted the IWM when they arranged their public exhibition of his surviving artefacts. He also collaborated with the author Ursula Harvey Robinson (nee Bloom) on her biography of him *He Lit The Lamp*. Ursula was a long-time friend of Archie and was given access to his papers and time to interview him. Her book is a key source to the details of his life. However, this book is far from comprehensive and most of what follows on A. M. Low had to be discovered through extensive research. Indeed, forty years after its publication, writing in the periodical 'The Automobile', Michael Worthington-Williams's review described *He Lit the Lamp* as 'quite the worst biography I have ever read and yet, among the most fascinating'. As to his criticism, these are his words, not mine, for without Bloom's biography I would never have started my research and would have missed the enjoyment of delving into Prof. A. M. Low's life and the times through which he lived. However, I echo Michael's concluding statement, 'I wish I had known him'. The story of drones is intricately interweaved with the life and work of A. M. Low.

CHAPTER 2

The War and Before

In most democracies, when not at war, peace reigns with an iron fist, demeaning all the reasonable voices cautioning against complacency. But when war arrives, military matters.

As Britain's memories of its Victorian wars dimmed and the series of social and welfare reforms begun in 1906 continued to tip the delicate balance of the class system, the edges of the European empires chaffed one against the other fuelling a growing network of alliances. British foreign policy was based upon the defence of its entire Empire and trade without which it could not prosper. The identification of vulnerabilities and the preparation of strategic resources were guided by advice from the Committee of Imperial Defence (CID). Here, Naval considerations had dominated the agenda for many years, driven by that need to protect commerce and to respond to the increasing capability of the German naval forces. The British Army and its new volunteer Territorial Force instigated in 1908 served for the defence of British soil and for liaison with the forces of the Empire. Levels of equipment, ordnance and supply provision were geared to the size of the force and only sufficient to sustain its training regime. In the alliance with France, Britain's main role ensured the maintenance of the supply routes on which both countries depended while denying the prospective enemies access to their material while France, unlike their performance in the war of 1870[1], expected to protect itself from invasion against which she had prepared over the preceding decades, finalising her latest mobilisation strategy known as Plan XVII in May 1914.

John (Jack) Edward Bernard Seely, a politician with military experience from the Boer War, chaired a CID Sub-Committee and in 1910 it had been tasked with addressing concerns expressed by Sir Frederick Bolton. Bolton was a former ship owner with considerable experience of business exposure to risks in times of war. He questioned the capability of the transport system to supply the British cities and industries from the west coast ports and simultaneously support the deployment of the army to the east coast should the North Sea ports be threatened.

In June 1911, just after the launching of the *Titanic* and just before the coronation of George V and Queen Mary at Westminster Abbey in London, Bolton's concerns acquired greater credence. Widespread strikes started in Britain causing transportation and supply problems and threatening civil unrest. Seely's committee secretly invited the individual railway companies to form a Railway Executive Committee to co-ordinate their networks under government direction should war be declared. This formed the model for the government's management of other crucial industries during the war, using an agreed formula that left the companies in the hands of their shareholders who were compensated fairly for losses incurred carrying out government business.

During their deliberations the CID uncovered the true complexity of a blockade on Germany. In 1911 Germany and the Baltic region supplied, mainly through Britain's east coast ports, 16 million tons of goods and Britain supplied them with 29 million tons, which in value terms for Britain was slightly over a quarter of all Britain's imports and over a fifth of its exports. Specifically, it accounted for over half of all the butter and margarine consumed in Britain and 70 per cent of all sugar; 30 per cent of the steel used came from Germany and, pertinent to the military, half of the electric motors were supplied by Germany. A blockade would place a great burden on alternative supplies from more distant sources routed exclusively into the country's west coast ports. Crucially, Germany had a virtual monopoly on some supplies such as optical quality glass.

The CID's tortuous process of assessment and reassessment repeated over many years led to the World War I strategy of waging war by imposing a total blockade of Germany despite the risks that could, in the extreme, have made this even more of a Pyrrhic victory for the Entente. In the end, in financial terms the only winner was America.

The development of military air power would become a defining feature of World War I, emerging rapidly and requiring a new industry to create and support it. However, political support was slow to acknowledge any need for funding. A statement in the House of Commons on 4th March 1909 by Mr. Richard Haldane gave the official position of the country's aerial aspirations:

> The Naval authorities are at present considering the pattern of the dirigible balloon they will order. The Army authorities are going in for dirigible balloons, and we are considering the best pattern. As to aeroplanes, we have begun negotiations with private inventors.... It will be a good while, however, before the aeroplane will be an efficient instrument in war.

Hence, British aerial capability until a few years before the war amounted to a limited number of these steerable airships and static observation balloons. These required supplies of expensive high purity hydrogen gas and the craft were unmanageable in windy conditions. Baden Fletcher Smyth Baden-Powell had recognised these limitations years before and had experimented with gliders and man lifting kites. On 23rd September 1895 he had patented a man lifting kite called the 'Levitor' and in 1901 radio pioneer Guglielmo Marconi had made the first successful transatlantic wireless (radio) tests, suspending the antenna from a height of 400 feet using a Levitor Kite.

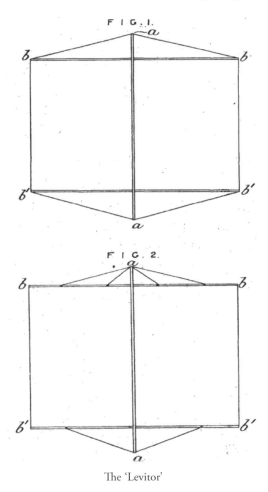

The 'Levitor'

The Edwardian progressive environment fostered the virtues of allegiance and duty. The Scouts, promoting a healthy moral lifestyle, caught the popular mood. Less welcomed by the establishment, the women's movements developed more assertive styles. Baden published *Ballooning as a Sport* in 1907 but he could not convince his brother Robert's Scout movement to adopt aviation themes.

John Theodore Cuthbert Moore-Brabazon was destined to become a lord of the realm with the title 1st Baron Brabazon of Tara but his friends and associates called him Brab and he made his name motoring with Charles Stewart Rolls and working at Darracq in Paris. He competed in road races on the continent where he also started flying in 1908 'on' a biplane made by the Voisin brothers Gabriel and Charles. Brab raced at the first meeting held at Hugh Fortescue Locke King's new Brooklands banked race track near Weybridge in the green and pleasant county of Surrey on Saturday, 6th July 1907. The following year he tested out his design of a glider at this racetrack.

The first aeroplane fatality did not occur until 17th September 1908 in a crash near Arlington National Cemetery in the US, at Fort Myer. This incident involved Orville Wright who was demonstrating the latest Wright aircraft to sell it to the Aeronautical Division of the US Signal Corps. when one of the aircraft's propellers split and tore through the rudder bracing wires. Orville survived but he had broken his ribs, pelvis and a leg and he was in hospital for seven weeks recovering from his injuries. Orville's passenger Lieutenant Thomas Etholen Selfridge was not wearing any head protection; his skull was crushed and he died shortly after the crash.

1909 was a momentous year. The newspaper aviation prizes offered by Alfred Charles William Harmsworth, Lord Northcliffe's *Daily Mail* were a great lure and encouragement to the private inventors the British government were relying upon. In July Marconi's company were at Cap Blanc Nez to radio to England that Louis Charles Joseph Blériot had left France to conquer the English Channel and win the £1,000 prize.

Brabazon won a second *Daily Mail* £1,000 prize in October flying a circular mile piloting an Albert Eustace and Hugh Oswald (the Short Brothers) biplane built at Shellness (Shellbeach) on the Isle of Sheppey in Kent. Looking for further records a week or so later he carried the first live cargo aloft by taking up a pig, just to show that they could fly! Brab and Rolls were awarded the first two British Royal Aero Club Aviator's Certificates on the 8th March 1910 and in June Rolls flew a Short-Wright machine across the channel and back again, becoming the first to complete this milestone.

Lord Northcliffe lived at Sutton Place near to Guildford in Surrey and aviators would often be invited to pay 'flying' visits to this Tudor manor house. It became popular when flying cross-country to make 'forced landings' near stately homes and country houses to be assured of lavish hospitality while 'the machine's problem' was being rectified.

After the death of Selfridge, only nine more aviation fatalities had been recorded in the whole world until Charles Rolls became the 11th at the aviation meeting in Bournemouth on 12th July 1910. The Brabazons witnessed the accident. Harry Harper, the flying enthusiast turned journalist who had been appointed as early as 1906 as 'the air reporter' by Lord Northcliffe, was at the meeting with his fellow journalist Sir Percival Phillips and they also witnessed the disaster. The competition required the pilots land as close as possible to the centre of a large marked target. Harry recalled that Rolls was above them at about 150 feet when the support on one side of the horizontal plane of the Wright biplane failed and the structure became entangled in one of the air screws. The aircraft crashed not far from where Sir Percival and he were standing and although there was a doctor nearby who attended to Rolls once he had been bought out from the wreckage, nothing could be done to save him and he died within a few minutes.

Brabazon's flying ended abruptly. Although Brab and his wife continued ballooning, he took up golf and machine flying was off the menu … until World War I.

The aeroplane had both actually and figuratively arrived in Britain by 1910. Aerial images, articles and even events increased dramatically in both frequency and popularity. While steam ships, railways, canal barges and horse-drawn vehicles were still the main forms of transport for passengers and goods, flying and motoring records and 'firsts' were always headline news and merchandising followed the public's fascination. 'Motor Ride' and 'The Aeroplane Race' (each priced at 9d.) appeared among the football, railway and more traditional board games in the department stores. Aircraft and cars were the marvels of the Edwardian age, both enabled by the creation of ever more viable and efficient internal combustion engines. Playing those aeroplane board games was definitely 'worth the candle' to light the room in the evening.

Some however clung to the age of steam. Frederic (Freddie) Coleman imported steam cars into England from America, supplied by the White Motor Company. He was a great champion and promoter of steam cars and he very generously placed two of these beautiful 1908 Model 'L' vehicles at the disposal of the Royal Aero Club to support the famous 1910 *Daily Mail* London to Manchester £10,000 Prize, the first cross-country air race. Harry Harper rode in Freddie's car chasing the first flight. The race was such a national event that the road had been cleared for the cars supporting the race and Harry recalled that they hared along, silent except for the rush of the wind, from Park Royal in London to Rugby. Freddie drove at every bend and turn at full throttle, braking and accelerating again, leaping on to the next hill or turn while his mechanic fine tuning the boiler controls of the magnificent vehicle. It had no gears and nothing could out pace it, all others giving way and following in the wisp of steam that trailed in their wake with Freddie's cry of 'pull over and let a real car get by' echoing in their ears. Many years later Harry said it was the most thrilling experience of his long career.

Competition prizes kept up the momentum of innovation. Claude Grahame-White's attempt at this London to Manchester prize started on 23rd April and met with no luck. He suffered very badly in the cold spring air on the first leg to Rugby. Claude's refuelled Farman III biplane and its revived pilot then took off for Manchester but its Gnome rotary engine failed and he was forced to land and give up on this occasion until the problem was fixed.

In the late afternoon of 25th April the Frenchman Isidore Auguste Marie Louis Paulhan took off from Hendon in London in his somewhat newer Farman III, cheered by huge crowds, to follow the specially whitewashed sleepers of the rail line towards Manchester. Later, the practice of following the railway lines and flying low

Louis Paulhan flying with a passenger (University of Southern California. Libraries. California Historical Society)

enough to read the names of the stations from the platform name boards would be called 'Bradshawing' after George Bradshaw's famous railway guides. Louis' entourage followed in a special train. Realising this, Claude, in his repaired aircraft, took off in pursuit. They both landed for the night. Claude, some 60 miles behind Louis, decided on the unprecedented strategy of taking off in the dark and flying into the dawn with all the risk that that entailed, but he did not overtake his rival who completed the challenge and won the £10,000 prize.[2]

On 28th January 1911, just seven months after the death of Charlie Rolls, the toll of flying fatalities had more than doubled to 28. *Flight* magazine in Britain published a detailed analysis of these fatalities, the first ever air accident analysis. It started, 'We learn by our friends' misfortunes is an old adage, and it is unfortunately very true in flight.' Of all the accident categories in the analysis the one titled 'Circus Feats' was singled out as the most avoidable. Six of the 28 fatalities fell into this group.

In the period immediately preceding World War I powered flight was challenging, difficult to achieve, very dangerous but, as the increasing casualty rate indicates, flying was becoming more popular and the machines more powerful. The majority of the activity was in France and of those killed in the 28 accidents most were French. Head injuries were always serious and often fatal but few of these early pilots wore safety helmets.

Arthur Walter Gamage, store owner and inventor, modelling his own design of aviator's safety headgear in 1912 (Grace's Guide to British Industrial History)

***

Jack Seely's CID Sub-Committee included the Royal Navy Commander Charles Rumney Samson, the engineer Mervyn Joseph Pius O'Gorman who was the Superintendent of the Balloon Factory and a staff officer David Henderson. A sub-group including Henderson and Captain Frederick Hugh Sykes proposed a structure for an air corps and views on the capability of aircraft in the military slowly matured. Sykes had gained a Ballooning Certificate in Africa in 1904 and in 1911 both he and Henderson gained their Royal Aero Club flying certificates Nos. 95 and 118 in June and August. At the age of 49 Henderson became instantly and simultaneously one of Britain's oldest pilots and probably the least experienced.

Exciting aerial reports from France at the time included a passenger using the 'emergency supply' to re-fuel their aircraft in flight. The French air exercises at 'Camp du Chalons' in August and their military aeroplane competition in Rheims that autumn, which Sykes attended, supported the case for a British Army aerial force. Then on 23rd October, the Italians demonstrated in Tripoli that, in a real conflict during the Italo-Turkish war, these frail early aircraft could prove invaluable. After some observation flights over enemy occupied oasis in previous days, on the eve of the battle of Sciara-Sciat, Capt's Piazza and Moizo of the Italian Army Aviation Corps, flying separately in a Bleriot and a Nieuport, reported about 6,000 enemy advancing in three columns. Without this information the massacre of the Italian force may have been even worse. On 5th November, the enemy were bombed by 1st Lieut. Gavotti who carried detonators in his pocket and flew over the enemy with four bombs in a leather bag.

On 13th April 1912 the Royal Flying Corps with its 36 aircraft was established by Royal Warrant as a Military Wing under Sykes, a Naval Wing under Samson, the Royal Aircraft Factory and the Central Flying School. The artillery's balloon and kite facilities established as the Air Battalion of the Royal Engineers on 28th February 1911 was merged with the RFC Military Wing on 13th May 1912. Their aircraft were not 'fighting machines' and most senior British officers still needed persuading that there was any need in *their* army for an air arm. 'Observation' was considered to be the only possible role for these fragile collections of wood, wire and fabric and reconnaissance was traditionally the preserve of the elite cavalry squadrons.

It was entirely logical that David Henderson should lead the newly formed RFC. During the Boer War he was appointed Director of Military Intelligence and his subsequent publications made him one of the army's foremost authorities on tactical intelligence. Reconnaissance being the sole role of the aircraft as envisioned in 1912, who better to head up this new embryonic force of scout aircraft.

The RFC utilised the complex of army establishments on Salisbury Plain in Wiltshire siting the Central Flying School at Upavon. They 'hosted' their military aircraft trials at Larkhill in August to choose which aircraft to buy. The RFC's third milestone in that first summer was their inclusion in Army Manoeuvres, the annual major military exercise.

The first of their aircraft fatalities occurred on 5th July. Captain Eustace Broke Loraine and his observer Staff Sergeant Richard Hubert Victor Wilson were flying a Nieuport Monoplane out of Larkhill on a routine morning practice sortie. They were executing a tight turn when the aircraft fell towards the ground and crashed. Wilson was killed outright and Loraine succumbed to his wounds not long after the crash.

In these first few months of the Corps a tradition was created when despite this tragedy the order was issued: 'Flying will continue this evening as usual.'

The Army Manoeuvres of September 1912 were staged in part to test the rapid concentration of the troops by rail to counter an invasion. Hence they were located in East Anglia. In these manoeuvres Sir Douglas Haig, an aircraft advocate, commanded the attacking Redland forces comprising 22,500 men, 9,000 horses, 7 aeroplanes and an airship. General Sir James Moncrieff Grierson in command of the defending Blueland forces had 25,000 men 8,000 horses, 7 aeroplanes, an airship and, crucially, his cavalry commander, Charles James Briggs. Briggs convinced Grierson to use his aircraft, which proved a success for the defending side, particularly on the first day, 16th September, when the 39-year-old Major Hugh Montague Trenchard as the observer in a Maurice Farman piloted by Lt. Arthur Longmore RN spotted Haig's forces. Playing upon Haig's faith in aircraft intelligence, Grierson had successfully 'hidden' his forth division of 12,000 men and horses from Haig by telling them 'to look as like toadstools as they could and to make noises like oysters.' Hence, Haig was misled into believing there was no threat due to the lack of intelligence from his aircraft, flying above the low mist that covered the forth division. This was a turning point in the attitude of the army and it prompted this statement from General Grierson on 27th November 1912: 'It is impossible to carry on warfare unless we have the mastery of the air.' Grierson, who was considered by many to be the more able leader, died on 17th August 1914. The history of World War I may have been different if Grierson had had a stronger heart.

King George V travelled down from Balmoral to witness the latter part of the manoeuvres and presided over the review conference held in the hall of Trinity College, Cambridge. In the course of a short speech, he said: 'The aerial work and the rapid concentration of the troops by railway, without dislocating the ordinary civilian traffic, and the use of mechanical transport have been the special features of these manoeuvres.'

On a more melancholy note, on their way to these manoeuvres Capt. Patrick Hamilton and Lt. Wyness Stuart had crashed near Hitchin on 8th September 1912. These brave solders are considered to be the first British airmen to be killed on active service.

A hymn was written for the funeral:

> Direct with thine all-seeing eye
> Watch each dread journey through the sky;
> Through every storm and danger zone,
> Bring each brave pilot safely home.

Their commanding officer Robert Moore Brooke-Popham (known as 'Brookham') addressed those that were criticising the erection of a memorial stone to the flyers in his speech to the mourners at the funeral service:

> Some people may think a memorial stone a waste of money and that it would have been more profitable to give it to the hospital or some local charity. I beg to differ. We should be a poor nation without recollections of noble deeds and heroic deaths to inspire us. The careless child and the weary wayfarer will pass along this road, look at this stone, read this inscription and realise that they, too, have a duty to perform. They will know that patriotism is not an empty word and that Englishmen are still ready to lay down their lives in the service of their country.

From the outset, the embryonic RFC was a facet of a horse-powered army that was just coming to terms with motorised transport. Aircraft were newer than new. The flying service proved to be fundamentally different to the army and the navy and as their activities intensified, the stress inherent in the military organisations become more and more evident. Through the course of the war more major adjustments were required, finally resulting in the separation of the air arm from the other two established arms. We might like to think that we would be more objective today with the concepts of the Revolution in Military Affairs (RMA) but the difficulty is as it ever was; once choices are made the lengthy and costly development and procurement process rarely results in a military capability entirely suited to the unfolding situation. In the event and in short, to some extent Britain prepared for the wrong war and in 1914, as a result, was unprepared when Germany successfully invaded and overran Belgium and northern France. Added to this, the British Liberal government, geared as it was to its successful peacetime programme of social reforms, proved ill-equipped to adjust to the changed circumstances.

The two-edged weapon of blockade, whilst causing supply difficulties to the Allies, was deployed, producing material shortage over which the modern alchemist sometimes triumphed and against which inventors fought for war-winning solutions. In aviation it wasn't just the 'back-room' aeroplane designers that produced an effective military aircraft. It required improvements in aerial firepower and communications, tactics, surveillance equipment and even, as with the Aerial Target, elements of automation.

As war loomed, the press thought that the British forces were inadequate and too 'modest'. In June 1914 the RFC 'Concentration Camp' at Netheravon had 70 machines, over 100 flying officers, 150 transport vehicles, and a staff of 650 air mechanics. Netheravon airfield is now claimed to be the longest continuously operated airfield in the world. It is not far from Upavon where the 1917 AT trials were conducted.

The RFC was then re-organised on 1st July 1914, just before war was declared, when the naval wing was transferred to Royal Navy control and renamed the Royal Naval Air Service (RNAS). The British Army found itself split down the middle, roughly half becoming the poorly resourced British Expeditionary Force (BEF) embarking for France while the Admiralty and elements of the government were to spend much of the war devising ways to use their substantial and under-utilised naval forces on new fronts in the Baltic and the East.

The size of General John Denton Pinkstone French's BEF in France was also described more elaborately as 'the contemptible little army', words attributed to the German Kaiser, Wilhelm II. However, the Kaiser could not have known that his words would be re-used with pride by the survivors in the regular army, 'The Old Contemptibles', before their re-organisation into the First and Second Armies at the end of 1914 and the subsequent rapid growth in their numbers.

According to Maurice Baring, when the RFC deployed to France, the administrative wing of the RFC under the command of Major Trenchard back in Farnborough consisted of 'one clerk and one typewriter, a confidential box with a pair of boots in it, and a lot of unpaid bills incurred by various officers in the Flying Corps, during the rush to the front.'

However, Lord Horatio Herbert Kitchener at the War Office had fantastic (but realistic) plans to build a force of 50 squadrons despite the lack of industrial capacity and the rather scant training facilities. There were questions asked; people used to say, 'where are you going to get the officers from?' Indeed, even in the first hectic days of the conflict personnel had to be spared from France (not yet stabilised into 'The Western Front') to return to Britain to organise the support facilities and train reinforcements and sadly – 'replacements'.

In a little over two years the RFC had been born, survived childhood and grown into what could be considered its adolescence and like a great many adolescents in 1914, they were sent to war. Many machines were lost before the end of the year including 16 that were wrecked in the storms at the end of December. However, by the start of 1915 the RFC had received 84 more aircraft to add to the 63 that had gone to France in the first deployment. The aerial vocabulary developed and 'scouts' became 'fighters' and their pilots became 'aces' deterring the enemy airship, bomber, balloon or spotter aircraft from doing their job or protecting their own more vulnerable assets.

Some early aerial observation reports proved to be wrong which eroded trust and reinforced prevailing prejudice. But gradually confidence in the reports was built up until they were accepted and finally, 'demanded'. Arthur Corbet-Smith, and others of his ilk, described the admirable skill and courage of the RFC that forged their identity and reputation as the war progressed. In the battle of the Marne, in September 1914, valuable information was obtained that no one would believe so the pilot took off saying, 'I'll go and have another look.' When he returned his aircraft was riddled with bullet holes. Lighting a cigarette, the pilot gave his second report: 'You're such a lot of unbelieving beggars that to make sure I landed in the field and had a look at the number on their tunics. Had rather a job starting again, but they're rotten shots.' Many such escapades occurred in the initial fluid phase of the war. On 22nd August 1914, a number of patrols including one by No. 3 Squadron's Vivian Hugh Nicholas Wadham and his observer Lionel Evelyn Oswald Charlton revealed, just in time, the risk to the BEF's flank by the approaching German Army. That evening, after a review of these reports, the BEF Commander John French amended his plans. After the initial battles in October the BEF GHQ was established in St. Omer. Soon this little British Army was all but spent in holding the initial onslaughts and required massive reinforcement that were achieved through voluntary recruitment.

The prevailing westerly wind would be a hazard to aircraft trying to get back over their own lines. George Frederick Pretyman soon discovered this when he and his observer took off at 11:10 a.m. on 26th August 1914 on an armed 'recce' – Number 57 – to Cambrai. They were lucky to glide back over the lines when their engine was hit by ground fire and having joined some retreating French cavalry were able to commandeer two bicycles and return to their base at St. Quentin about 11:30 p.m. On a sortie on 15th September, George took five photographs of the enemy artillery positions on the river Aisne on his camera. Their only significance lies in the fact that they were the first RFC wartime aerial images. Cases of friendly fire on the RFC aircraft were partially attributed to the St George's Cross being mistaken for the German Cross so the French model of a suitably coloured cockade was introduced and by mid-December this roundel was formally adopted although its application took months.

Meanwhile, urgent aid was required for the maimed, injured and sick. Brabazon took his own car to use as an ambulance and travelled 'back' to France with the Red Cross. Realising that the war was not going to be over by Christmas, the idea of joining the RFC occurred to him when he saw the distinctive 'maternity' tunic of an RFC officer passing through their location. He decided to motor over to the main RFC base at St. Omer to see his friend Colonel Frederick Sykes, Commander, RFC in the Field, and join up. In no time he was no longer a civilian and because of his previous experience, he was awarded his wings without completing the mandatory courses. On 5th March 1915, Brab joined others who were already working on aerial photography such as Frederick (Freddy) Charles Victor Laws, William David Corse and Charles Duncan Miles Campbell, becoming a back-room boy commanding the unit advancing the RFC's aerial photographic technology and with Campbell produced a purpose-built aerial camera. However, as a pilot travelling back and forth between France to England this was hardly a 'back-room' activity. Convincing the army hierarchy and the surveyors who made the maps that aerial photography was of value as a mapping tool and source of intelligence was greatly assisted by an impressive mosaics of prints produced by Charles Curtis Darley. Further re-organisation followed just a few months into the war when, to foster closer co-operation with other army units, a divisional structure was adopted. Sykes, opposed to this change, moved to the naval air services and Henderson took the opportunity to take over the field command in France and delegate the work in Britain to subordinates. Brab had a little incident involving an unauthorised two-day trip to liaise with a technical section of the French Army based near Versailles. They had a mutually productive exchange of ideas and techniques and he came away with one of their gadgets. Hugh Trenchard wasn't called Boom for no reason. He was tall and broad and by all accounts, 'resonant'. Brab said that he didn't know he needed permission to go but got the full dressing down from Boom who specialised in verbally trouncing the misguided. A few weeks later Boom went down south to host an inspection by the French. The device Brab had been given was now in service and was demonstrated to one of the visiting senior French officers who had no knowledge of its origin and begged for a copy to be supplied to his units. The requested 'gift' was solemnly presented and later, when Boom's urbane aid, Maurice Baring, told him that the device had originally come from the French, Boom was delighted. This story shot round the mess and the wider RFC causing great delight. Brab's shadow on that particular carpeting faded quickly.

One of their main problems was creating the RFC photographic capability from scratch, including the design and production of lenses. Britain had cause to lament the decline of its internationally acknowledged leadership in optics that had been demonstrated as far back at The Great Exhibition of 1851. In Jena in Germany, Carl Zeiss with the inspiration of Ernst Abbe had started improving his microscopes. Then Ernst got a young glass maker Otto Schott to relocate to Jena. Here, these three, Schott, Zeiss the instrument maker and Abbe the scientist were joined by Paul Rudolph. A ground-breaking company model was developed in which all the workers were involved as a co-operative that took a modest profit. This Zeiss company assured its pre-eminence when it designed and produced the first anastigmatic lens in the 1880s. As they would supply their glass at such competitive prices to one and all, British and most other countries optical glass-making capabilities dissipated. The war bought this situation into 'sharp focus' so to speak. All manner of high-class optical products were needed, from field glasses and cameras to range finders and gun sights. There were appeals such as the Countess Roberts Field Glass Fund. But these were short term solutions and production of new items was required but the glass wasn't available. Parra-Mantois et Cie in France using coal from Durham in England produced a small amount of this precious product. But then they were instructed to use French coal and such was the sensitivity of the chemistry, it didn't work. Chance Brothers Glassworks in Smethwick near Birmingham were to supply much of the demand but Brab worked with Wood Brothers Glass Co. of Wombwell Yorkshire who, after many trials, reproduced the formulae. The shortage of quality lenses was a graphic example of the nature and importance of strategic supply. This had been a crisis of materials science and once solved, supply could begin but Brab said that he lived every moment of this drama. He certainly wasn't the only customer so there was a scramble to get the first batches. In 1914 after the declaration of war, Woods had been making electric light bulbs but in 1915 they extended their works and were full engaged in making this 'new' glass for scientific and laboratory uses.

The legacy of the RFC's aerial reconnaissance capability created by Brab's unit includes the work of Danesfield House – RAF Medmenham that ranks alongside the Bletchley Park code breakers and its ULTRA product for intelligence gathering throughout WW2.

Later in life, after World War I, Brab obtained a 'FLY 1' number plate for his car. He had by then got to know Archie Low though their motor sport interests. As RFC technical officers, Brab and Archie worked in separate 'secret' worlds.

Aerial photography was being developed before Brab joined this development group. Similarly, Archie joined the RFC when it was already endeavouring to design an Aerial Target. The first steps towards an AT had been taken at the Royal Aircraft Factory at Farnborough in 1914. Contributors to the work on these designs may have been Henry Folland and even Geoffrey de Havilland who was at the factory until May 1914. Surviving drawings are dated October 1914 but these would have been under consideration for some time and thus may well have involved de Havilland. These include A4794 shown below. This design is very similar but of a smaller scale to that of the first drone that was flown in 1917 … and that AT was designed by Geoffrey.

Thus, as the war stagnated along the new muddy boundary in German-occupied Belgium and France, the RFC and many aspects of its capabilities such as aerial photography and even the idea of the drone grew rapidly from adolescence into serious maturity.

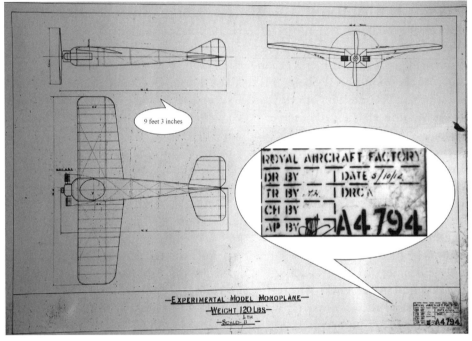

Royal Aircraft Factory drawing of a 10-foot wingspan unmanned monoplane fitted with a 6 h.p. A.B.C. engine, dated October 1914 (FAST Archive 2018)

CHAPTER 3

The Making of Archie

Of all the many characters in this story, Archibald Montgomery Low or Prof. A. M. Low as he later signed himself, is the principal. In later life Archie was considered a true treasure. He was without doubt a prolific and productive inventor and one who some thought only lacked the application and persistence to be one of the greats. To a large extent he was, in both temperament and style, the archetypal British inventor of popular imagination. He became sufficiently famous to be mentioned in public without further explanation or introduction, as on 7th June 1944 when the president of the Board of Trade referred to '… no less an authority than Professor A. M. Low …' in a debate in the House of Commons.

Archie's branch of the Low family were definitely middle class although they were struggling most of the time to maintain this position. His father's side of the family were from Dundee in Scotland and their moderately comfortable position in society derived from shipping interests that had passed down the paternal line. Archie's great, great, grandfather inherited the family business from his father who according to family tradition was one of the founding partners of the 'Perth and London Shipping Company'. The shipping inheritance passed down to Archie's grandfather Andrew who was not one to be content to just live off his inherited assets. He added insurance to his business interests, got married in 1846, had six daughters and three sons and moved to London. By the 1860s, Andrew, with his brokerage business, his wife Elizabeth, the children and their maid were residing in Camberwell, in the diocese of St. Giles, south of the River Thames in Surrey at 90 Grove Lane.

Archie's father was the middle son of the three boys, born on 18th February 1854 and given his great grandfather's and his mother's family names. He was John Smith Low. The three brothers all inherited interests in shipping and the two youngest, Archie's father John and Edward Hunter, Uncle Ted, both subsequently developed engineering careers.

Archie's maternal great-grandfather, Joseph Arthur Allen, was in the British Colonial Office and in 1842 was appointed Receiver General of Trinidad in the West Indies. Joseph married Martha Mogg in 1849 and their daughter,

Martha Mogg Allen, married a merchant, Alexander Stewart. There was still money to be made in Trinidad, unlike many of the Caribbean islands whose economies were in decline, and the family's income was most probably derived from trade rather than from direct plantation ownership. Alexander and Martha had six children and all of them, including Archie's mother Gertrude Anne Duncan Stewart, were, by 1871, lodged with their Aunt Eliza Allen at 16 Arlington Villas in the Clifton area of Bristol. It was common practice, almost a tradition, to lodge children with a relative 'back home' to secure their education and health. This was usually a mutually beneficial arrangement that gave the host an income. In Eliza's case this arrangement and source of income lasted for decades.

Eliza moved from Bristol to London with her 'foster brood', living at 29 St Lawrence Road in North Kensington (which has since been renamed St. Lawrence Terrace). Gertrude Stewart and John Smith Low both had a Scottish heritage and they were now both in 'the smoke', aka London, moving ever closer to their first meeting.

In 1881, Eliza Allen had a household comprising the Stewart children and their 22-year-old servant Christina West. From oldest to youngest the children were Amy 26, John's future wife Gertrude 24, Alexander 22 who was studying theology, Florence 18 and Alice 16. Their brother James aged 19 had flown the nest by now. Subsequently, Eliza moved her household again, this time to 14 Colet Gardens in Hammersmith in West London.

By the early 1880s John Smith Low had moved from his childhood family home into the Battersea area of London. His and Gertrude's lives were converging and by now they were living less than four miles apart, albeit on different shores of the River Thames. John had moved into accommodation provided at his new place of employment as the laundry secretary and manager of 'The Provincial Steam Laundry Company' located at 152–154 Battersea Park Road.[1] This industrial laundry would have been a noisy, busy and crowded place to work. Living in this area of London was not ideal but the laundry was a modern and large facility, employing 20 men and 150 women as operatives and handling 80–90,000 pieces per week.[2]

John and Gertrude may well have met over some business with her Aunt Eliza's laundry account. Whatever the circumstances were of their first meeting it led to a happy and adventurous life together. They were married and Gertrude had to make the adjustment from her leafy quiet abode living with her family in Hammersmith to the accommodation on the laundry premises. This new branch of the Low family with their one live-in servant was soon joined by their first son Kenneth who was born on 7th August 1884 in South Kensington.

In 1888 the weather was weird. There had been a lot of snow on the North Downs south of London in July while October was the warmest on record (a record not beaten until 2005). On Wednesday 17th of that hot October, Archibald Montgomery was born in Purley in Surrey, not far from his grandparents' home. On the same day Thomas Edison filed a patent for the optical phonograph, a device for viewing motion pictures which is of no importance to this history other than the coincidence related to Archie's Televista.

Archie was not a strapping, overly healthy or particularly strong specimen. He was devoted to his mother and would remain emotionally close to her throughout his life and even after her passing. When Archie was three, John and Gertrude were still living at the laundry with their young live-in servant Caroline E. Walkey. They probably felt the need to move from Battersea to a more suitable area to bring up their two precious boys. In Battersea, Gertrude was sensitive to the continuing evident poverty. When he was older, Archie could remember that she told him about the street beggars, the men without shoes and she described the squalor that still persisted. London's provision of hay and fuel outstripped its capacity to export the residue. Dirt, soot and smoke caused the famous pea-soup fogs that shrouded the city. Gertrude was probably old enough before leaving Trinidad to have witnessed the social problems on the islands. In England she recognised the powerful effect on attitudes of Charles Dickens' published works and also of his charitable work; his direct involvement at Urania Cottage the 'home for fallen women' in Lime Grove near Shepherds Bush, an area she knew well. Many others were to have an impact on the growing social conscience, but they were less well known. Emmeline Pethick-Lawrence and Mary Neal with their Espérance Club inspired the overworked girls in 'the rag trade'; Mary introduced them to English folk song and dance during its Edwardian revival; Constance Georgina Bulwer-Lytton, known as Constance Lytton, provided financial support to the club and with her husband became a champion of the women's suffrage movement.

In the early part of the 19th century, Erith, along the south coast of the Thames estuary towards the North Sea, had been a rural community of somewhat over 2,000 souls and was for a time a haven of peace for busy Londoners. It boasted a pier that provided a suitable mooring for the river ferries and had hotel accommodation. Then it experienced a staggering growth rate to which the Low family eventually contributed. Heavy industry in the area bloomed, causing stress to such an extent that in 1848 Chartist movement disturbances required the authorities to enrol special constables. Erith was by now a town and in 1849 it acquired a railway link to London. Within a few decades, with the nearby Woolwich Arsenal and the availability of electrical power, large companies such as Easton and Amos established their businesses there. They opened their new Erith works in 1865, manufacturing large pumps and boilers. Erith became a busy place. The town was significant enough in 1884 to host the touring Australian XI in a match against the local cricket team. This fixture was repeated in 1900. As a sign of the changing times, in 1893 the last Thames Sailing Barge race left from Erith.

In 1877, Thomas Octavius Callender set up a branch of his father's company in Erith and started shipping refined bitumen from Trinidad. This was most suitable for cable insulation. With the growth in the telegraph and then the telephone, demand for cables knew no bounds. Trinidad's bitumen was from the Pitch Lake, the largest natural deposit of asphalt in the world. In 1887, an American businessman Amzi Lorenzo Barber aka 'The Asphalt King' paved the roads of New York City, Washington D.C., and other eastern US cities with deposits shipped from this lake. In Britain, road building moved from the macadam construction to sealing the surface with tar making it pitch macadam until in 1902 Edgar Purnell Hooley patented tarmac, which was then used extensively. In 1880, Callenders Bitumen & Waterproof Co was established in the Belvedere area and in 1896 this became Callenders Cable & Construction Company (and later BICC).

After some years of great effort, the development of the oil fields in Trinidad were eventually producing commercial quantities. From 1911 onwards these fields gave companies such as United British Oilfields Trinidad Limited, a subsidiary of Shell and Duckhams, their crude oil supply. They also gave the Royal Navy a secure source of fuel at a critical time just prior to the World War I by which time much of the fleet burned oil instead of coal. Alexander Duckham was a great supporter of aviation and a personal friend of Louis Blériot and he erected a memorial at Dover 'to the Aero Club of the United Kingdom' to commemorate the channel flight. Duckhams' lubricants eventually passed into the hands of British Petroleum.

It would be nice to think that it was Gertrude Stewart's family connection with Trinidad that caused the move of the Low family to Erith but it is much more likely that John, as the manager of an industrial steam laundry, will have developed expertise and contacts related to the machinery of his business. He may have found a position with a company in the area. Around 1894, when Easton and Anderson of Erith, a major manufacturer of boilers, was 'rearranged' and became Easton, Anderson and Goolden, positions will have become available that would have attracted John. It would have been one such company that John joined in the early 1890s when the family moved to Erith.

The factories were fascinating places for a young enquiring child and Archie remembered 'trotting beside his father round the large workshop' and that Maxim's was close by. Much later Archie met Hiram Stevens Maxim, remembering him as a kind old man who loved roulette. Many thrilled at 'Sir Hiram Maxim's Captive Flying Machines' at the Earl's Court exhibition in 1904 and one of these still operates in Blackpool. It is a turntable from which 'aircraft' are hung for the public to ride in. As examples of 'on the shoulders of giants', turntable devices were conceived a long time before Maxim 'as a method for investigating the forces on objects moving through fluids. In the 1840s Benjamin Robins had used his paddle windlass to investigate the drag force on various shaped bodies in the 1840s during his early fluid dynamic research into the ballistics of cannon ball flight, from which he described and explained the force that 110 years later became known as the 'Magnus Effect', named after Gustav Heinrich Magnus. This effect can be observed in the curved flight path of a spinning ball. Orville Wright also acknowledged the influence on the brothers' work of George Cayley, another early researcher, who also utilised a windlass to investigate the forces on wings.

Archie never had a robust constitution and so it was a blessing when they moved from the city to the countryside of Kent, even though Erith itself was becoming ever more industrial. In London he was always sick, most especially in the stuffy jolting confines of the horse bus. The peace in Erith for the Low boys was rarely disturbed, except when the family home caught fire and the local fire brigade had to be summoned. He remembered their parlourmaid Emily who would carry the lamp when it was time to go to bed. He remembered this because he feared the dark, a phobia that would last his lifetime and was so extreme that he would send companions to the house to turn on a light before leaving the car at night if he could.

After a pleasant and comfortable childhood in what was still a relatively rural area, the young Low brothers experienced their first major change of circumstances. At this time, the source of all that was going on in the world that wasn't spoken in your presence was written on paper. There was no other conduit for information. Gossip, the paper boy and public announcements were the only social media of their day and, therefore, the church and the public house were important venues to obtain 'the news'. Letters were delivered twice in the morning and five times in the afternoon.

Literacy was key. Therefore, schooling loomed large in Kenneth and Archie's lives. The 1870 Education Act had great significance for the education of the poorer working-class children so schooling was now an accepted and valued stage for all. However, the education of Kenneth and Archie was to be a higher standard than most. At seven years old they took entrance exams for the preparatory school Colet Court and the exams to join St. Paul's were taken at eleven years old.

Archie had quite a few uncles and aunts, which at this time was not unusual. Now they were going away to school it proved convenient to have relatives in the right area. Great Aunt Eliza Allen's house was to be the boys' home as they attended Colet Court and St. Paul's School. However, as well as going away to school, the boys had an even more significant separation as their parents embarked on business to Sydney, Australia. Gertrude's own childhood colonial background may well have influenced her decision to support her husband and leave the children. In New South Wales, as with most of the world, the long depressions of the 1870s, 80s and 90s were still in evidence. Despite this, in October 1897, Archie's father joined two other partners as a director of the Paddy Lackey Deep-level Company, mining for gold. The company headquarters were in the imposing and prestigious Equitable Buildings on George Street and their mine was 120 miles inland at a place called Dark Corner. A report on this gold-mining venture in *The Sydney Morning Herald* on Saturday 27th August 1898 stated:

> The only draw back at present is the want of steam power, but that difficulty will soon beat an end, as a powerful Lancashire boiler is now on route and will be placed in position as soon as

it arrives. Giant rock drills are at work, and three shifts of men are kept continuously going. As to the probability of striking the reef, I think there is very little doubt. Deep level sinking in New South Wales is the exception and not the rule, and if this company is successful in locating the reef at 950 ft it will be one of the deepest gold-mining shafts in the colony.

The Lancashire boiler referred to in this report was a particular type of boiler. Its power derives from using two flues and, therefore, producing a greater furnace grate area relative to the volume of water than other boiler designs. John almost certainly worked for one of the firms in Erith that made these and his expertise in this area would have been the principal reason for his inclusion on the board of this company.

While his parents were doing well on the other side of the world, Archie suffered. Being four years younger than Kenneth he felt the absence of his mother more keenly. Adding to this burden was his dislike of school, both Colet Court and then St. Paul's. Archie's weak constitution and lack of sportsmanship did not help him blend in. He complained about the uniform's itchy vests and even about the 'rather dull' boy who had the next desk to his for a couple of years. This was Bernard Law Montgomery. In later life and despite his blunt school assessment of this classmate, Archie quoted a number of complimentary stories about General Montgomery's abilities as a commander. He liked the story of a soldier in World War II who, not knowing of his school connection with the general, told Archie before the second battle of El Alamein that 'Monty will be unlucky if he losses, but he will be damned well unbearable if he wins!'

In common with most of his generation, Archie was becoming interested in the early motor cars that were appearing in increasing numbers on the streets of London. At this relatively young age he was taken on the epic journey to Sydney for a visit. Here he records that he learned to swim and he talked about the steam trams on the street and was amazed at the number of homes with telephones (which probably reflects more on the standing of his father's business associates and their households than the general level of private telephone ownership).[3]

Back in London, around the turn of the century, a girl caught Archie's eye. Her father was the local bookie and for a time as he entered his teenage years he was besotted with her. The family, whose disapproval of this rather innocuous liaison was evident, would always refer to her rather disparagingly as the 'Bookmaker's Daughter'. Archie described her as very untidy with long grubby legs and dressed in her pink frock.

John and Gertrude finally returned from Australia to Scotland and by 1901 John was the manager of an engineering works in Renfrewshire. Just as they were returning from Sydney there was an exceptional cause for concern. In 1900, Glasgow had a small outbreak of bubonic plague and Australia suffered its first in what was to become a series of outbreaks. These were in Sydney, and the source of each outbreak generally occurred in the areas around the docks. Smallpox was also a public health issue but was being successfully addressed.

On finishing school in 1901 at 16, Kenneth started his engineering apprenticeship in Scotland where his mother's side of the family had connections and his parents now lived. He worked at Edward Chester & Co in South Renfrew. This may well have been the works that his father managed. A report at this time described these works as remarkable:

> Everything of the newest, the buildings of iron framework with corrugated iron covering, everywhere the most recent and attractive engines and tools, and buildings conveniently arranged with sidings from the Glasgow and South-Western main line.

When their travelling was over, the reunited Low family settled into a new home back in London, near to Eliza's, at 3 Luxemburg Gardens, Brook Green. This was an expensive and desirable area and their home was an elegant three-storey terraced property. This move indicates that John and Gertrude's Australian and Scottish adventures must have been justified in financial terms. However the costs of bringing up children and educating them was still a concern.

Gertrude indulged Archie's passion for science, encouraging him in his quest for understanding and listening to him intently when he became obsessive about his latest experiment or invention. Her attention to her youngest son's 'hobbies' was a great spur to Archie's development from an early age. She was also sufficiently equipped with her own enquiring nature and knowledge to grasp the basic details of the Archie's current project so her support to him was an active participation and not just an accession to his needs.

At an early stage in their new residency, his mother suggested that Archie needed a shed for his 'stinks', her generic term for the noisome and noxious concoctions cooked up by his inquisitive nature. It was said that as he grew older the neighbourhood became scared of him. His bible at that time was Cassell's *Book of Sports and Pastimes*. In such boys' books of the time he would have found intriguing items such as a spark gap transmitter. Of course, like the telephone, it isn't much fun if you don't have a receiver.

Early 20th-century society placed, as a necessity, a value on thrift. As a result of this, Archie would have found local suppliers of the raw materials and preparations intended for household repairs and even for small-scale manufacturing. Home cooking included some very different recipes. Cleaning products and medicines were regularly made up to the customers special 'family recipe' that had no doubt been used for generations. Or they were made at home from readily available, often nasty, toxins or highly reactive compounds from either end of the litmus paper. Controls on drugs and poisons had been introduced but these were very loosely enforced.

So, for Archie and many like him, the wherewithal to experiment was not hampered by laws on drugs, poisons, chemicals or material supply, handling or storage. Money, however, was an ever-present constraint. He was not idle in his

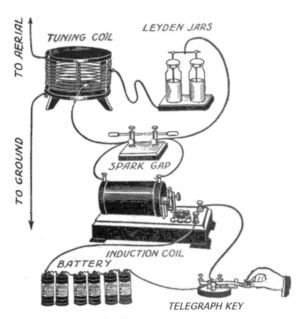

TO AERIAL

TUNING COIL

LEYDEN JARS

TO GROUND

SPARK GAP

INDUCTION COIL

BATTERY

TELEGRAPH KEY

Spark gap transmitter

school holidays when, he said, he learnt to drive steam cranes and stoke boilers in the hope of a little reward. Long before he was 'learned', Archie made notes, jotted down his thoughts and recorded his most fleeting ideas. And he kept them all; profuse volumes of mail and notes. Whilst busying himself with his inventions and experiments and preparing for his entrance into the realms of high education, Archie was also developing his interest in girls. The Low family still had a servant, Mary, but she did not live with the family. Despite Archie's shed acquiring labels such as 'Keep Out', 'Don't Sit Here' and of course 'Danger', it may not have been off limits to Mary. However, we are told, any 'goings on' were all really fairly innocent.

In 1903, aged 15, Archie passed his examinations for further education but he could not start until he was 16 when he finished at St. Paul's. He was off to the 'Old Coll', The City and Guilds College which in 1907 became, while he was still studying there, the Imperial College of Science and Technology.

Since the 1830s, educational choice had blossomed. Oxford and Cambridge universities were the only real options prior to this but by the time the Low boys reached higher education there were many more institutions available. The student body at Imperial College numbered just over 400 when Archie Low was there and although the fees must have been a significant consideration to his parents, they did not constitute more than about half of the income of the College. Endowments, treasury grants and public fund raising provided the rest and helped to hold the fees down.

Archie was now a commuter. The Great Northern, Piccadilly & Brompton Railway (GNP&BR) opened on 15th December 1906 with a terminus at his local station in Hammersmith. In 1907 South Kensington station opened on this line but for his journey to college this did not appeal to Archie. South Kensington was not very convenient for Exhibition Road and the college but his avoidance of this form of transport may have been more to do with his achluophobia than the walk from the station. One alternative public transport, the steam bus, had become more common but Archie said they were unreliable. Freddie Coleman, as well as driving his beautiful Whites Model 'L' steam motor cars, also introduced a fleet of 'White Steamers' in London which Archie thought had the potential to be explosively dangerous, operating on super-heated steam. Archie loved steam engines and had made a Hero engine in his earlier days. Later he produced a steam turbine in his shed so he understood the danger and avoided Coleman's buses. However, the cars were successful and continued in production until 1911 when the company changed to the internal combustion engine. Despite his aversion to dark, confined, airless spaces, Archie commuted to 'the Coll' on the horse bus.

As Archie started his college life the motor car had become a more common sight. Attempts to get both lift and thrust from bird-like motion of the wings had proved too complicated for early flying machines and the ornithopters had given way to the air-screw driven concept but the motors of these early machines still had barely enough power to propel them to flying speed. However, by 1906 in France, Louis Blériot with Gabriel and Charles Voisin were demonstrating powered flight and had already established the world's first commercial aircraft factory which was located in Paris in the commune of Billancourt. Until just before the war, the world's total output of heavier-than-air flying machines was small and they were generally one-off, custom-built designs or designs licenced for manufacture at a facility near the customer.

At college Archie worked hard, probably at times by candle light or oil lamps if the desk wasn't under one of the wall-mounted gas lights. Occasionally he overworked and, being a sensitive lad, was unwell. But he was obviously inspired by a number of the academic staff at Imperial and in particular he wrote about his professors. He studied civil engineering with Andrew George Ashcroft and Archie also remembered Professor Henriques, the Jewish mathematician. Armstrong's acid was named after Low's chemistry Professor Henry Edward Armstrong.

Archie railed against the pursuit of qualifications, obtained in his view by boys who achieved great feats of memory but who had gained no depth of understanding of the subject under study. This prejudice may have arisen from a personal frustration and perceived failure when sitting formal examinations but, as we will see, it probably matured into his cavalier attitude to the use of academic 'handles' used by him in later life.

Professor Ashcroft's explanation of a local transport hub involving the intertwining of roads, railway lines and a canal and the intricate curves required to achieve this

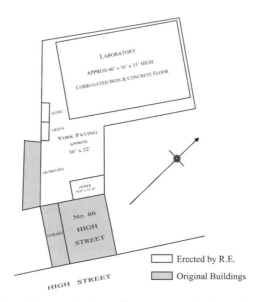

The Feltham Works layout from a National Archives sketch

inspired Low to invent his 'Low Flexible and Adjustable Curve' as a drawing aid for draughtsmen. With the help of his father he made this bendable ruler and it went to the market as part of the range of drawing instrument supplied by A. G. Thornton's of Manchester. This was probably one of his first successes in what was to become a lifetime of inventing. Other professors Low mentions with some affection include William Cawthorne Unwin, John Perry and William Edward Ayrton.

In the period when Archie was being educated, Edwardian social change was in full swing. Despite the prevailing institutional prejudice, disadvantaged men and women could and did reach academic heights. Women fought for recognition as hard as they did for the vote and those with academic aspirations and ability had many prejudicial hurdles to negotiate to gain their voice and influence in the male-dominated establishment.

Professor William Ayrton's second wife, Hertha Ayrton (they married in 1885, after the unfortunate death of his first wife), is one such example of this. Ayrton supported her in her election as the first woman member of the Institution of Electrical Engineers. She had an extraordinary career for a women of the mid-1800s. She took out a patent in 1884 for a drawing aid, the first of many patents and decided on a life of study and invention. She enrolled at Finsbury Technical College, where she met Professor Ayrton. After they married she had a successful career in electrical research both independently and in co-operative projects with her husband and others. In 1902, Hertha's comprehensive book *The Electric Arc* was published, bringing together many papers she had presented separately since the first in 1885.

The publication of this book coincided with the start of her fascination with sand ripples on the beach at Margate. The learned paper 'The Origin and Growth of Ripple-mark' appeared in 1904 and she became the first woman allowed to read a paper at the Royal Society when she presented it that year. Although as a woman she was not eligible to apply for membership, the Royal Society awarded her a Hughes Medal in 1906. Her new-found standing and a bequest from Barbara Leigh Smith Bodichon, her benefactor, allowed Hertha to offer financial support to the Women's Social and Political Union and on Black Friday, 18th November 1910, she was in the lead delegation of the WSPU at the Houses of Parliament. She continued to campaign and helped to form the Jewish League for Woman Suffrage in November 1912. She had not finished inventing and submitting a number of patents, continuing to do so throughout the war.

In 100 years, the total population of England and Wales had leapt from 8.34 million in 1800 to 32.53 million at the turn of the 20th century, with over three quarters of them living in the towns and cities. Much of the celebrated Victorian ingenuity and inventive flair was a response to the challenges of living in the newly booming cities. By 1850, London had become the biggest city the world had ever seen, and such enormous concentrations of people posed brand new problems of feeding, watering, transporting and housing the masses. There were plenty of opportunities to create new products or develop a new enterprise with the means and the need crying out for a solution, it only needed the spark to complete a triangle of invention.

Children in London learnt to dodge Hansom Cabs manoeuvring in the traffic jams or admired an elegant Clarence, especially if it had the owner's emblem on the door. Growlers were popular family vehicles, but the slower heaver commercial carts and buses dominated. London was not just a human city as it housed about 50,000 horses, each of them requiring hay and creating around 25 pounds of manure per day, to say nothing of the urine. Most of this excrement was deposited on the streets of the capital and the rest in the stables. Added to which their working life was short. The provisioning of animals and their eventual removal along with the supply of hay and removal of waste was carried out mainly along the river by the Thames barges. To keep London moving was then, as now, a major undertaking. In 1914, everyone was familiar with the sight, sound and scent of horses and probably even more so in the cities than in rural areas. But they were slowly becoming just as familiar with motor transport. Thankfully, for the health and continued growth of the urban environment the internal combustion engine had arrived, without which the major cities of the world would eventually have come to a grinding halt. By the eve of war London's population was over seven million, one and half that of New York or Paris and close to twice that of Berlin.

Great Britain was a much smaller and homogeneous nation than we would recognise today but it had seen enormous and accelerating change. Before the war

The Franco-British exhibition of 1908 – the White City, featuring 'The Flip Flap' (James Valentine and Sons Company)

the majority of its people would have been more familiar with the process of 'turning on the gas tap', 'lighting the lamp' and 'turning the wick up' than 'switching the light on'. Indeed we often still refer to 'turning the light on'.

From the 1890s onwards the area around Archie's home acquired a number of notable public buildings and with a growing Irish labouring population, a new Catholic church. From Archie's particular viewpoint the two new public libraries would have been a great asset. Archie had lived in this area throughout his school life and saw it becoming more developed and urban. Just two miles away in the north of Shepherd's Bush towards Wormwood Scrubs prison and the military area it was still green and open farmland. The area was protected by an act of Parliament granting 'the perpetual use by the inhabitants of the metropolis for exercise and recreation.'

This became the location for the massive Franco-British exhibition in 1908 with its famous high Flip Flap attraction, from the top of which visitors were said to be able to see Windsor Castle twenty miles away. The Exhibition buildings were all painted white so the site was dubbed the Great White City. The name stuck and when the Great Stadium was opened by King Edward VII for the London Olympic Games, the 68,000-seat building became the 'White City Stadium'. It only took ten months to construct.

Archie was still living close by when the Japan-British Exhibition was staged at the White City in 1910 and he would have been aware of the Brennan monorail. Louis Philip Brennan was already well known for his guided torpedo that in 1877 was one of the first practical guided weapons. The gyroscopically balanced monorail would have intrigued engineers like Archie. The vehicle ran on a circular track at 20 mph carrying 50 visitors on each trip. One of those who was thrilled by the experience was Winston Leonard Spencer Churchill and H. G. Wells considered it might be used to traverse over the water on wires strung from pylons. The power of the gyroscope as a 'Means for Imparting Stability to Unstable Bodies' as it was described in Brennan's 1903 patent, was well and truly demonstrated.

Just after his 19th birthday Archie applied for a patent. It is dated 7th November 1907 and it states that he was still a 'student'. The subject was for 'Improvements in and relating to Hydraulic Clutch Mechanisms'.

Archie applied for two more patents soon after, one of which was a spark plug and in this he declared that he was an engineer (that is, no longer a student but an 'old centralian' as the alumnae of the engineering school within Imperial College are known).

Archie's Imperial College records (see Appendix 1) appear to have been supplied by Archie himself, as most of its content clearly occurred much later in his career after he had left Imperial. Indeed, it seems to be complete up to World War II, as his book *Science in Wonderland* is included but was not published until 1935. He gained his membership of the Magic Circle in 1950 and this would certainly have been mentioned had the listing been updated again as he was very proud of this honour.

Archie's use of the title 'Prof.' was frowned upon by many but his doctorate never seemed to have been questioned. He claimed, or it was claimed for him, that he was one of the youngest in his generation to gain such a distinction. His doctorate of science was the principal qualification upon which his subsequent career hinged and it would seem to be a qualification that could have been readily confirmed. However Imperial's records list this as a science doctorate awarded by the Chicago Law School, an institution that is now defunct and was never affiliated with the University of Chicago. The Chicago Law School was founded in 1896 and existed during the time period that Archie would have studied. It was located at 64 W. Randolph Street and it is believed that it offered correspondence courses, so that might explain how he was able to get a degree from there without living in the US. Whoever recommended him to the school and verified his research stated to have been on 'Internal Combustion Engines with methods of infra red photography' remains a mystery.

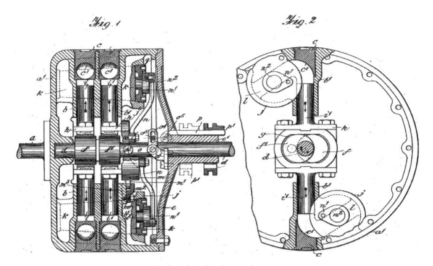

Hydraulic clutch mechanism

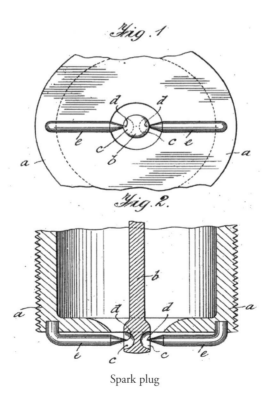

Spark plug

CHAPTER 4

Work, Cars and the Woods Next Door

Archie finished his formal schooling in 1908 and it is interesting to note on his Imperial College records (Appendix 1) that he worked at Edward Chester in Refrew, just as his brother Kenneth had. This may well have been his father's attempt to place his sons into an established engineering firm to earn their living. If this is so, it didn't work because neither of them stayed there. Archie did not fit into large industrial organisations. His working practice involved the tenacious pursuit of a solution to his latest interesting project until, and only until, that solution was within reach and then he would flit on to the next project. This was his great joy but also his great failing. He rarely saw a project through to its conclusion and would be looking over his shoulder for the next big idea as soon as his current work seemed to be succeeding and did not require his full attention.

1909 was a momentous year for Archie. On his return from 'work experience' in Refrew, he went to work for his father's affable and portly 52-year-old younger brother Edward Hunter Low. Ted Low lived with his three sisters, a niece and two servants in a substantial 11-room property in Hazlewell Road, Putney. He ran his engineering business but listed his occupation as a 'Shipowner' as the family's Perth & London Shipping Company connection continued and still operated from Dundee Wharf. Their steamer sailed for Dundee in Scotland every Wednesday and Saturday carrying goods and passengers. Dundee was a thriving port; the jute capital of the world.

Uncle Ted had a good friend, Robert Fleming, who was also from Dundee. Robert was 64 and his career was legendary. He had worked from the age of 13, initially at Baxters, a Dundee manufacturer of jute fabrics. Their product sold very well in the US for making such items as sandbags and with the American Civil War raging at this time, demand was insatiable. Managing this business took Robert to the US and eventually to the creation of his Scottish American Investment Trust launched in 1873, the start of Fleming & Co., the merchant bank that was simply known by the populace as 'Flemings'.[1]

Robert was a regular visitor in Edward Low's offices, sipping 'Rosie Lee' (tea) and being content with his life's work, with his reputation assured on both sides of the wide Atlantic Ocean. On the other hand, Edward's business, the 'Low Accessories and Ignition Company', was not so rosy. His was the second oldest engineering firm in the City of London, located at 15 Great St. Helens Street and it was just around the corner from Fleming's headquarters at 2 Princes Street and close to the famous Leadenhall Market.

The financier and philanthropist Robert had a firm friendship with Edward, as well as with Kenneth and Archie. Edward managed to get Robert involved in Archie's development of the car coal engine which had its furnace inside the boiler at the heart of the engine to prevent heat loss thereby increasing the efficiency. They built an engine but it was 'troublesome' and the development proved too much of a financial strain on Archie's meagre resources. He also designed a selector gear, which when he built it, 'worked the clutch and changed the gear like winking!'

It may have been through Robert Fleming's American connections that Archie qualified as a doctor of science from the Chicago Law School. However, it is also possible that it was Professor Ayrton who arranged Low's enrolment, as he had been to Chicago in 1884, before Low was born, to present a paper. He may still have had connections there.

In addition to Fleming, there were many other visitors who discovered the hospitable musty old offices at the top of the ancient crooked stairs and they added to the lively atmosphere. Sadly, few bought along commissions and business was always a bit fraught for Ted. There was always his personal 'wolf at the door'; his nadir just around the corner. Archie was encouraged to persevere with his innovative projects by Robert and connections with men such as this must have been a great assistance to the young engineer.

Uncle Ted would occasionally receive a windfall from his stock market investments, which would lighten the mood of impending financial doom and be another topic to discuss with Fleming on the next visit. Archie was given a salary of £120 a year, equivalent to £14,000 in 2019. Luckily he didn't fritter his money away on smart clothes and he cultivated a unique style that most classed as shabby. He thought it rather amusing that he was once offered 6d by a lady to look after her dog.[2]

Nobody forgets their first vehicle, and Archie was no exception. He acquired a Motor Manufacturing Company (MMC) Panhard which cost him £22 10s, partly funded by his mother. MMC had gone out of business in 1904 and the car was old when he got it, so he put in a great deal of work and effort to get it running. He was just 20 and very proud to be the owner of such a vehicle. He told one story about people's assumption that amused him. It concerned an outing to collect the newspapers. He was approaching his car with his purchases when a 'lady' hailed him. She was initially affronted at being ignored by this young 'paperboy' and then open mouthed when he got into his car and drove off.

But car ownership is onerous. Firstly, Archie had to find somewhere to keep it while he stripped off the tonneau body and got the vehicle running. Mary, his mother's maid, assisted him and was with him on the first 3-mile run to Barnes Common. At one point in this excursion Mary saved the day by putting her foot over the cap of a can of petrol that caught fire. Their relationship, such as it was, progressed to her sitting on his knee and the occasional kiss.

Among the big car problems and the smaller issues, Archie gained a great deal of practical knowledge while running his car. Sometimes this experience came at some cost and it could prove expensive. For example, the vehicle's rear lamps had a bi-metallic strip that operated a bell if the strip got cold because the lamps had gone out. However, this alarm system consistently failed to work and on one occasion he got a two-shilling fine for driving without a light which severely affected his lunch fund for a few weeks.

Motoring was a very expensive and prestigious pastime and still fascinated the general public. The Panhard was his pride and joy and it had an illustrious lineage. In the 1900 One Thousand Mile Trial, which included the steep portion of Shap Fell in the Lake District, Charles Rolls had driven one to gain the gold medal for the

1912 'cup' plug advert (Grace's Guide to British Industrial History)

most meritorious competitor. In those early days the people turned out in thousands to see the cars pass, and the police had to keep the streets clear for their passage.

Archie had needed some way of stopping the engine on his Panhard when it got so hot and continued to run after the ignition was turned off. He had designed a water injector to address the problem but this caused his ignition to get damp, giving him another problem. However, in the process of solving this new problem he designed, developed and marketed his 'cup' spark plug.

He invented gadgets like the whistling egg-boiler which he christened 'The Chanticleer' and with the help of his uncle and using 'their' business premises, Archie set up 'The British Low Accessories Co. Ltd' marketing his 'Famous 'CUP' plug'. Along with a great many young men, Archie was obsessed with the new miracles of his age; those motors and their petrol engines. Regardless of background and means, such devotees were almost addicted to the sight, sound and smell of the garage and track. The motoring mecca Brooklands was the most significant market place for innovative motoring products and Archie became involved in the administration of the clubs and the events on this course. Racing was not his forte partly due to his impaired vision and, anyway, it was well beyond his financial means. It was a sport for the upper classes as entrants' fees for a race were about 30 gold sovereigns, when just one of these worldwide accepted coins was the weekly wage for a well-paid 'man in the street'. The site, which was a second home to many like Archie, was looked upon with great affection by its loyal following. His love of and association with Brooklands lasted up to its closure for motor racing at the start of World War II and its motoring community was a very significant part of his life.

Meanwhile, in part of the huge area bounded by the banked track, a flying community developed. Louis Paulhan arrived at Brooklands in October 1909 and the shed that housed his machine was the first to be erected on the south westerly end of the 340-acre race course site on the far side of the sewage works from the clubhouse near one of the original farm houses. This was to become the flying village. In Whitsun the following year, this shed No 8 became the 'Blue Bird' restaurant (more of a tea-room and cafe) which was opened by Eardley Delauny Billing with his wife Ada Millicent and run by them with their experienced cook, Mary Hughes, and their two young servant girls. The Blue Bird was the only communal building and it quickly became the beating heart of this flying community. It developed rapidly from a few tables and chairs and a makeshift counter to boast a fire and a piano. Its name was immortalised when Malcolm Campbell named his famous record-breaking land speed 'Blue Bird' cars after it although some say Campbell chose the name from the 1908 play *L'Oiseau Bleu*. Edwin Alliott Verdon (A.V.) Roe once quipped of the Blue Bird cafe and the sewerage farm that he wasn't sure which one he had spent more time in![3] This flying village would be loved by its familiars just as the motoring village community was by its devotees.

Archie's brother Kenneth was by now an experienced civil, mining and mechanical engineer. He and Archie set up a consultancy business together at 10 Paul Street, near St. Paul's Cathedral in London, in 1911. Kenneth referred to Archie, his BSc. and

ACGI (Associate of the City and Guilds Institute – Graduate of Imperial College, London) and said that between 1911 and 1914 they 'did a good deal of work in the design of internal combustion engines and also mining and metallurgical machinery.' It is notable that he does not mention Archie's doctorate.

Archie, the unusual car-owning boy with his dark eyes and thick, straight, black hair, began to show more than a passing interest in the girls next door at number 5. Amy, the older sister, was forward enough to enquire about his car when Archie was trying to start the engine and she got herself covered in exhaust soot at their first introduction. She was small and slightly plump but very pretty. She had been educated in Freiburg and Lausanne and spoke a number of languages and her whole family were musical. Amy had also won medals as an amateur figure skater and was probably as excellent on roller skates which was a very popular pastime in her youth.

Amy's father, William Frederick Woods, was 43 when he married Emily Eleanor Oakes on 25th March 1888. Emily was only 26 when they wed and the couple went on to have seven children between 1890 and 1906 during their 30 years together: William, Amy, Eleanor, Thomas, John, Richard and Edward. Their first children were born in the seaside town of Dovercourt in Essex and then the family moved to Rochester in Kent, a short distance from Chatham Dockyard. Bill Woods, a purser, retired as a Paymaster in Chief from the Royal Navy and the family moved to Brook Green.

Amy and Eleanor, being a purser's daughters, were expected to behave conventionally but they became co-conspirators rebelling against this. Amy and Archie, aided by Eleanor, were able to engineer a liaison despite the formal cool relationship between their families. Archie called Amy 'Teddy', she called him 'Three' and an example of this engineered relationship was a construction of Archie's design that gave the couple some privacy. The contraption was set to work in the room at the Woods' house that contained a table tennis table. It was designed to make enough of the right sort of noises so that the senior members of the Woods family did not realise that a somewhat different game was being played in the room.

Archie was more intense than usual at this time, and with the certainty of youthful knowledge he became prone to forceful statements. When he was 'explaining' to an unreceptive audience of family representatives that men would leave this earth in the not-too-distant future, and that logically the first place they would investigate was the moon, even kindly old Uncle Ted said he would 'end up in Colney Hatch'.[4]

Ursula Bloom's biography of Archibald Low may be a little hard on William Woods, describing him as such an unapproachable character. Archie, whose opinion she also records, thought Bill fair and even kind, considering what transpired. Archie seems to have been egged on in the relationship with Amy by his Uncle Ted's more ribald remarks about the situation but the Low family in general disapproved of the match. In 1911, when Archie announced his intended marriage to 'the girl next door', his brother's comment, with reference to the beautiful summer weather, was 'If you ask me, the heat's gone to Archie's head.'

Amy was just 19 and 'with child' when they married, a long way from Brook Green, down at St Giles Church in Dallington, East Sussex on 14th June 1911. The parson's family were friends of Amy's from her time in Lausanne and Archie stayed the night before the wedding in the rectory where he remembers he had a friendly welcome, although the parson was also opposed to them marrying. William Woods escorted Amy into the church for the ceremony but Archie said that Aunty Flo (Florence) was the only representative from his family who attended.

From the church it wasn't a great distance through Battle, passing its famous abbey, for their short honeymoon in Hastings. Then they returned by rail to Greenford and took a pony and trap for the journey from the station to their newly rented house, 'Avoca' in Greenford Park. Only 843 people lived in Greenford when the Lows arrived. The summer of 1911 was exceptional, one of the warmest on record. Just over a week after the Lows' wedding, the nation celebrated George V and Queen Mary's coronation on 22nd June and the subsequent Festival of Empire in London. That summer heat must have got to Archie's brother Kenneth as well, as he was married on 12th September.

The Lows' first son, John, was born on 16th December 1911. The baby had a very difficult time in early infancy, survival being in the balance at times. As recounted in Bloom's biography, his father thought him:

> Such a funny little boy with a good head and blue eyes. I thought it absolutely wonderful. Never in my life had I known before that a woman's character is worth many times her appearance. Women are so remarkable ….

The baby slept too soundly and was too feeble to suck. Nobody thought he would live and Archie said he sat and stroked his tiny fingers as stimulation in his sleep. However, John soon grew stronger and another, Alick, arrived 11 months later, on 15th November 1912.

Archie and Amy hated living in Greenford Park, with the drains being in an appalling state. On their income, economy ruled as an ever-present constraint on their life together. They had lost, for the first time in their young lives, the close family support, the servants and Archie's Panhard. The long commute, life on a budget, in a house that they hated, that had poor sanitation and was a dreary long walk from the station, all took a toll on their marriage. Archie remembered how his wondering instincts leaked back into his life at this time; the face of the sophisticated lady who gazed at him in the tunnel of the old steam underground had set him on a diversionary course from his marriage. In recounting this simple but significant moment in his personal life it seems typical of Archie that he felt the need to explain why he was on the train and to supply considerable detail about the invention for making tea chest rivets he was going to demonstrate at a works near the old Tidal Basin station. Another embryonic extramarital excursion ended when he was asked by a girl's mother if his intentions were honourable. Archie and Amy separated in 1912 although they never lost touch. Amy and the boys went to live in Richmond.

A 1907 Fiat Taunus like Archie's (Wikimedia commons)

In 1910 the Austrian 'Petroleum War' increased the popularity of the light car and the cyclecars. They were a more affordable alternative to a motor car and a year or so later Archie was able to acquire a fairly new Bedelia tandem cyclecar. His Bedelia became the test bed for his latest project, his 'Low' forced induction engine. With this new engine the vehicle was over powered and the cyclecar collapsed when cornering at speed leaving Archie's unfortunate passenger stuck in a hedge.

By 1913 Archie's financial circumstances improved and he moved to Pellew (sometimes written as Pellow) Lodge at 281 Goldhawk Road, back in the Shepherd's Bush area near his parents' home. He also acquired the property at 86 High Street in the village of Feltham in Middlesex and a newer motor. Fiat had won the race that had been held at the Taunus Circuit outside Frankfurt in 1907 and so, despite the fatal crash that had occurred during the race, they named their new 1907 model after the circuit. Charles G. Lane, who had his flight training school, Lane's British Aeroplanes Ltd., at Brooklands, had a Fiat Taunus and sold it to Archie for £30.

In his Fiat he once covered the 70 miles to the seaside at Bognor Regis in only 1 hour 45 minutes, ignoring the time taken at an enforced stop for a speeding fine in the London suburbs at Priory Lane, Roehampton. In later life, Archie declared that this Fiat was 'the most glorious monster that I have ever handled, not excepting Sir Malcolm's BlueBird.'

Archie was beginning to meet like-minded people, those with a technical knowledge due to their business interests or simply their joy of speed in fast motor cars. He obviously spent time at the local garages picking up parts along with the latest motor trade gossip and was now familiar with many of the motoring establishments in West London from his work on his own cars and marketing his new accessories.

Other patents sparked new businesses and products and Low's business interests expanded over a wider portfolio of wares. For example, he setup his Low Generator & Engineering Co. Ltd lighting business based at Craven House, 121 Kinsway, London.

Archie's life was always about his next invention.

Acetylene gas generator (Grace's Guide to British Industrial History)

CHAPTER 5

Televista

It was most probably the work of Archibald's old college masters, Professor Ayrton and Professor Perry, on visual image transmission in the 1880s that 'sparked' his early development of television with its matrix detector (camera) and mosaic screen (receiver). A plethora of other system designers used devices to scan the image and 'paint' the screen. Perhaps Archie had a digital TV system 80 years before the advent of digital TV in the 1990s.

When Archie started, a number of investigators were publishing their findings and thoughts on the subject of capturing, transmitting and displaying quality still and moving images. Progress on telegraphic facilities were providing techniques that could be applied to the transmission of such images. Archie would have been aware of these developments and with his insight he knew that it was only a matter of time before moving images would be transmitted to remote audiences. But this conviction was based upon very new technology that had only been developed over the previous few decades.

The 'filter of time' usually condenses history, extracting only the essence from the complex compound of the past. This usually simplifies entries in our collective chronicle, associating a development or event with a single representative personality. Unfortunately, it is not always a very precise process. If history had a different bias then Karl Ferdinand Braun would be more famous than Marconi (who 'borrowed' inventions from Braun and others). Braun and Marconi were joint winners of the 1909 Nobel Prize for Physics 'in recognition of their contributions to the development of wireless telegraphy' but in addition, Braun gave us the first practical cathode ray tube, the phased array directional antenna and the semiconductor diode crystal detector. Semi-conductors were not given a collective name until 1910 when the German term 'Halbleiter' was coined.

Maybe we should also remember the pioneering French physicist Édouard Eugène Désiré Branly, whose invention was used to detect Hertzian waves (electromagnetic radio waves) and remember Oliver Joseph Lodge who named detectors, like Branly's, 'coherers'. After all, Marconi himself acknowledged Branly's contribution to his success in 1899 when the first wireless message was received from the other side of the English Channel.

In Britain, many ascribe the invention of television to John Logie Baird in the mid 1920s, but the first application under the 'new' British Patent Office 'Television' classification was granted on 24th December 1908, long before Baird developed his system. Of course, if history was fair, Baird would not be so famous but we would all know of Paul Julius Gottliebl Nipkow and Alan Archibald Campbell-Swinton. The same may be said for Philo Taylor Farnsworth, Vladimir Kosmich Zworykin and Manfred von Ardenne. There were so many contributors to the development of television that ascribing the invention to a single individual is a fool's errand.

In 1908, a system of television described as 'an apparatus for remotely transmitting images of animated objects and views', was patented (390,435) by Georges Pierre Édouard Rignoux of Charente, in France. In 1909, Georges and Professor A. Fournier demonstrated their system in Paris by using 64 selenium cells in an 8 by 8 matrix to detect an image. These cells were individually wired to a rotary switch which connected each of the detector cells in turn on to the transmitter output. In the receiver, a type of Kerr cell modulated the light and a series of variously angled mirrors attached to the edge of a rotating disc scanned the modulated beam onto the display screen. The image was scanned at a rate that was said to be 'several times' each second.

Archie, inspired by his new television project, envisaged a different form of rotary switch to Rignoux's. He developed a rotating roller for his moving picture detector. In May 1914, Low gave his first demonstration of what he called 'Televista'. This demonstration was given to the Institute of Automobile Engineers and was entitled 'Seeing by Wireless'. The main performance deficiency was caused by the selenium cell used for converting light waves into electric impulses, which responded too slowly thus spoiling the effect to some extent.

He was able to demonstrate his Televista at a number of events in London during the glorious hot summer of 1914. These demonstrations included an appearance at Selfridge's in one of the store's most famous special exhibitions.

This was 11 years before John Logie Baird took his system to this iconic London store and became famous for inventing television, when in fact he achieved some firsts in its development but definitely did not invent it. The demonstrations of Low's Televista were widely reported and garnered a lot of media interest. On 29th May 1914, the *Daily Chronical* reported: 'Dr. Low gave a demonstration for the first time in public, with a new apparatus that he has invented, for seeing, he claims by electricity, by which it is possible for persons using a telephone to see each other at the same time.' The *Times* on 30th May reported: 'An inventor, Dr. A. M. Low, has discovered a means of transmitting visual images by wire. If all goes well with this invention, we shall soon be able, it seems, to see people at a distance.' The *Daily Sketch* said it ominously pointed to 'a new terror for those who do not want to be found out.'

A much more informative report was published in the US in a consular report from London provided by their Deputy Consul General Carl Raymond Loop. He describes the transmitter as a screen divided into a large number of small squares cells of selenium, the resistance of which element varies according to the light that touches it. Over the screen is passed a synchronously running roller consisting of a number of pieces, which are alternating platinum conductors and insulators. The roller is driven by a motor of 3,000 rpm. The receiver is made up of a series of cells operated by the passage of polarized light through thin slats of steel, and at the receiver the object before the transmitter is reproduced as a flickering image.

Televista's large matrix of selenium cells would have provided a reasonable resolution but the image still flickered due to the slow reaction time of selenium. The outputs of these 'camera' detector cells were routed by the 'many wires' to the contacts that were scanned by his high-speed rotary switch (the roller). There are no details of its construction but it is tempting to think that Archie had developed a process of coating and machining to produce the pattern of isolated platinum contacts on his roller. Each cell's output would have been 'sampled' in turn as the roller rotated. This produced a signal for transmission comprised of the stream of the output amplitudes of each sampled cell as a continuous and repeating sequence; each cell's amplitude added to the output in exactly the same sequence on each rotation of the roller. It had a fast frame rate (50 times a second, derived from the 3,000 rpm speed) all of which would have been a considerable improvement on the Georges Rignoux system.

Ursula Bloom states that the Televista system employed 'electronic guns, which are used in televisions of our time.' This implies Archie used a cathode ray tube (CRT) or Braun tube as the display but this has to be in doubt as it would have been expensive to make one and commercially produced CRTs were not available until the 1930s. Loop's report also contradicts this, implying that it used a mosaic display technology based perhaps upon the Kerr effect, using polarised light with the 'thin slats of steel' acting as a filter.[1]

The textbooks on the history of television concentrate on the two systems of television, namely the mechanical Nipkow disk systems and the electronic CRT/ Vidicon tube televisions. With its element matrix 'camera', Low's cellular flat screen Televista was more like our post-1980s digital television systems than any of the other early systems but 70 years before its time. Ronald Frank Tiltman's book *Television in the Home* was published in 1927. The book concentrated to a significant extent upon J. L. Baird as he was very active in his work at this time but Tiltman chose Professor A. M. Low to write the introduction. In this Low does not mention his own work or Baird but he does predict that 'we shall be able to see and speak to our relatives as they fly in safety around the world.' However, Tiltman acknowledged Low's work, referring to his various related patents with an apology that they were of 'too technical a nature for inclusion' and confirming the press interest in Low's television demonstrations in early 1914.

A 'wirelessed' footballer image (Ursula Bloom's *He Lit The Lamp*)

Archie raised Patent 191,405 in October 1917 for an image transmitter. This had a transmitter with selenium cells and a roller closely matching the description of his Televista invention but the receiver used bi-metallic strips, which, as they heated and cooled, bent to regulate the light in each display cell. This would not have been suitable for his moving picture Televista as the response time of these metal strips would have been even worse than that of the selenium cells in the transmitter but it seemed to work well on still subjects. Ursula Bloom's biography includes a transmitted 'still' image taken in 1918 by Archie. A figure taken from a photograph of a group of footballers was 'wirelessed' by means of the apparatus Archie Low produced. This was produced direct from the copper base on which it was received in 1918.

In 1922, Low Engineering advertised their 'Wireless Sets for Broadcasting' that were made at their works in Feltham. At this time Low was also in business with his acquaintance from his MID days, Sir Henry Norman, a highly placed engineer with a 'radio' background. Archie did not resume this work on Televista after the war. However, he did not give up his desire to use his techniques to improve television. His later patent of 1938 (491,011) stated:

It has been proposed in connection with television apparatus … a mosaic of photo-electric elements is produced by coating one face of a carrier plate of conducting material such as copper, with a coating possessing photo-electric properties, such as caesium alloy; applying a backing of non-conductive material … such as resin … to the reverse face of the said carrier and sectioning said carrier with its coating by cross cuts extending completely through the carrier and the coating to form a mosaic of separate photo-electric elements … of comparatively small size ….

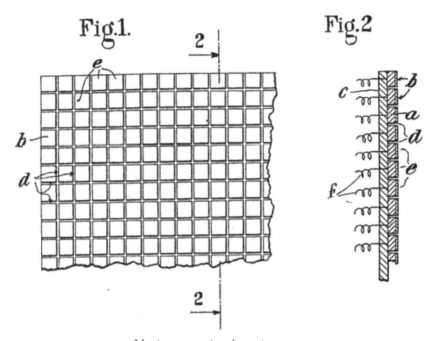

Matrix construction shown in patent

This patent goes on to suggest a number of ways such a screen could be used:

…such a screen being disposed inside an electric discharge tube, and an image of the object to be televised being projected by a suitable lens system on to the photoelectric elements whereby the latter acquire a small electric charge in proportion to the light stimulation; the elements are scanned by a ray in the tube and the resultant signals are transmitted. … the elements of the mosaic being each connected by a conductor to a commutator.

Low's control system for the Aerial Target also included a plate coated with a conducting surface and an insulating surface. Televista's contribution to the development of the first drone is clear.

The early development of television post-WWI continues to be a murky mix of inventors and claims. Many inventors were also involved in work to improve radio and telegraphic communication after the war. In 1922, George William Walton and William Samuel Clouston Stephenson were working on a 'mechanical' television system at the Twyford Abbey Works in Low's area of London. It would be gratifying to assume that Low and Stephenson knew each other in the early 20s as they were both ex RAF officers, they lived in the same area of West London and they were involved at the time in common areas of technical investigation. Walton and Stephenson's system was the technological basis of the company 'Scophony Limited' which operated a commercial form of television right up to the start of World War II, something that was not achieved by J. L. Baird.

Using valve (tube) technology, their Patent 213,654 submitted in 1922 describes the signal between the television transmitter and the receiver as a carrier signal modulated with both the low frequency synchronising signal and the picture data. After amplification at the receiver, a suitable filter separated the synchronising signal and from the picture data carrier.

William Stephenson became famous a number of times in his life. His secret British Intelligence activities in World War II have been told and retold in stories that first appeared in the early 1960s. They all tell of this small, quiet Canadian code-named

PATENT SPECIFICATION

Application Date : Dec. 30, 1922. No. 35,481 / 22.   **213,654**

Complete Left : Oct. 30, 1923.

Complete Accepted : March 31, 1924.

PROVISIONAL SPECIFICATION.

Improvements relating to Means for Synchronising the Movements of Two Rotating Bodies.

We, WILLIAM SAMUEL STEPHENSON and GEORGE WILLIAM WALTON, both British subjects, of Twyford Abbey Works, Acton Lane, Harlesden, N.W. 10, in the County of London, do hereby declare the nature of this invention to be as follows :—

This invention relates to means for maintaining two rotating bodies

station by means of suitable filter circuits the modulating component of the received waves is separated out and. is employed to drive an alternating current synchronous motor coupled with or geared to the rotating drum at the receiving end. It is most convenient to have the drums at both ends actually on

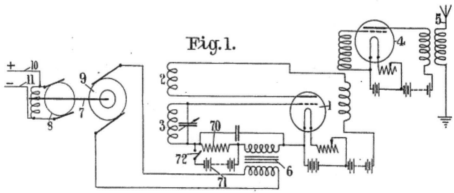

Fig. 1.

Diagram in Stephenson's patent

'Intrepid' who had amassed a fortune in the inter war years from his interests in many branches of industry. He had networks of operatives garnishing information and influencing events in Europe before he brought his skills to 1940s America on behalf of the British War effort. Often cited as the Head of British Intelligence in the Western Hemisphere during World War II and guardian of the ULTRA secret in North America, some say he was the inspiration for Ian Fleming's James Bond.

Fame also reached Archie to some extent in 1914, after the public demonstrations of his work on Televista exposed him in the media. The provincial press reported two attempts by enemy agents to kill Archie. The stories were widely circulated and repeated. They were part of the anti-German sentiment building in the country and referring directly to the Hun, the Teutons and other such terms. On Saturday 24th October 1914 the second attempt was documented in the *Birmingham Daily Gazette* and the *Birmingham Mail*, the *Aberdeen Press and Journal* and other newspapers. The *Derby Daily Telegraph* report was typical, extensive and detailed. Under the banner 'A Second Attempt which Failed' it said that since the beginning of the war two attempts have been made upon the life of Dr. A. M. Low, the accomplished young scientist who has been experimenting with a rifle of which German agents wished to obtain control. The first attack was in the latter part of August when two shots were fired at Archie and his brother while they were working in their laboratory in Paul Street. The second much more subtle and complex attempt involved a cigarette laced with strychnine chloride.

It would be easy to dismiss such reports except that we know that Archie and his brother Kenneth did work together at this time. In 1912, Archie filed a patent for rubber using 10 Paul Street as his address. At this most sensitive time in 1914, the rifle fire would have been big news in John Elvin's 'Fox' public house at 28 Paul Street which was just down the road from the Lows' premises. The clientele would also have known that Archie was rarely seen without a cigarette.

Maybe Kenneth and Archie Low made the composite roller for his Televista in this laboratory and it may have been the place referred to in this *Flight* magazine's note, 'Dr. A. M. Low, the eminent consulting engineer, writes: "It might interest you to know that I had several doors in my laboratory some years ago which could be opened by whistling a certain note to them."'

The notoriety accruing from these lurid reports of attempted assassination in the German agent stories put Archie's name and capabilities in the minds of military men and aircraft designers with ambitions to get their ideas realised.

Through the latter half of that hot July and into August Britain anticipated the impending confrontation brewing on the continent and many people waited up for the declaration of War to be confirmed. Before the German undersea telegraph cables were cut by the Royal Navy, the Central Telegraph Office in London sent their 'G.N.' ('Good Night') message to Berlin which would be the last message by this medium to that destination for four long years.

CHAPTER 6

Three More Generals

The pre-war airplanes were only just manageable when controlled by their fearless and often fearful pioneer airmen. However a few unorthodox thinkers and those most concerned by the threat posed by airships believed that a machine might be built to be controlled by pilots on the ground. If so it might offer a means of defence against these seemingly 'impregnable' Zeppelins.

These senior officials would discuss such schemes in the mess or at the club, seated in their favourite firm deep buttoned leather library chairs in the slightly dusty, shadow infested reading room that had been coated down the years with an aromatic 'patina' of fine tobacco residue and lamp soot. We can envisage the scientists and engineers meeting in the less salubrious surroundings of their cluttered labs and draughty flight sheds now becoming more commonly referred to as hangars. These men were serious professionals dealing with death at home and abroad on a daily basis. Open to public and political scrutiny in the highly charged emotional climate of the world war they were unlikely to support schemes that they did not believe in.

The aerial branch of the army was novel and – like Jack Seely, Sykes and Henderson – the officers in Britain's emerging air services included many open to untraditional concepts. Who were these mavericks in the vanguard of British military aviation that would become involved with the Aerial Target? Four of them would be directly involved in supporting the development of the AT – or at least not shutting the enterprise down. Apart from David Henderson who was their commanding officer, the other three were all long-serving army officers in their mid-thirties and older at the outbreak of the war. They were Walter Buckingham Caddell, Duncan le Geyt Pitcher and William Sefton Brancker.

Caddell became involved in aviation in the first full year of the conflict and was Low's immediate superior officer on the AT project. The fourth of nine children he was born in 1879 in Dundalk, Louth in Ireland. His father fought in the 2nd battle of El Teb on 29th February 1884, one of the last battles fought in an infantry 'hollow square'. By the 1900s his family home was in Dublin when he got his commission in the Royal Artillery. 1906 was quite a year for Walter; he married his Welsh bride Harriet Hughes Jones and by 1907, Walter had an heir, Henry, and by 1912, a daughter Mildred Sheila. He was serving in Bermuda before being transferred to France in 1914.

The Bermuda Contingent. Officers and senior enlisted men of the Bermuda Contingent of the Royal Garrison Artillery drafted to the Western Front, during the Great War

Walter was an ornithologist and a fellow of the Zoological Society of London which may have influenced his move to the RFC in 1915. In March 1916 he became Deputy Assistant Director of Military Aeronautics at the War Office in London, in effect the chief assistant to the Canadian, Brigadier-General Duncan Sayre MacInnes, the Director of Aircraft Equipment (DAE). Walter retired from the RAF on 28th May 1919 with the honorary rank of Brigadier-General.

The next general was destined to reach the rank of air commodore in the Royal Air Force and, would, in due course, recommend Low for work on the Royal Navy 'drone' boats. Pitcher was born on 31st August 1877 in the British hill station at Nainital, Uttarakhand in India, the sixth of seven children.[1] An officer in the British Indian army, he was in England when he learnt to fly. He got his certificate No 125 on 29th August 1911, just before the British and Colonial Aeroplane Co. offered the army and navy pilot training for 250 officers in each service at discounted rates to create a pool of trained pilots. He was posted back to England in 1913 to study the Central Flying School's system of training in order to instigate a similar establishment back in India. Duncan did not get back to India before the start of hostilities. The encouragement and inducements available to increase the number of pilots had not extended to training observers and at the start of hostilities, as an expedience, the RFC resorted to reassigning pilots. So Duncan along with three other qualified pilots, Lt Hugh Lambert Reilly from the Indian army and Lt Kenneth Reid Van der Spuy and 2nd Lt C. F. Creed from South African were assigned as observers. This would have been a serious blow to these men as they could not practice their trade as pilots but would, as observers, encounter the same risks from accident, aerial combat or anti-aircraft fire for less status and less pay. Duncan was assigned to No. 4 squadron as an observer and crossed the English Channel to France in August 1914.

In October, the War Office requested the return of Captain Pitcher for service in England but Brig-Gen Henderson who was commanding the RFC in the field noted that Duncan had been 'employed exclusively on observation duties and could only be released if a replacement were found.' Capt Harold Wyllie of the 9th (Cyclist) Battalion, Hampshire Regiment had just arrived in France so London merely assigned him as the required replacement observer and Duncan returned to Blighty.

Duncan was posted to the Central Flying School and became its assistant commandant in early 1915, having as it were, been trained for the job two years earlier. Duncan's career progressed. In its 26th July 1917 edition, *Flight* magazine noted that General Pitcher, controller of the technical department of the Air Board, was recently nominated as an additional member of the Advisory Committee for Aeronautics. He gained his permanent promotion to air commodore on 5th August 1919.

Two factors dominated military aviation at the start of World War I. One was the dire shortage of aircraft and engines. The other was the competing roles of the British Army's and the Royal Navy's aerial forces. Having shown their potential, aircraft and airships provided a newly accessible third dimension to the area of conflict over which both the army and the navy would lay claim. The entwined history of the British air services started when the RFC was formed. It comprised 133 officers and by the beginning of 1913 it had 12 manned balloons and the three dozen machines referred to earlier. Due to the strains on the RFC's men and machines in support of the armies in the field on the continent of Europe and in other theatres of the war, British home defence and long-range bombing became the province of the RNAS. However, demarcation issues between the RFC and RNAS and their competition for the limited resources would continue.

Britain was not the only country with these issues of resource management and repeated re-organisations. The German Air Service was just beginning a 'comprehensive re-organisation' when their ace Max Immelmann was killed on 18th June 1916 and General Maurizio Moris the head of Italian military aviation admitted, 'There exists a certain want of harmony – a certain occasional, shall I say, friction? – between the military and naval branches of our flying service.'

For the Royal Naval Air Service, Frank McClean generously provided the training facilities and aircraft needed to literally get the establishment off the ground. Frank had been flying as long as Brabazon. He was an amateur astronomer and an early pioneer of aerial photography. He also had an eye for pubic exhibition and had flown his flimsy Short seaplane through Tower Bridge and under the other bridges on the Thames in August 1912 just two years before the war.

Frank McClean on the Thames in August 1912 (Flight Global)

Frank McClean flying through Tower Bridge on 10th August 1912 (Flight Global)

This RNAS supply difficulty became an inspiration to Lt. Charles Samson and his Eastchurch Squadron who experimented with arming their private cars. Samson had served on Seely's sub-committee of the CID (Committee of Imperial Defence) before the war. In Belgian and France, during the first German advances and with too few aircraft, the frustrated RNAS squadron used their 'armed cars' and, with guidance from locals, harassed the aggressor to great effect, or at least to their own satisfaction. Encouraged by these successes, two of the vehicles were fitted with protective plating. 'Poor little Belguim' was to become the rallying cry on recruiting posters and the RNAS irregular response was an inspiration to those resisting the German advance. Thus the first British armoured cars were operated by the RNAS. With Churchill's assistance (and maybe, insistence) more armoured cars were produced by the navy and the RNAS Armoured Car Section was formed, just as 'entrenchment' started which prevented their deployment in France. Churchill championed unconventional innovation and of course, he had created the Royal Naval Division, 'Winston's Little Army', that fought alongside the army on the Western Front.

Before all of this, Charles Samson had gained his Royal Aero Club Aviator's Certificate No 71 on 25th April 1911 and in May 1912 he had taken command of the RFC Naval Wing. He attempted to teach Churchill to fly but had more success being the first ever to take-off from a ship on 10th January 1912 and a few months later on 9th May he flew off a moving ship.

Throughout the war, the qualitative attributes of their aircraft would see the fortunes of the warring powers wax and wane as new designs and innovations gave one side or other the advantage for a time. For the British, this aerial inter-service arms race and rivalry matured, frustrating all attempts at a working accommodation and reaching a festering furuncle that would only be finally lanced by the creation of the autonomous Royal Air Force.

The quantitative shortages would be resolved moderately quickly for the Royal Flying Corps thanks largely to the leadership of the third general Low mentions in connection with the AT. General William Sefton Brancker became more widely known than either Walter Caddell or Duncan Pitcher, at least during the war and throughout the 1920s. Indeed, to this day athletes from the services and civil service still compete annually in Britain in the 'Sir Sefton Brancker Competition'.

Brancker did not tolerate waste in any form; not of time, nor money nor resources and he had the opportunity and to some extent a strong case to terminate Low's work but he didn't. Therefore, he obviously considered the work at the Feltham establishment of value and the AT a potentially viable weapon.

Brancker was born in Kent on 22nd March 1877, the son of an established military family. Initially a successful military career did not seem very promising as he was a small, moustached man, standing at only 5 feet 7 inches with brown hair and grey eyes. He possessed enormous energy and a twinkle in his eye that was apparently not only due to his distinctive corrective eyeglass. He was renowned for his joie de vivre as much as he was for his monocle. He fought in South Africa and was wounded on 13th October 1900 at Geluk farm in the continued fighting that followed the final pitched battle of the second Boer War, the battle of Bergendal. He witnessed the entrenched warfare in Manchuria in 1905 that involved all the elements to be repeated on the Western Front including the enormous casualty rates. He married May Wynne Field in 1907 and together they had a number of adventures including a trip to Tibet. Their next big adventure in 1909 was the birth of their son, John William Sefton Brancker, which was no doubt celebrated in style in the mess by the proud father and his associates.

Sefton was in Calcutta (Kolkata) in November 1910 when a team from the British and Colonial Aeroplane Company arrived with three 'Bristol' boxkite biplanes to undertake experiments with the army. General Douglas Haig ordered the participation of these demonstration aircraft in the army exercises and Sefton, with his previous experience in observing from tethered balloons, made his first flights with them.

The 1911 Durbar for King George V and Queen Mary in Delhi was a huge undertaking. It had an official directory which, with its maps, ran to 388 pages. This directory detailed all of the aspects of the events, the guests, the participants, the parades, the sports, the circus and other entertainments. A coal-fired power house was built to provide lighting for over 100 miles of roads. A number of elephants arrived to be paraded in the associated festivities in Calcutta. Sefton's sense of fun, which was infectious, spread to his fellow officers. Three of them borrowed one of the largest beasts and went for an evening ride in town. The most senior of the group awoke the next day to his incoming correspondence that contained a summons on official letterhead accusing him of the offence of endangering the public on an elephant. For such a senior officer this was a serious matter. During that fraught day of consultations with his lawyer they finally discovered that the magistrate named on the summons did not exist and that Sefton was behind the ruse, having obtained the letterhead stationery in advance of the evening in the howdah that he had instigated. Needless to say, once the ribbing in the mess died down, the butt of the joke and Brancker remained the best of friends, one of the few who could call him 'Blotto', a name he reserved for his closest chums.

Sefton was posted back to Britain in April 1912, to Edward Bailey 'Splash' Ashmore's Battery of the Royal Field Artillery close to Farnborough. This posting required him to visit the area near the new aviation camp at Larkhill and he started to fly with the RFC in the first months of its existence. He was prevented from transferring to the RFC at this stage as he was short sighted, not well off and being of junior rank, without much influence.

Born into an Anglo-German family and speaking excellent German, he decided in December to visit Hamburg to update his vocabulary and refine his knowledge of German culture. This visit reinforced his conviction that conflict was likely in

Europe in the near future, a view to which a growing proportion of the population of the whole of the continent subscribed, as the imperial ambitions of the European nations intensified.

Sefton was one of the few general staff officers who could tell the front from the back of an aircraft and he found himself purchasing aircraft, any aircraft in whatever state, on the direct instructions of Colonel Seely, the secretary of state for war to satisfy a government undertaking given in the Army Estimates Debate on 19th March 1913 where he stated 'we have 101 at this moment, and if there is no further delay in supply, we shall have, on the 31st May, 148.'

Despite his poor eyesight and strained finances Brancker managed to obtain his Royal Aero pilot's licence on 18th June 1913 at the Vickers Flying School in Brooklands. Other short-sighted pilots, such as Charles Gordon-Bell and Francis Thomas Courtney also slipped through the system of checks.[2]

It became quite the thing in early 1914 for British officers to take their 'private' holidays touring Belgium and northern France. Sefton reconnoitred the area between Charleroi to Ardennes looking for likely bases and potential airfields. Unsurprisingly, with his striking appearance as a bicyclist in his tweeds and with his distinctive eyeglass, he was twice questioned about his activities by the local constabulary who were obviously suspicious that he might be a spy. He probably looked every inch an imposter masquerading rather poorly as an eccentric Englishman. When the war started, those with German-sounding names were targeted and their shops and business were attacked. More insidious social pressures came to bear. The German Shepherd dog was renamed Alsatian, Battenberg became Mountbatten and finally the Royal Family became Windsors. But Sefton remained a Brancker.

Lord Kitchener, Sefton's boss at the War Office, was one of a very few who acted on the assumption that the country was in a very long, very aggressive hard fight. He had at the outset, when the meagre force of four squadrons had departed with the BEF to France, told Sefton 'that a large number of new squadrons would be required to equip that army'. So it was that Brancker at the War Office and Trenchard with his administrative wing in Farnborough were tasked with creating from scratch a complete and very large air force. From the small training structure that existed they provided the personnel and from the tiny industrial base that had up to this point only created small numbers of experimental aircraft they obtained the huge numbers of machines the war required.

The search for suitable equipment took many turns. Captain James Valentine, who had been the Officer Commanding the British aviation depot in Paris, went on a special mission to Italy to collect an Italian Caproni Ca 1 bomber for evaluation in Britain. On 12th February, Valentine took off from Milan and after 3 months he had reached Dijon where the aircraft was abandoned. James, who had obtained his ticket No 47 from the Royal Aero Club in December 1910, later died while serving in Russia in August 1917.

On 9th March 1915, Sefton was promoted to deputy director of military aero-nautics and became increasingly involved in the political shenanigans of the various re-organisations of the air services and through 1916 bore some of the emerging criticism that concerned the aircraft supplied to the RFC. The introduction of the R.E.8 suffered considerable from bad publicity and was never universally accepted as a great aircraft. Sefton had much to do with the promotion and supply of these aircraft and felt that his meteoric rise through the ranks and his status were in jeopardy.

By March 1916, Noel Pemberton Billing, a monocled ex-RNAS officer, had resigned his commission to become an MP. The growing ascendancy of German air power during what was later dubbed the 'Fokker scourge' of late 1915 and early 1916 gave Billing his platform to rile against the performance of the Royal Aircraft Factory and its products. It was determined that this 'RFC scandal' should be investigated by an Inquiry Committee. Sefton summarised the trouble caused by these accusations and the investigation: 'Never was there a more useless waste of time and energy in the middle of a great war.'

Early in 1917, Sefton found himself in the Hotel Cecil with the rest of the hierarchy of the country's air organisations. They were bought under one roof in what had been one of London's largest hotels. The political overview provided by the Air Board, the army War Office elements, the navy organisations under the new Fifth Sea Lord, specially created to represent naval aviation, and the research elements of the Ministry of Munitions were confined in an explosive mix in what became known as Bolo House aka the Hotel Cecil. Although this was intended to foster co-operation and liaison internally, it couldn't withstand the concentration of inter-service rivalry and the sustained attention of the press while the German large bombers rained a new campaign of terror from 18,000 feet upon the innocent civilians of the country's cities.

Access to the war zones by more critical 'voices' was being reluctantly allowed in order to counter this negative press, resulting in part from the repression of news. In April 1917, Christopher Richard Wynne Nevinson was appointed as an official war artist, one of the more than ninety who contributed over the course of the war. Sefton took Nevinson aloft at Hendon by way of an introduction to aircraft. A little later that year Nevinson went to France and was based near Caen in the press centre at the Château d'Harcourt. Nevinson was able to fly with the RFC over the front and went up in observation balloons. He made much of these adventures in the press and was scorned by some for his self-aggrandisement. However, his images of the war are some of the most remarkable and at the time, very controversial. He, like Paul Nash, had critical views on the constraints placed upon them. Emotions stirred by Nevinson's 'Paths of Glory' were not those invoked by the original text of Thomas Gray's 'Elegy Written in a Country Church-Yard' and although the painting was censored, for depicting two British soldiers face down dead in the mud, Nevinson still exhibited it. Paul Nash expressed his feeling at the time in this way, 'I am no longer an artist. I am a messenger who will bring back word from the men who are fighting to those who want the war to go on for ever. Feeble, inarticulate will be my message, but it will have a bitter truth and may it burn their lousy souls.' In World War II Nash produced his 1941 allegorical painting 'Battle of Britain'.

In his introduction to Alan Bott's book *An Airman's Outing,* dated 1st August 1917, Brancker referred to the maturing of aerial power and the effect of indiscriminate bombardment from the air:

> The importance of the aerial factor in the prosecution of the war grows apace. The Royal Flying Corps, from being an undependable and weakly assistant to the other arms, is now absolutely indispensable, and has attained a position of almost predominant importance. If the war goes on without decisive success being obtained by our armies on the earth, it seems almost inevitable that we must depend on offensive action in the air and from the air to bring us victory.
>
> We in London have had some slight personal experience of what a very weak and moderately prosecuted aerial offensive can accomplish. With the progress of the past three years before us, it needs little imagination to visualise the possibilities of such an offensive, even in one year's time; and as each succeeding year adds to the power of rival aerial fleets, the thought of war will become almost impossible.
>
> War has been the making of aviation, let us hope that aviation will be the destruction of war.

Sefton was at odds with the mood for change. He was opposed to the proposals to create an Air Force separate from both the army and the navy as championed by Pemberton Billing, recommended by General Jan Christiaan Smuts and now being formulated for implementation by David Henderson. So Sefton found himself posted out of the Hotel Cecil, goaded into a move to command the RFC in the Middle East where Alan Bott was also posted. In October 1917 Sefton travelled down through France en-route to Alexandria. He passed through Italy as it was reeling from the events in Venetia after the breakthrough by the Central Powers in the battle of Caporetto. On arrival in his new command he was then engaged on the job in hand. Leaving his staff in Cairo to 'hold the fort' he joined General Edmund Henry Hynman Allenby's Headquarters controlling the RFC's support to operations at the front.

After the British successes against the Ottoman forces and their supporting German airmen in the advance from Beersheba to the fall of Jerusalem, Sefton visualised that he would have time for visits to the further reaches of his extended command. At the end of December he dreamed of returning as the distinguished leader to his old haunts in India that he had left as a lowly ranker. This was not to be as he was summoned back to London. He did however manage some flying excursions, despite his dubious skill in the cockpit. On one occasion he ended up 'on his nose in a ditch' and on another, arriving at the outpost he was to inspect, he overheard an assessment of his landing by someone unaware of his rank – to summarise the spectator described it as 'Bloody awful!' One joke going the rounds at the time was: 'How long did it take you to learn to run an aeroplane?' 'Three or four.' 'Three weeks?' 'No, aeroplanes?'

After this short but eventful eastern excursion and probably with some sense of restored self-esteem, Sefton was back in London. The new appointees to the Air Council were chaired by Lord Rothermere (Harold Sidney Harmsworth, 1st Viscount Rothermere, Lord Northcliffe's brother) and at the start of 1918, meeting in Adastral House in the Kingsway, Holborn they had exactly three months to plan and instigate the consolidation of Britain's air services into the proposed new independent organisation; the Royal Air Force along with the Women's support organisation, the WRAF. Brancker was appointed to the role of Controller-General of Equipment. Boom Trenchard could not work with Rothermere and he resigned, an event that attracted huge press interest. The Royal Air Force, the world's first independent national airforce, was created on schedule on April Fools day when the anticipated German 1918 Spring offensive was in full flow. By the 11th Haig issued his 'Backs to the Wall' order and on the 15th it was announced that Trenchard was to be replaced by Frederick Sykes, the officer who in May 1915 had been moved to the RNAS. The newborn RAF and the air services lost some of its leadership, as following the departure of Boom, within days the Hotel Cecil would see the departure of David Henderson and Lord Rothermere. William Douglas Weir took over.

On the front Britain was stretched and, having been obliged to extend its Western Front, were in the depths of an army manpower shortage as they faced the German divisions with resources flowing in from their now near quiet Eastern Front. The government priorities were to maintain the needs of the forces with the production of ships, tanks, aircraft while supporting agriculture, transport and all the other demands for resources. The government controlled the supply of men and had already forced the army to restructure, reducing every division to 9 battalions from 12. Of the many resignations at this time George Lambert MP on 6 March 1918 was moved to say:

> Our army and navy to-day – and I say it with no disrespect to the present occupants – are directed by second-rate soldiers and sailors. The people do not know of these things. We are still rocked in the cradle of complacency. The Press is either controlled by the Government or controls the Government. We are drifting in the conduct of this War, drifting so that, unless we mend our ways, we shall have the bitter humiliation of a peace on German terms.

The prospect of retaliating to the German bombing of Britain's civilian targets with a serious, significant and above all, a sustained bombing campaign had been mooted in the autumn of 1917. The prospect became reality in the spring of 1918 as suitable aircraft became available and by June, with Trenchard back and in command, the long-range air capability was re-organised as the 'Independent Bomber Force'. This Inter-Allied Independent Air Force (IAF) was part of the Smut's recommendations; in effect the strategic Bomber Command of World War I and although it was only formed in May and was in action for a matter of months, it delivered a significant amount of ordnance on German cities.

At the start of 1918, when the war was considered to be far from over, Sefton led a mission to the US to improve co-ordination with the US forces. When Brancker's mission arrived in the US the threat of the German main 'Michael' spring offensive breaking through in the British sector had passed a week or so earlier and the US, who had been at war with the Imperial German Government for just over a year, was now beginning to build up its forces in Europe.

Brancker was impressive during his 1918 mission. Workers at a presentation at a plant in Buffalo, New York were fascinated by Sefton's monocle and laid bets on how long he could wear the eye-glass without moving it or blinking but when the speech concluded their estimates had all been greatly exceeded. His constitution, energy and capacity for socialising was at times taken close to excess but this never affected his concentration on his work. This was a man who got on extremely well with most of the US officials and the press he met but this personal accord did not translate to any significant agreements. As recounted in Basil Collier's (1959) biography of him, *Heavenly Adventurer*, he did however comment later on claims that 'America won the war', saying that 'during 1918 a large body of Englishmen on commissions in America were frankly preaching that the Allies were exhausted after three and a half years' fighting; that we had not sufficient men or material left to win a decisive victory and that therefore every patriotic and right thinking American must shoulder his pack, come over and do it for us in the name of liberty and civilisation. Surely there is some justice in their claim!'

Back in London, he found 'the fear of a German victory stalked the streets of London' and the end of the war in whatever form this might take was far from certain. Soon after his return, on 22nd August 1918 he was given a new RAF post as master-general of personnel.

The Hotel Cecil had not reformed itself in Sefton's absence. Lady Gertrude Eleanor Molyneux (Crawford), know as GEM to her friends, had not stayed long in her post as the first commandant of the Women's Royal Air Force that was created in 1918. Violet Douglas-Pennant took over and fared little better in the role. She said her time at 'Bolo House' had been spent in her office which she described as a small, dark room on the top floor of the hotel next to a men's lavatory. There was so little furniture that she was forced to keep her papers and files on the floor. She said that she was not given an Air Ministry pass, meaning that every time she entered the building she was forced to fill in a form before being escorted to her office 'presumably to call on myself'. She was in office until 27th August when Sefton, only 11 days into his new personnel appointment, summoned Violet to his office and informed her that she was dismissed and would have to leave the following day. This was 'Not', as he stated, 'because you are inefficient, as you are very efficient, but as you are grossly unpopular with everyone who has ever come in contact with you'. This dismissal, taken under the direction of his new boss Lord Weir, put Brancker in the eye of a storm that blew for some time, subsided and would then gust again every now and again over the next few years.

At issue was the manner of her dismissal and her subsequent claims that it was politically motivated to cover up immorality in the WRAF ranks. Her case was championed in parliament on 29th May 1919 which led to a judicial enquiry. Violet's case did not fare well in the enquiry but it did not go away. As late as 1926 she made her case again in the 13th February edition of the *Spectator*.

This first WRAF organisation was disbanded in 1920.

Sefton Brancker's Royal Aero Club certificate portrait (Royal Aero Club Trust)

525

BRANCKER, William Sefton.

    General Staff, War Office, S.W.

Born 22nd March, 1877, at Woolwich
Nationality British
Rank or Profession Major, R.F.A.
Certificate taken on Vickers Biplane
At The Vickers School, Brooklands
Date 18th June, 1913

Sefton Brancker's Royal Aero Club certificate certificate (Royal Aero Club Trust)

LEARN TO FLY
. . . at the . .
VICKERS FLYING SCHOOL
BROOKLANDS.

Thoroughly graded tuition from slow Biplane to fast Monoplane

Special Terms to Naval and Military Officers

VICKERS, Limited,
Aviation Department,
VICKERS HOUSE, BROADWAY, LONDON, S.W.

An advert for Vickers Flying School, where Brancker qualified (Courtesy of Aviation Ancestry)

Sefton had been a great driving force in the first years of the RFC but his remaining RAF career did not last long. When he resigned in 1919 his departure was reported all over the world. The enormous growth of the British air service in the four years of the war shown in the following table was due in good measure to the work of Sefton Brancker. He was knighted in January 1919.

The growth of British air power

	August 1914			End of 1916			October 1918		
	Officers	Others	Machines	Officers	Others	Machines	Officers	Others	Machines
RFC/ RAF	147	1097	179	5982	51915	3929	27906	263842	22171
RNAS	50	550	93	2764	26129	1567	–	–	–

By the end of the war his duties had consumed his domestic life and he was living permanently at 13–15 Little Grosvenor Street in the Mayfair Mansions and not with his family. Sefton had become a 'Club Bachelor' seeing less and less of his wife May and his son.

In this fresh, less formal civilian society he was called 'Branks' and his capacity to work long hard hours and socialise into the small hours served him well in his new roles. Dining, drinking and dancing were undertaken with the same gusto and energy as work. Preparing for a night out that might involve dancing he was girded with at least three changes of starched collars in his supplies, as these were the items that suffered during his sessions of raucous (and probably embarrassing) 'hop' dancing. Following the new fashion he shaved off his moustache. He was still somewhat of a schoolboy at heart but a perceptive and visionary schoolboy who saw aircraft like stagecoaches not ocean liners, requiring proper commercial pilot status and pay, airports and all that that entailed. He embarked on his successful and illustrious career in the growing field of civil aviation.

He collected comments people made about him and took delight in them. His favourite was a report that the chauffeur of the embassy car in Paris (who knew that Brancker had had a fortunate escape by not boarding a flight that crashed) said 'You can'ardly believe 'e's an important man – I bet they talk more about his eyeglass than 'im when he dies.'

In 1922 Sefton formed a liaison with Auriol Lee, the very popular stage actress. Sefton sought divorce and was angered when May refused, although it did both him and Auriol the service of not having to commit to and face a formal relationship. Self sufficient, Auriol was not a strain on Sefton's income or his financial obligations to his family and so on a practical level, as long as he lived at the Club, no social norms were strained.

After Charles Augustus Lindbergh collected his brand new unique 'Spirit of St Louis' from Ryan Aircraft in California, he flew it to St. Louis for his backers to see their investment and then flew it on to New York. He took off for his solo flight to Paris in the morning of Friday 22nd May 1927 and later that day the Boeing 40A, the company's first passenger carrying aircraft, completed its first test flight. However, the single seat Douglas M-2 was ordered as the replacement for the

De Havilland DH 4 mail plane services. America had, finally, completely woken up to the age of aviation. Everybody in the world wanted to meet Slim, the Lone Eagle. And, of course, Sefton Brancker was at Croydon on the Sunday 29th to welcome Lucky Lindy when he arrived in England. While Charles's flight was an amazing success in an aircraft with a periscope as the only means of forward vision, it is strange that the feat of one man flying across an ocean 7 years after two men flew across that same ocean should be considered so extraordinary and that the later event should totally eclipse the former.

There were also those wishing to be critical of the aerial policy and potential. Charles Grey Grey, the aeronautical journalist who was known as CG to one and all would repeatedly question policy while Marion Whiteford Acworth as late as 1927, in her book *The Great Delusion* which was written under the pseudonym 'Neon', questioned the potential of aviation, to which Sefton Bracker quipped 'it is widely read and given a great deal of publicity but I doubt it has cut much ice, Neon is a particularly good non-de-plume – a light which attracts a lot of publicity but gives no illumination.'

Sefton, 'W.S.B.' as he often signed himself, championed women pilots, assisting Amy Johnson before she became so famous with important introductions during her preparation for her epic Australian flight. He was at times ferried to various engagements by Winifred Evelyn Spooner and saw women pilots as better than many men. Sefton was a close family friend of the Blackburns, knowing them for their Leeds-based aerial activities before World War I. Jessy Tryphena Thompson (Jessica Blackburn) was flying before the war and became the wife of Robert Blackburn of the Blackburn Aeroplane and Motor Co. They met due to their common interest in aviation. Indeed Robert's first government contract to build aircraft was announced in a telegram from Winston Churchill at their wedding reception on 31st October 1914 and they postponed their honeymoon to finalise the aircraft order in London. At the beginning of October 1930 Jessy drove Sefton to Cardington, Bedfordshire, England for him to travel in the largest airship the world had ever seen, the R101, on its maiden flight to India. Together with the Air Minister Lord Christopher Birdwood Thomson, Brancker was killed when the R101 crashed near Beauvais, Allier, Auvergne, France on 5th October 1930. He is buried in the churchyard of St. Mary's, Cardington.

This famous and tragic story of the R101 and its fateful flight is the subject of many books. It underlines how simple a steerable streamlined gas container supporting engines and passengers sounds to the layman but how technologically difficult they can be to produce and operate. Some of the scrap metal salvaged from the wreck of the R101 was bought by the Zeppelin company and it is possible, just possible, it was reprocessed and used in the construction of their 'Hindenburg'. In the anguished wake of the R101 crash, the second dirigible to be lost was R100, which featured Barnes Neville Wallis's geodetic structure on which Nevil Shute Norway worked and that had flown to Canada and back. It was broken up for scrap.

At the beginning of World War II Nevil worked on the design of a gliding bomb. Of course he dropped his surname and became famous as the writer Nevil Shute and not as an engineer. With the Hindenburg disaster on 6th May 1937, the era of these hydrogen passenger airships ended.

So those were Low's three generals, Caddell, Pitcher and Brancker. In contrast to these three career soldiers, Archibald Montgomery Low, the least likely military man, was destined to be the one who served in all three branches of the British armed forces and in a number of weapons development organisations. In later life he was proud to say that he had served in the British Army, the Royal Flying Corps, the Royal Air Force and in the Royal Navy Volunteer Reserve. From first to last he was an inventor. He knew invention to be an illusive concept that required the right conditions to grow. He had experienced the frustrations of the brilliant idea without the wherewithal to produce a marketable end product. At the outbreak of the war it became desirable to 'invent' a role in the services to suit your talents before the services chose one for you. Abstaining from service became less and less socially acceptable. In Archie's case, in a happy coincidence, the military imperative and the personal preference converged.

These generals that Low recalls were the principal officers involved in and controlling the various resources involved with the AT development, in common with their brother officers running the rapidly expanding RFC had great responsibilities that they were overseeing at this time. It is remarkable that, in the midst of fighting an existential war, the Army sanctioned and supported the development of drone technology when it was still experimenting with and being criticised in the country for the lack of performance of its earliest aircraft designs being provided to its airmen. So let us not forget that the first drone was a British Army project.

CHAPTER 7

The Aerial Threat Over Britain

At the start of the 20th century the world was being exposed to the implications of flight, initially by the authors of science and future fiction. One of the themes that emerged was the military potential of this new dimension. Many examples exist such as LeRoy (Roy) Elisha Norton's book *The Vanishing Fleets* that appeared in 1908.

In Britain at the start of the 1900s, the English Channel had ceased to be the historic first line of defence for the country. Airships became more capable and from 1909 after the Channel flights of Blériot, Rolls and others, aircraft were added to the potential threat. The islands had lost their isolation and Britain was vulnerable like never before. That same year, 1909, the film *The Airship Destroyer* was released. Like most titles produced at the time, *The Airship Destroyer* is a short film. It contained an animated portrayal of aerial bombing from airships and a missile attack on them. Quaint and unsophisticated by today's standards, these visions of aerial bombardment were shocking at the time for a public that had probably never seen a flying machine of any sort – or seen a moving picture for that matter. In the film, a fleet of airships bomb the homes and kill civilians until the hero launches his guided missile and brings down the foe. It also depicts another imagined invention; a form of armoured car. In his 1907 book *The War in the Air*, H. G. Wells had a similar horrified reception to the concept of aerial bombardment by the more bookish section of society.

Meanwhile and back in the real world outside the cinema, 'sausages' (balloons and dirigibles) had not previously been thought by the public to have significant military potential. They had been flying for many years and were a growing force for good which offered the possibility of faster worldwide travel without the rigour of a sea voyage. There were many successful craft built in the 1880s and 1890s. On 22nd September 1885, 'La France' was the first to demonstrate sufficient control to complete a circular flight. For the wealthy few in the inter-war years, airships fulfilled this promise of faster travel with their timetabled routes rivalling the great liners in comfort and service.

In Britain, Laffan's Plain in Farnborough, adjacent to the British Army head-quarters at Aldershot, had in 1897 been a suitably large and vacant site to assemble the 27,000 troops for the review by Queen Victoria as part of her Diamond Jubilee celebrations. It was decided that this would be a good site to research, make, test and exercise military balloons. By the time of this decision in 1907, the 'Plain' had reverted to type and become a wooded area. To clear it in a reasonable time the General Officer Commanding, General Sir Horace Lockwood Smith-Dorrien decided to exercise the artillery. The forest was bombarded for 6 hours which created a cleared flying ground for the Aldershot complex. The whole area between the Swan Inn on the Farnborough Road across to Eelmore Flash on the Basingstoke Canal was made available and this is now the site of Farnborough Airport.

In their efforts to match the German technology, it was here that the army built their balloon factory, using hundreds of surplus ancient virtually indestructible teak wood naval gun carriages in the foundations because of the boggy conditions. British military airships were designed and built in this facility and it was where Samuel Franklin Cody (Cowdery) built the British Army Aeroplane No 1 biplane that made the first sustained powered flight in the United Kingdom on 16th October 1908.

From discovering new compounds and novel uses of the properties of existing materials, to the formulation of processes making affordable new materials, developments in materials science have always underpinned the march of innovation. Balloon making was a specialised business and James Lethbridge Brooke Templer was in the army's vanguard of balloonists. A Trinity College man he was a senior army officer, an inventor and innovator; added to which he engaged in the unconventional. He recruited to his cause a family with a particular skill in the manufacture of balloons. In the 1800s London's poor eked out a living in whatever way they could and many laboriously processed skins and pelts for the clothing industry and other uses. A specialised product was gold leaf which required Goldbeater's skin, the cleaned outer membrane of ox intestines, for use in the beating process. This skin was an impervious, tough, tenuous, light, tear-resistant material, ideal for making gas-tight bags for the niche market in toy and decorative balloons. In the 1850s in Islington, Ann, a London lass in her twenties, fed herself and her children by working as a balloon and globe maker. Her husband, Casimir Frederick Lewis Weinling was born in 1807 in Pfettisheim in the Alsace in France and he had joined in the great economic exodus from the region in the early 1800s, bringing his Goldbeater's skin process to Britain. He and Ann married on 20th August 1843 at St Pancras Parish church, Camden.

The method of producing gas-tight joins between the skins became a family secret. Templer first employed the Weinlings around 1890 at the small Royal Engineers balloon section at Chatham and then at Farnborough. Ann had trained her children and grandchildren in the art and this family's labour was needed at Farnborough in 1907 to make the Nulli Secundus II, the factory's first successful airship that was officially designated British Army Dirigible No 1. To build it, the gas cells required three layers of very thin Goldbeater's skins.

The unusual attracts rumour and in this all-male security-sensitive army balloon factory myths grew around the tight knit civilian 'French' family that ran the skin shop almost as a private domain and resisted all attempts to disseminate their knowledge and skill with the skins. Some said that they originally came from the infamous lawless old sanctuary area of Alsatia in London. While they were employed by the Royal Engineers in Hampshire, they lived at the rather less fanciful address of 3 Prospect Place in Cove, Farnborough. Ann's grandson Robert had enlisted in the Royal Navy when they were at Chatham and had served for seven years before being invalided out and returning to work in the skin shops. Indeed, they were not such an unusual family, except for the historic place they deserve in Britain's aviation history. By 1915 the family had moved back to London and Robert's father Fred and mother Elizabeth resumed their balloon business at their home in 94 Rhodes Street in Holloway. Robert, who then lived in Camden Town, joined the Territorial Force with service number 4890 on 16th July. Occasionally, Weinling's ornate globes still appear in the fine art auction rooms.

By 1912, the Germans had also adopted this material for their Zeppelins, exhausting the available supply as about 200,000 sheets were used for a typical World War I Zeppelin. Unfortunately, the other main large-scale use of ox intestines was to make sausages, which put a strain on the available supply. This was especially noticed by the public in the German-administered areas where, as a result of priorities for airship production, the authorities choose to introduce a ban on the use of these skins for sausage making.

Under the British Aerial Navigation Act of 1911, the Home Office was made responsible for the protection of people on the ground and the Board of Trade assumed responsibilities relating to the registration and certification of aircraft and pilots. The aviation press assumed that this was a panic measure to implement controls before the coronation of George V. Mr. Churchill spoke of the regret that would be felt over anything which would 'hamper the development of this vast new science, which the government believed was fraught with immense consequences to the future of the people of these islands.' He repeated that the bill must be regarded merely as a temporary measure.

The Aerial Navigation Act of 1913 was passed earlier in that year when control was transferred to the secretary of state for war indicating which way the wind was blowing. It was portrayed in the press as 'Legislation Against Hostile Aircraft' and was largely concerned with defence matters, introducing prohibited areas, corridors of entry into the country's air space and compulsory landing grounds. The legislation described signals to be given to aircraft flying in from abroad or those flying over designated areas requiring them to land and allowing them to be fired on if they did not comply. Some of the press questioned why foreign visitors flying aircraft should be controlled as it would mean that British flyers abroad would be controlled. They also mused on how aircraft would be signalled, sarcastically suggesting such things as smoke signals. On 22nd September 1913, a ban was placed on flights over London within four miles of Charing Cross.

The King's Counsel, Roger William Wallace, who was the chairman of the Aero Club of the UK, presented a paper on 19th November 1913 titled 'The Right To Fly' to the Aeronautical Society of Great Britain at the Royal United Service Institution in Whitehall, questioning the adequacy of the three-mile limit to provide sufficient protection for any nation under sudden attack and pointing out that a 20-mile limit would hardly give sufficient security. He concludes that the position of Great Britain and France at Dover would be difficult for diplomatists to settle and that the international community was only just waking up to this new reality and starting to address the complications accompanying this technology.

Germany's progress in aerial capability was of great interest. By 1909 their military operation of dirigibles was centred in Metz but routine exchanges of technical detail across national borders still took place, with the reporting of details such as the speed of 75–80 km/h achieved by Z8 on its flight from Friedrichshafen to the military base at Potsdam on 7th February 1914, the details of the major redesigns approved by Admiral Alfred Peter Friedrich von Tirpitz in March following the destruction of the naval airships L1 and L2 and the delivery of Z7 to the German military authorities.

The programme of the summer meetings of German naval architects was opened by the King of Württemberg on 27th May 1914. All of their meetings were comprehensively reported in Britain including the 11th meeting on Thursday, 28th May which was held at the Zeppelin Works in Friedrichshafen with papers read by Count von Zeppelin and Herr Claude, Claudius Honoré Désiré Dornier.

Dornier went on to become a pioneer of stressed-skin monocoque aircraft construction and Zeppelin soon became a generic name for all German airships although the Luftschiffbau Schütte-Lanz Company designed and built some of those used during the war. Professor Johann Schütte was the designer and Dr Karl Lanz had the manufacturing facilities, including a wood supply business providing the material for the framework of these vessels.

Following Britain's declaration of war with Germany on 4th August 1914, British war measures included a ban on civil aviation except for flights within three miles of a recognised aerodrome.

From 1915 onwards, Dr. Ernst H. Ludwig Dürr was Zeppelin's technical director and the chief designer of their airships. He would remain with the Zeppelin company until 1945. The biggest of these German airships was truly gigantic, adding to the feeling of impotence and fear by those below. A Boeing 747–400 Jumbo Jet is nearly 71 metres long but for instance, the Zeppelin L57, launched in 1917 was more than three times longer at over 742 feet (226 metres). All of those launched after 1913 were over 500 feet (152 metres) long, and there were a great many of them.

An early attempt in the war to thwart the airship threat indicates how aware the British Flying Services were of the German airship facilities and the threat these craft posed to their nation. On 22nd September 1914, Charles Herbert Collet, flying one of a number of Samson's Eastchurch RNAS Squadron aircraft that took part in a raid on Düsseldorf and Cologne, dropped several bombs on the Zeppelin sheds at Düsseldorf. The RNAS mounted another raid on Düsseldorf on 8th October. Then, in the first clear weather following fogs and gales when parts of Flanders were flooded, the raid on the Zeppelin facilities at Friedrichshafen was widely reported in the British, French and German press. Unsurprisingly, the various accounts of this 21st November 1914 attack were somewhat contradictory. One from the *Daily Chronicle* correspondent at Basle was most encouraging from the Allied viewpoint. It did however report the downing of one of the British raiders flown by Commander Edward Featherstone Briggs. He was taken prisoner and needed hospital treatment for severe head and hand wounds.

Realising that a practical seaplane needed to be transportable, in 1913, from their London address at 56 Prince of Wales Mansions, Queens Road, Battersea Park, all three of the Short brothers including Horace Leonard patented their folding wing mechanisms. A hinge design on the rear wing spar and a tongue and socket connector arrangement on the front spar allowed the wing to be folded back or locked securely in its flight position. The cut out behind the hinge that was essential to allow folding was automatically filled when the wing was swung forward by a wire connected across the gap at the trailing edge which supported a fabric gusset covering the gap. With their wings folded back along the fuselage, the aircraft could be transported but rapidly deployed and recovered with these build-in patented devices. The Royal Navy were able to mount their first ever shipborne aerial attack on Christmas Day 1914. During the operation, ships in the supporting fleet were attacked by a Zeppelin and by German aircraft but they were not damaged. Seven Short Folder seaplanes were deployed from tenders into the sea and took off on a reconnaissance and bombing mission over the German naval and airship facilities in Cuxhaven. Three aircraft returned and were recovered. Three others were lost but their airmen were picked up by one of the ten submarines accompanying the force. The seventh aircraft and its pilot was posted as missing, to the great distress of the mother who had taught its pilot to fly. The boy was Francis Esmé Theodore 'Cecco' Hewlett, the son of Hilda Beatrice Hewlett, the first British women to gain her flying ticket number 122 on 29th August 1911. She owned and operated a flying school and in 1912 opened the Hewlett and Blondeau aircraft factory at the Omnia Works, at 2–16 Vardens Road, a disused ice-skating rink in Battersea, London. The firm built a new factory at Oakley Road, Leagrave near Luton in Bedfordshire and moved there in 1914. 'Cecco' Hewlett had ditched in the sea near a Dutch trawler on which he was obliged to stay until it finished its fishing trip. When news came that he was safe in Holland, he received a telegram: 'I am delighted and greatly

relieved to hear that you are safe, and heartily congratulate you.—GEORGE R. I.'
Francis returned to England on Sunday 3rd January 1915 and he was perhaps lucky
not to have been interned in Holland. 'The Hague Rules of Air Warfare' weren't
formulated until 1923, seeking to clarify the status of downed airmen who found
themselves in a neutral state but, even then, subsequent cases occurred where their
status remained questionable.

Despite the risk to the precious aircraft and crews, the perceived level of threat
posed by the Zeppelin weapons warranted these two operations on Düsseldorf, the
one on Friedrichshafen and the Cuxhaven raid. The experience gained in this first
engagement of the British fleet with the German aerial forces and the intelligence
gathered by the RNAS aircraft over Cuxhaven was thought to have been of great value.

In the scramble to equip squadrons at the outbreak of the war two prototypes of
the Bristol Scout aircraft had been despatched to France for evaluation. These were
rechristened 'Bristol Bullets' when they got to France. These were used for other
attacks on Zeppelins and their ground facilities. One of these involved Lanoe George
Hawker who had learned to fly before the war and was one of the first pilots in the
war on either side to engage an enemy in combat, along with of course the German
he attacked! He was with No. 6 Squadron and on 22nd April 1915 he was awarded
the Distinguished Service Order for consistent bravery and for his action on the
18th of that month when he attacked a German Zeppelin shed at Gontrode, near
Ghent, by dropping hand grenades at low level (below 200 ft) from his B. E.2c.
He had mistakenly believed that the three-engined type 'M' LZ 35 was there. He
used a tethered German balloon to help shield him from enemy ground fire as he
made successive attacks.

Hawker became the first British ace. On 26th April 1915 he was wounded but,
although he had to be lifted into the cockpit, he insisted on flying the next day
as these early days of the second battle of Ypres had become so critical. With his
engineering bent, Hawker and Air Mechanic Ernest John Newell Elton modified
his Bristol Scout aircraft by fitting a Lewis machine gun firing obliquely, strapped
on the side of the fuselage. Another pilot in the same squadron, Felton Vesey Holt
had had two rifles mounted in similar fashion on his aircraft.

On 25th July, the day the Germans' new secret weapon flame thrower was
used for the first time in the war, Hawker was flying alone when he attacked three
German aeroplanes in succession, all of which were armed and had two crew. The
first managed eventually to escape, the second was driven to ground damaged, and
the third, which he attacked at a height of about 10,000 feet, was driven to earth
on the British lines, the pilot and observer being killed. For this action Hawker was
awarded his Victoria Cross, the first given for combat between aircraft. After his 7th
victory on 7th September he returned to Britain to form No. 24 Squadron where
he issued his operational order 'Attack everything'. Flying in a DH2 south of Ligny
on 23rd November 1916 he became the 11th victim of that most famous German

ace, the Red Baron, Manfred Albrecht Freiherr von Richthofen's Albatros. After a half hour duel Hawker's engine began to fail and he dived for the British lines but was shot in the head before he could escape.[1]

Another opportunist attack on the airship menace had a tragic post-script. On 7th June 1915, Reginald Alexander John Warneford, an officer of the RNAS flying a Morane-Saulnier Type L chased the German airship LZ 37 from the coast of Belgium near Ostend to Ghent where 'Reckless Rex', as he was known, succeeded in dropping his bombs on it. LZ 37 crashed but the airships explosion stopped his engine. He landed behind enemy lines and 35 minutes later he managed to restart the engine and return to base. He won the Victoria Cross and the Légion d'honneur but just after receiving the French award on 17th June 1915 he was killed when his aircraft broke up after take off.

The German aerial campaign against the British was approved by the Kaiser at the start of 1915. The Kaiser and the Crown Prince were vilified in Allied countries, accused in what we would now call the tabloid press, of the most heinous war crimes. The first air attacks on Britain were on 19th January when airships LZ 24 and LZ 27 bombed King's Lynn and Great Yarmouth. A third Zeppelin involved in this raid, LZ 31, had to turn back.

Warneford's memorial (Grace's Guide to British Industrial History)

Warneford's fame outlived him. His picture was so well known his name did not need to be on this recruitment poster (Library of Congress, Prints & Photographs Division, WWI Posters LC-USZC4-10972)

The Admiralty were responsible for the defence of London by dint of the tasks assigned to the RNAS. In September 1915, the Zeppelin raids over London prompted Arthur James Balfour, who had taken over from Churchill as The First Lord of the Admiralty, to order the creation of the London Air Defence Area under Admiral Sir Percy Moreton Scott, the gunnery expert who also invented coding machines.

LADA inherited the Metropolitan Observation Service (MOS) and the Air Bandit Reporting System (ABRS) organisations.

Subsequently, in February 1916, the army assumed the responsibility for the defence of Britain's skies while continuing to support their troops overseas. The RNAS then concentrated on controlling the seas and carrying out longer-range operations.

Effective defence against the Zeppelin raids was very difficult in 1915 and into late 1916. Aircraft were not much faster than these dirigibles. It took First Lieutenant Warneford 45 minutes to catch up with LZ 37 before he could attack. These ships of the air relied upon their engines to maintain steerage and control. They flew at over 10,000 feet but they could be terrifyingly silent if atmospheric effects deflected the noise of their engines and they were so gigantic that they could appeared to be menacing close overhead. Their shape was hard to distinguish in the night sky and it was just luck if they were caught by a searchlight and could be engaged by the anti-airship guns. Added to the difficulties of location and altitude was the lack of defensive aircraft as most of the available machines were at the front in Belgium and France. Initially, even if a fighter could intercept an airship, its guns were not effective, merely punching holes in a gas cell that could easily be patched and sealed by the crew.

The authorities and many private organisations operated blackouts that gradually became more widespread and effective. For example, some railway authorities required the passengers to close the carriage blinds when the train left the station. The night raids were announced by the police and special constables rushing around the streets and later in 1917, by the firing of warning rocket maroons. Youth organisations like the Boy's Brigade and the Scouts would give the warning on their bicycles, and their bugles later on would sound the All Clear. As to the effectiveness of the warnings, the London City Coroner remarked at one of the multiple air-raid inquests that 'he had never heard the syrens [sic], and the previous day he heard no sound signals, nor saw any coloured smoke.' As to the suggestion of the Lord Mayor for the tolling of St. Paul's bell, when it had been rung the Coroner said, 'he had sat at that court for sixteen years and had never heard the bell.' London did whitewash the line of the kerbstones 'to form a safe and sure mark to the unwary pedestrian using the darkened streets.'

The public were made aware with information notices and the raids were used on posters to bolster recruiting but WWI air-raid precautions never approached anywhere near the formality and legal obligation of those of WWII. The spring of 1916 was hard. The fatherly face of the war in Britain, due to his appearance on the recruiting posters, the prominent Field Marshal, Lord Kitchener had been killed. Conscription had to be introduced, having been unnecessary up until March 1916 due in most part to Kitchener's success in recruiting volunteers.

From 7th August 1916, the British public were exposed to the reality of the war in France. The cinemas, now such a part of the social fabric, were showing the

MILITARY SERVICE ACT, 1916

Every man to whom the Act applies will on Thursday, March 2nd, be deemed to have enlisted for the period of the War unless he is excepted or exempt.

Any man who has adequate grounds for applying to a Local Tribunal for a

CERTIFICATE OF EXEMPTION UNDER THIS ACT

Must do so BEFORE

THURSDAY, MARCH 2

Why wait for the Act to apply to you? Come now and join of your own free will. You can at once put your claim for exemption from being called up before a Local Tribunal if you wish.

ATTEST NOW

1916 military service act poster (Library of Congress, Prints & Photographs Division, WWI Posters LC-USZC4-10943)

footage taken by Arthur 'Geoffrey' Herbert Malins and John Benjamin McDowell (Mac) that had been compiled into the film of the Somme Offensive, *The Battle of the Somme*, a battle that would continue until November. The film, which ran for over an hour, had an immense social and political impact. Its effect, combined with other factors such as the ability of the 'Sausage Eaters' to bomb the British population with apparent impunity, made this second autumn of air raids hard to bear.

The mood change was reflected in popular song and the literature. The poetry took on a more sombre mood. People had quipped lightly of 'sausage and mash' to describe an airship manoeuvring through the clouds, but no longer. To top it off, the weather had been poor all summer and apart from the odd few days was now showing every sign of entering into an early winter. Things were at a low ebb.

Sixteen airships, twelve from the German Naval Airship Division and four from the Army Division, took part in a mass raid on England on the night of 2nd September 1916. One of these was the wooden-framed Schütte-Lanz SL 11 which had just bombed St. Albans when it became the first raider to be shot down over England. It was intercepted over Cuffley in Hertfordshire by Lieutenant William Leefe Robinson in his B.E.2c night fighter. This first successful use of aircraft against Zeppelins attacking

The New Empire,
MARKET THORO'FARE, BURY ST. EDMUND'S.

6.30 TWO PERFORMANCES NIGHTLY. **8.30**
Full Matinee, Variety & Pictures, Wednesday,
And Picture Matinee Saturday, at 2·30.

Showing MONDAY and all the week,

THE BATTLE OF THE SOMME

The most wonderful film ever produced.
KING GEORGE says: " It shou ld be seen by EVERYBODY."
In addition to the above, other in teresting films will be shown, viz. :—

MONDAY, TUESDAY, and WEDNE SDAY,
OUR FIGHTING NAVY (Drama).
THE INDIAN ARMY AT THE FRONT (War Topical).

THURSDAY, FRIDAY, and SATUR DAY,
SONS OF THE SEA (1,000 feet Drama).
MILITARY SKIERS (War Topical).
THE WRECKED ZEPPELINS IN ESSEX.
GAUMONT'S GRAPHIC NIGHTL Y.
For Times, etc., see small bills.
As many seats are already book ed, if you wish to avoid disappoint-
men, book your seats at once.

The Battle of the Somme advert

Britain was emphasised by the immediate celebrity accorded Lieutenant Billy Robinson after the event. He was awarded the Victoria Cross just 2 days after the action.

Initially SL 11 was mistaken for the Zeppelin L 21 (with a tactical number LZ 61). But the demise of LZ 61 occurred later on 27th November 1916 when it was one of a ten airship raid and on its departure for the homeward flight it was attacked by three RNAS aircraft, burst into flames and crashed into the sea east of Lowestoft.

Knowing about a threat is one thing; devising an effective defence against the threat is quite another thing entirely. Most Londoners had become aware that the practice of firing the anti-airship guns and the testing of searchlights at dusk occurred on nights when an air raid was likely. The British authorities knew when the Zeppelins were operating and in July 1919 Lord Weir explained that the German wireless stations radioed the airships their exact positions based upon direction finding (DF) by the ground stations from the airships' own regular transmissions. He did not reveal that they were also being tracked by the British DF system.

So it was that thousands were alert to the danger and witnessed the SL 11 descend in flames, seeing at last the results of an effective weapon being used against the airships. There were many reports of the downing of the airship in the media reflecting the psychological effect the two years of raids had on the seemingly defenceless population and recognising the significance, so soon after the event, of this new vulnerability of airships to attack by aircraft. These reports attempted to describe the sight of the SL 11 lighting up the darkness across a large part of London's dark night sky and they contained many eye-witness descriptions of its plunge to earth. As reported in C. S. Peel's *How We Lived Then,* one of these eyewitnesses said she

Wreckage of the German airship near the Plough Inn at Cuffley (Central News)

heard 'an odd chunkety, chunkety noise. It sounded as if a train with rusty wheels were travelling through the sky. I ran out on to the balcony and saw something which looked like a large silver cigar away to my left, and I realized that it was a Zeppelin. Almost immediately it burst into flames and the sky turned red. Then came the sound of cheering. It seemed as if the whole of a rather far-away London was cheering, and almost unconsciously I began to cry, "Hooray! hooray!" too.'

Another pilot said he was nearly at 10,000 feet and with two other aeroplanes getting close to the airship which was making frantic efforts to get away, producing a cloud of black smoke and firing its guns. The airship rose a couple of thousand feet and Robinson headed for the raider. The huge sheet of flame created a scene of terrifying grandeur. The 21-year-old Robinson concluded his report: 'I quickly got out of the way of the falling, blazing Zeppelin and, being very excited, fired off a few red Very lights and dropped a parachute flare.'

On that night it had taken young Robinson 53 minutes to reach his operational patrol height of 10,000 feet or put another way, it had taken him 21 years via India; public school; the Royal Military College at Sandhurst; wounds received while flying over Lille (France); the loss of both his close cousin and older brother in early 1916; pilot and operational training and the support of his base at Sutton's Farm airfield to reach this point. An elaborate early warning system of air raids, anti-airship ground

Zeppelin in heaven (Flight Global)

defences and routine night patrols by specifically designed single-seat night scout versions of the Blériot Experimental 2c had combined to put the lonely RFC pilot in his dark, cold, exposed cockpit within striking range of the raider. He had reached 12,900 feet in pursuit of the German machine that was being tracked by the search lights and bombarded by the ground forces. He had been in the air for 3 hours when he engaged the enemy, clad against the cold in bulky layers of cumbersome clothing, operating and reloading his upward firing Lewis gun while still having to control his plane. The airship was taking evading action and firing at him with its considerable weaponry. With very little oil and petrol left it was a further 30 minutes before he navigated the blacked-out countryside to land in the dark at his base where, on examination, his aircraft was found to have sustained significant damage from the airship's guns. Following this airship's demise, five more airships were destroyed before the end of 1916.

At last the tide turned against the airship raids on London and by the autumn of 1917 the German tactics had to change. The Luftstreitkräfte used aircraft, attacking with fleets of large Gotha and Giant bombers, but by then the improvements in British ground observation and the introduction of improved radio communications enabled interception by the defensive fighters. Nevertheless, the German aircraft raids proved far more deadly than the airships had been. The maroons continued to be fired to warn the population of further German airship attacks as they continued their operations in long range raids on Britain. Hull was bombed by two Zeppelins in March 1918.

German airships made their last attack on Britain on 5th August 1918 with a raid by four Zeppelins over the Midlands.

On a warm, sunny day in peacetime, an airship could have been described as graceful or majestic but for the watching public threatened by these impudent intrusions of seemingly invincible 'sausages', the overriding emotion was a deeply felt anger. Shot at by anti-airship guns from the ground and attacked by little aircraft, they had looked unaffected. These seemingly lethargic aerial slugs appeared almost ignorant of all attempts at defence from those they surveyed from their lofty vantage.

The truth, however, for those in the Zeppelins and Schütte-Lanz craft was somewhat different. In bitter cold conditions when flying high to avoid attacks, they had to navigate through the searchlights and patch holes created by wear, chaffing, frame movement and enemy action. Manning the defensive guns, finding targets and manoeuvring their giant weightless vessels in the turbulent void required skill and dedication while the cold and lack of oxygen sapped their concentration and strength. These were a different type of serviceman, enduring freezing temperatures for prolonged periods, clad only in their greatcoated uniforms. They had more affinity with their brother sailors than with airmen. It wasn't until 1917 that they were issued with fur-lined jackets. Hot drinks, particularly chocolate in Thermos flasks fortified, when allowed, with schnapps would have helped a little. Sandwiches were the only food consumed on their patrols. They were the first to fly and work for long periods at their operating heights around 11,000 feet; about the elevation of the world's highest communities where visitors usually require periods of acclimatisation. Later in the war they would fly even higher at up to 17,000 feet and not all of these Zeppelins carried oxygen. During the war, long periods at these altitudes would exhaust airmen of all the conflicting nations, producing cases of frostbite, severe headaches and light-headed dizziness. These conditions were tiring but off-duty airship crewmen could at least relax and sleep in hammocks. Most of the larger German airships in World War I had about 20 in the crew operating in two watches. These included the commanding officer, an executive officer and a warrant quartermaster-navigator, a warrant engineer, a sail maker and the machinists for the engines, with the remainder manning the helm and flight controls, guns and radio.

They were not fooled by any illusion of invincibility. They were very aware of the true flimsiness of their apparently 'solid ships' and were reminded, by the copper tools they used to maintain her, that fire was only an errant spark away. Airships were lost to structural failures and fire. Airships were fickle beasts and unforgiving to the inattentive helmsman. They rode the breeze if correctly trimmed but bucked and buckled if not gently handled.

In very different circumstances to those 'sailors of the air' and on the opposing side were the talented home-defence pilots facing the withering fire from the airship guns and the perils of night operations with rudimentary instruments for navigation and landing. These were not novice pilots on cushy home duties but some of the best, as night flying was a hazardous activity, generally to be avoided and only attempted by experienced pilots.

As recounted in Bloom's biography, Archie gave his personal account of a flight as an observer and of those training for night landings:

> On one occasion, I recollect, we had difficulty in getting back to the flying ground and as we hung in the wind at our maximum speed of about 90 m.p.h. I was able to watch the ambulance coming from its shed in readiness for our landing. Actually we alighted safely, but I found it extraordinarily difficult to concentrate … I can still see painted on the roof of a little chapel near the aerodrome the ominous words—'Prepare to meet thy God'! Those were very experimental days. Before practising night landings pilots used to tip the stoker at a local factory to make plenty of flame.

Backing up the Allies' anti-airship defences were the back-room boys assessing the aerial threat and devising systems of detection, targeting and engagement. Every opportunity to examine and understand the performance of the enemy's equipment was seized upon. Today we have named the process of analysing captured equipment 'reverse engineering' but it was a sophisticated process even in World War I and they called it 'common sense'. As an example, detailed drawings were made of the Maybach engine parts that were recovered from a Rumpler two-seater· biplane crash site. When the Maybach engines on the SL 11 were examined it was found that they were fitted with White and Poppe carburettors made in Coventry, England.

This process of examination yields estimates of the performance of the enemy's equipment but it also has the potential to indicate much more. For example it may expose strategic information such as material shortages that have forced the adversary to use less suitable substitutes or it may suggest improvements applicable to your own equipment.

Analysis of enemy weapons usually involved dissecting and documenting damaged remains. However, occasionally captured weapons were intact. On its third attempt to cross to France, a disastrous navigation error delivered a new undamaged Handley Page O/100 twin engine heavy bomber, its crew of five and all of its performance documentation onto the German airfield at Chalandry on the 1st January 1917.

In another example, crude deflector plates devised by Raymond Victor Gabriel Jules Saulnier and championed by the French ace Eugène Adrien Roland Georges Garros, when fitted to his aircraft's propeller blades enabled him to fire forwards

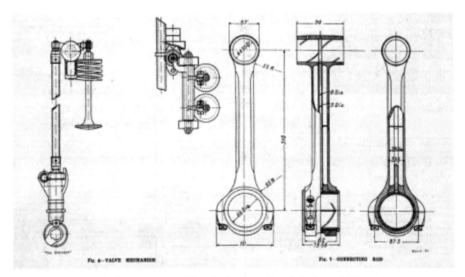

Maybach engine parts (Grace's Guide to British Industrial History)

through the propeller. The capture of his aircraft was probably responsible for the German forces realising that they had a proposed synchronising mechanism in their files. The use of this device contributed to the extended period of German air superiority known as the 'Fokker scourge' when Anthony Fokker's Eindecker scout 'fighter' aircraft, fitted with this system, were able to fire forward through the propeller while the Entente powers' aircraft could not.

On the Allied side there were the various inventors who developed and promoted their solutions to the problem of shooting down the German airships. Aircraft could just about reach the enemy's operating altitude but without an effective weapon, even if they got 'up close and personal' they were impotent. A weapon was required that would disrupt the airship's gas cells sufficiently to mix its hydrogen with air and to also supply a substantial source of ignition. That triangle of fire had to be created for the weapon to be effective.

In December 1915 the Royal Navy's Lieutenant Commander Francis Rankin patented a combined explosive and incendiary dart and a 'Dropping Box' containing 24 darts arranged in groups of three. When dropped from an aircraft, hoops on the dart's tail part deployed to snag onto the outer surface of the target. This tail housed the incendiary charge. The penetrating head separated from the tail part on impact and proceeded until a tether wire from the tail tightened and triggered its explosive charge deep inside the victims' structure. Francis was a wing commander in 1922 when he was awarded £2,250 for his dart invention after it was stated that the Airship L15 (Production Number LZ 48) was downed over the Thames Estuary on the 1st April 1916 by a Ranken dart (although it appears L15 had been hit and was descending before the dart attack).

The French Lieutenant, Yves le Prieur of Paris, invented his plane-mounted Fusées Le Prieur, allowing an airplane to fire a volley of rockets with cutting points to bring down observation balloons. To get his system accepted and overcome objections regarding the fire hazard to the attacking aircraft, he demonstrated his system by mounting a wing section armed with his rockets on a Piccard Pictet (Pic-Pic) automobile that could achieve a representative speed. These rockets were first used in April 1916 at Verdun. The British also used them and they proved to be remarkably effective against the German observation balloons but against airships they were not successful. Their use was only phased out when tracer rounds and incendiary bullets became widespread among the Allied air forces, and by 1918 they were fully withdrawn from service.

In this war of attrition and blockade, the provision of materiel and manpower was crucial. The supplies needed to make munitions was just one demand. In October 1916, the Empire Resources Development Commission was created. Its chairman was Alfred Bigland, the instigator of the Bantam battalions for shorter volunteers that had supplied additional manpower to the British Army. The ERDC became tarred with the brush marked 'exploitation' by the nationalist movements that were to emerge in many countries of the British Empire after the war but in the war it organised supplies of crucial commodities for Britain. The ERDC was involved in the procurement of fats and oils used in soap, foods and, of course, for lighting. A significant source of glycerine, with its many uses including munitions, came from the whaling industry in the South Atlantic where the humpback yielded the high glycerine content in its 'whale' or 'train' oil in which Britain had a virtual monopoly. A very large number of whales died in World War I.

Germany also needed supplies of glycerine. The Kadaververwertungsanstalt (Corpse-Utilization Factory) newspaper stories appeared in Britain in April 1917 purporting to explain where the Central Powers were obtaining their high explosives, oils and fats. They are considered to be baseless propaganda that may have originated as misinformation from John Charteris in British intelligence but were more likely to have originated as rumours that the British establishment did not quell. These 'Tallow Factory' stories were used by the Nazis in World War II to illustrate that the Allies always tell lies and thus to discredit the rumours of their atrocities when these started to circulate.

A number of explosives and propellants were available. In the mid 1800s, Alfred Bernhard Nobel concocted his more manageable nitroglycerine compounds; dynamite and then gelignite but he was then so stung by the premature publication of his obituary which stated 'Le marchand de la mort est mort' ('The merchant of death is dead'), he is said to have been prompted to create the Nobel prizes. Somewhat less well known is the lengthy acrimonious court action that Nobel fought and lost when he sued Frederick Augustus Abel over the patent for the low explosive propellant 'cordite' which Abel and James Dewar had patented.

John Fletcher Moulton was a barrister, and by the time the appeal was dismissed in 1895, he had acquired an intimate knowledge of the chemical industry over his years working on this Nobel patent case. When war was declared, Britain's reliance on imports from Germany of medicines and other chemicals became clear and Lord Moulton, as he was by then, chaired the committee advising on explosive supplies. His pragmatic approach during the initial years of the war involved forcing the maximum out of every source of supply for explosives production and to develop new sources. New mixes were formulated for particular needs, changed to speed up production or refined simply to substitute a more available ingredient for a scarce one; sometimes, this was done against the wishes of reluctant military customers, who were initially unwilling to compromise for the common good on the recipes for their particular explosives. In this period, the building of new factories and facilities, the training and employment of many thousands of new staff and the purchase of products from overseas put a great stain on the government's finances. It also put enormous stress on the workers in this dangerous industry and those scarce, crucial chemists in the back-rooms.

In 1892, Dewar invented the vacuum flask for his experiments and these became popular in the decade before WWI and enabled the Zeppelin crews to have warm drinks on their long cold missions.

Chaim (Charles) Azriel Weizmann was a chemist of Russian Jewish descent who arrived in Britain in 1904. He registered many of his papers and patents under the name Charles Weizmann. At Manchester University he developed an acetone–butanol–ethanol fermentation process which was bought to the notice of the Minister of Munitions, David Lloyd George, in 1916. Plants were then set up to produce acetone, a key ingredient for the cordite factories, from cereal crops and when these were in short supply, from acorns and chestnuts. In the autumn of 1917 children were organised through their schools and youth organisations to collect this unusual harvest of nuts in return for a small bounty paid by the government.[2]

While Britain still had its sea routes to the Americas, obtaining nitrogen products was not a problem and they could continue importing guano and saltpeter for the Allies' agricultural fertiliser and munitions needs. Germany was cut off from this supply by the blockade but they had Fritz Haber. In 1909 Fritz was working with Robert Le Rossignol, a British chemist from Jersey, and together they patented their process for making ammonia or in more dramatic terms 'making bread from the air'. By 1913 Fritz's method of nitrogen fixation had been turned into a cost-effective 'industrialised' process to create commercial quantities of ammonia. Haber was one of the 'Manifesto of the Ninety-Three' German scientist who supported their war from the beginning. Robert Le Rossignol had married a girl from Karlsruhr and stayed in Germany throughout the war. Fritz Haber became the 'father of chemical warfare' for his work on chlorine gases and also won his first Nobel prize for chemistry just after the war. Low declared in his book *Benefits of War* that Haber's high-pressure process to combine nitrogen and hydrogen was 'the greatest weapon in Germany's armoury.'

Even before the war it was a military and political imperative to devise defences to prevent the German airships bombing Britain with impunity. Every possible method to achieve this was explored, again and again. The RFC's Aerial Target was instigated on the premise that it would put an end to the airships' dominance of the skies over Britain. The solution to the Zeppelin threat in the end was a combination of early warnings prompting the dispatch of waiting patrol aircraft armed with suitable weapons – tactics that were developed under 'Splash' Ashmore's command and echoed 24 years later in the Battle of Britain.

Despite airships being full of highly flammable hydrogen and therefore being extremely vulnerable to even the smallest spark, they were incredibly difficult to shoot down. Just like invention they needed the right spark; a device that introduced enough heat and oxygen into the gas for it to ignite. Just like invention, the fire triangle needs all three sides to be present, in this case fuel, oxygen and the spark. A great and momentous blow could at last be wrought on the foe but it wasn't just a question of having the right weaponry. It was the right mix of incendiary and explosive ammunition concentrated at one point on the gas envelope coupled with a set of well-conceived and executed tactics that finally ended the terror of the mighty Zeppelins.

What was different about the first successful attack on a German airship bombing Britain to all of the previous encounters was the use of special ammunition developed by three inventors, Buckingham, Brock and Pomeroy. James Frank Buckingham was educated as a boarder at Kelly College, Tavistock in Devon and then gained a great deal of experience working in the motor car manufacturing industry in Coventry. He was 27 years old when he took out his patent in December 1914. It begins:

> This invention relates to incendiary shells, bullets, and the like, and it has for its object to provide a construction which will be safe to handle, simple to manufacture and effective in use.

By August 1916 he had filed three patents for improved versions of his bullet; the end result being an incendiary ordinance that was safe to handle with soldered windows in the casing that, when fired, were mechanically and thermally disrupted by the forces created by the rifling in the barrel of the weapon which exposed the phosphorus charge enabling it to react with the oxygen in the air during flight.

After the war James was rewarded with an OBE and continued as a very successful businessman emphasising his contribution to the war effort in his company's advertising. In 1920 the Royal Commission on Awards to Inventors granted him £10,000 for the incendiary tracer bullet.

However, the Buckingham bullet, as it came to be known, did not ignite the airship's gas. As the bullet flared on firing, its phosphorus charge was largely exhausted before reaching the target. It was still a useful addition as a tracer bullet.

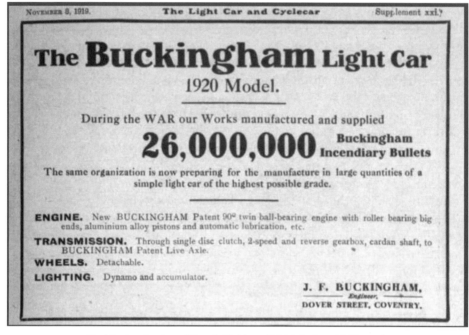

November 8, 1919.   The Light Car and Cyclecar   Supplement xxi.?

The **Buckingham** Light Car
1920 Model.

During the WAR our Works manufactured and supplied

26,000,000 Buckingham Incendiary Bullets

The same organization is now preparing for the manufacture in large quantities of a simple light car of the highest possible grade.

ENGINE. New BUCKINGHAM Patent 90° twin ball-bearing engine with roller bearing big ends, aluminium alloy pistons and automatic lubrication, etc.

TRANSMISSION. Through single disc clutch, 2-speed and reverse gearbox, cardan shaft, to BUCKINGHAM Patent Live Axle.

WHEELS. Detachable.

LIGHTING. Dynamo and accumulator.

J. F. BUCKINGHAM,
Engineer,
DOVER STREET, COVENTRY.

Buckingham's advert (Grace's Guide to British Industrial History)

Frank Arthur Brock was a director of the Brock family firm C. T. Brock & Co. which was founded in Islington, London in 1698 and was the oldest firework manufacturers in Britain. He served for a short period in the Royal Artillery before transferring to the Royal Navy where he joined the RNAS and was involved in the planning of the raid that bombed the Zeppelin sheds at Friedrichshafen. Frank was only 4 months older than Archie Low, was born within a few miles of Archie's birthplace and, like Archie, he served in all three services, the army, the navy and the RAF. Both he and Archie were involved in the military's experimental works, although Frank's was a navy establishment.

The Navy and the Ministry of Munitions were particularly interested in Brock's use of high explosives such as trinitrotoluene (TNT), amatol, ammonal and of course nitroglycerine and propellants with lower brisance, such as cordite. He was appointed as a member of the Admiralty Board of Invention and Research and was one of the founders of the Royal Navy's Experimental Station at Stratford in the East End of London.

Being very familiar with the use of compounds such as potassium chlorate employed in the manufacture of fireworks, he used a mixture of this in his design of an explosive bullet to down the German airships. The resulting ordnance was the Brock bullet, produced as a '.303' round and this was effective against the German airships.

Later in the war Brock's experimental unit was responsible for smoke screens and other distractions to be used on the Zeebrugge raid. The aim of the raid was to block the port of Zeebrugge to deny the use of this North Sea port to the Imperial German Navy, the Kaiserliche Marine. Operations in the Baltic and the bombardment of the ports on the Flanders' coast by the big guns of the British Monitors in 1917 had failed to significantly curtail enemy activity.[3] Operation *Hush*, the planned major offensive to advance up the Flanders' coast and take these ports was not pursued. From late 1917 onwards the German land forces had been greatly enhanced by reinforcements from their Eastern Front when Russia's involvement in the war effectively ceased. The threat of a major defeat in the anticipated German 1918 spring offensive was a great concern and the German U-boat operations were expected to intensify after the winter storms subsided.

The operation aimed to sink block ships filled with concrete in the canal and to destroy the lock gates, making the port and canals in Bruges tidal. On 23rd April 1918, over 200 British servicemen were killed in the raid and, although two block ships were sunk in the canal, they proved to be only a minor inconvenience to the Germans. In his *Flight* (1952) magazine article, Low talked about the assistance his Feltham Experimental Works gave Brock in his preparations for the raid, recalling: 'Rocket experiments were conducted under my own patents with the help of Cdr. Brock, a truly great man who lost his life at Zeebrugge. For that Mole attack I had prepared a radio-fired bomb device by which any one of a number of floating buoys could be selected and exploded by radio.'

When the RNAS merged with the RFC forming the RAF, Brock became a wing commander and a few weeks later he was granted permission to go on the Zeebrugge raid to examine a German range-finder that was on the Mole. At the age of 34, he was killed on 23rd April 1918 during the raid. The control of devices like these radio-fired bombs was subsequently defined in Patent 244, 498 'Control of Switches', submitted on 3rd September 1918 by 'Low, Captain in His Majesty's Army, of Royal Air Force Experimental Works, Feltham, in the County of Middlesex'.

After the war, the award commissions obviously attempted to minimise the cost to the treasury of all the claims that it considered. The Brock bullet, although it was not patented, did receive an award. Like Archie, Brock had been employed within the inventions departments so, had he survived the war, he would not have been entitled to claim. However, in this case, because the Zeppelins had represented such a threat to the public and Brock's sacrifice at Zeebrugge had been of such public interest, it had to consider the claim. The birth of Brock's daughter in November 1918 may also have been a consideration. The claim was successful and his estate received £5,000 plus a further £7,000 from the Admiralty. Sixty-year-old Mr. Herbert Dickinson of 144 West Green Road, Tottenham, who had raised patents in 1915 on a fusing mechanism for exploding bullets, also made a claim. His submission was based upon tests carried out on his invention to which Brock had access. Herbert considered this knowledge

PATENT SPECIFICATION

Application Date: Sept. 3, 1918. No. 14,314 / 18.

244,498

Accepted: June 2, 1919 (but withheld from Publication under Section 30 of Patents and Designs Acts, 1907 and 1919).

Authorised to be Published: Nov. 17, 1925. Date of Publication: Jan. 14, 1926.

COMPLETE SPECIFICATION.

Improvements in the Control of Switches or the like.

I, ARCHIBALD MONTGOMERY LOW, Captain in His Majesty's Army, of Royal Air Force Experimental Works, Feltham, in the County of Middlesex, do hereby
5 declare the nature of this invention and in what manner the same is to be per-

Figure 6 is a developed view on a smaller scale of Figure 4.

In carrying my invention into effect in one convenient manner as, for example, 45 in its application to the selective control of switches provided, for example, in

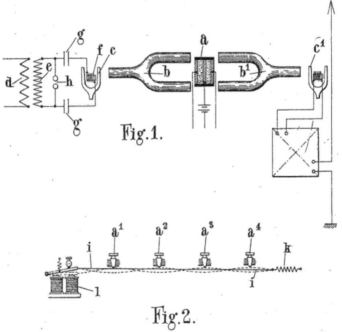

Fig.1.

Fig.2.

may have influenced Brock's bullet design. After due investigations, his claim was not successful although he did receive £100 from the Admiralty.

Along with Buckingham's incendiary tracer bullets and Brock's explosive bullets, Leefe Robinson's Lewis machine gun magazines also contained Pomeroy's explosive bullet. All of these three different types of bullet were considered to have contributed to the successful attack on SL 11 and subsequent downed airships. The RFC Feltham

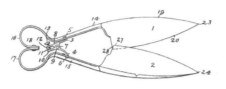

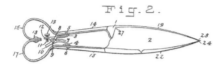

Pomeroy's shears patent

Pomeroy's bullet

Experimental Works undertook many tasks and one of these involved this Kiwi's invention. John Pomeroy was from the Southland in New Zealand's South Island and he invented various improvements to domestic items in his youth. He was living in Catherine Street, North Invercargill in 1902 when he patented an improvement to his country's most used tools; sheep shears. In that same year he read an article about balloons and airships and developed an exploding bullet to be used against these. Like the Buckingham bullet, Pomeroy's used the action of the rifling in the barrel to activate the round. The rifling spins the round as it is fired and Pomeroy's invention used the resulting centrifuge forces during flight to separate the mixture of nitroglycerine and the stabilising absorbent (such as Fuller's Earth). The nitroglycerine which was 74.6% by weight of the charge collected on the walls and thin front face of the round rendering it highly explosive and very sensitive to the slightest contact with the target, even, as his patent confirmed, an oblique contact.

Pomeroy, like the Wright Brothers, was unsuccessful for many years in getting any governments to buy his new development. In 1914, at the outbreak of war in Europe, John, who was then living in Australia, sailed to England in another attempt to sell his bullets. Unsurprisingly, as the prevailing view was that the 'war would be over by Christmas' and the Germans hadn't mounted any air raids on England, he was unsuccessful. When the war intensified in 1915 and the first bombs were being dropped, he finally succeeded in piquing the British Army's interest. Major Clarence Christopher Colley at the Ministry of Munitions, who was based at the Royal Artillery Mess in Woolwich, was so impressed with the bullet he arranged to test this ammunition on 'a range at Ealing'.

Archie Low remembered the experiments, as he reported in *Flight* magazine (1952):

> I ... made various experiments with the Pomeroy bullet, that very clever missile so constructed that it would explode on striking even the fine envelope of a Zeppelin. Some of these bullets had an unpleasant tendency to explode in the rifle breech, and I used to lean round a piece of boiler-plate before touching them off and hoping for the best. Pomeroy was a marvel; he made all his own materials with the help of his wife, working in the kitchen at home.

Archibald's Experimental Works at this time were 3 miles from Ealing so the range used by Colley and Low to test Pomeroy's bullets was probably the Haddon Engineering Works in Honeypot Lane, Alperton.

Working with Pomeroy, Major Colley's account is that they designed a number of modifications to the .303 bullets to accommodate the explosive and his Number 6 design became the production prototype. The design went into service in a slightly modified form as the 'PSA' (Pomeroy Small Arm). In the early summer of 1916 the RFC ordered 500,000 PSA bullets that were produced at the Nobel's Explosives Factory, Farm Hill Road, Waltham Abbey. Colley was nearly 'sacked' for distributing unauthorised ammunition while working on these bullet developments, whilst simultaneously being mentioned in Despatches for his valuable work in connection with the war. We saw this same pattern of compartmentalised discipline applied to Brab by 'Boom' Trenchard; chastised for the manner in which he achieved his objective but also, praised for doing it. Nevertheless, the Pomeroy bullet was deemed to be successful.

An alternative narrative of these events was given by Pomeroy who said his bullet was tested in 1908 by Lieutenant Ralph George Dinwiddie of HMS *Encounter* which was visiting New Zealand. When the war broke out, he travelled to London and on 27th August 1914 he submitted his bullet to the War Office at Adastral

House on Victoria Embankment as an anti-Zeppelin weapon but it was rejected and he returned to Australia. When the Zeppelin raids began he returned to England, with his wife Amy, by way of America. In trials at Fort Grange, Gosport on the South Coast in June 1915 it destroyed all the aeroplane wings against which it was directed and Colonel Ashmore at once reported the results. Eventually, at the end of the summer of 1916 he received an order from the government and his wife made the first 5000 bullets in a room at the top of Adastral House, which was lent for the purpose. He was awarded £20,000 for the invention (half of which went to pay off his expenses) and his wife received £5000 for her services. He said that 10,000,000 of the bullets had been made.

Perhaps a little of both accounts occurred, one being associated with the army and the RFC while the other was for the navy and the RNAS. This dichotomy may be another example of the growing rivalry and jealously guarded independence of these two services.

Mrs Amy Pomeroy was awarded the MBE for her services in filling the bullets with what her husband referred to as his 'dope'.

When the bullet went into production, Mrs Pomeroy worked with Kathleen Hamilton Devonald and 500 'girls' producing it. Kathleen, aged just 18, married Private James Henry Passfield in late 1916 and she was awarded the British Empire Medal for supervising this dangerous work.

The Pomeroy's story continued after the war. In February 1919 the papers all over Britain published reports about the theft of Pomeroy bullets being put up for sale to the Sinn Feiners and revolutionaries. This was followed within weeks by the report of John in the Old Bailey being acquitted on the charge of stealing a Ford motor car.

John went to America with the £25,000 award for his bullet design which was also the amount he received in 1919 for the sale in the US of his 'elixir of life' called puratone.

Back home in Melbourne, Australia in the 1920s, the Pomeroys went into the hotel and catering business. Outside Flinders Street Station, the world's busiest passenger station at that time, they ran an all-night pie-stall. 'Pop's Pie Cart' was drawn by a white horse and became a Melbourne institution. John 'Pop' Pomeroy, described as plump, round-faced and silver-haired, sold his pies, pasties, coffee, steak and kidney on toast and plates of peas through the night to the commuters and night owls.

In 1941, when he was approaching 70 and living in New Haven, Mitcham in the hills east of Melbourne's centre, he and Arthur William Parfitt of Stafford House, Norfolk Street, London raised a patent for 'Improvements in Explosive Projectiles'. You can't beat the spark of a dinkum idea when there is a war that needs it and an army to use it! There is that invention triangle again.

Pomeroy commented on the many years it took before his bullet was accepted. However, the questions of efficacy and legality were not simple.

This Is The Pomeroy Bullet

Mr Pomeroy with one of his bullets (National Library of Australia)

In addition to the technical approval of the newly developed .303 incendiary and explosive ammunition there were of course the Hague Convention agreements of 1899 and 1907 to consider before such ammunition could be sanctioned for use. John Hartman Morgan, the eminent lawyer, had considered the legality of the use of such bullets in 1915 in a section on unlawful weapons in *War: Its Conduct and Legal Results*. In the autumn of 1916, the RFC forbade the use of incendiary ammunition for air-to-air combat with another aeroplane. Their use against personnel was considered to be a violation of the St. Petersburg Declaration of 1863 that underpinned the Hague Conventions. However, the aerial weapons of the first months of the war included such rudimentary missiles as the 'flechette,' a small steel arrow used by French, Russian, and German aviators. When dropped from above on an unsuspecting soldier it could pierce his body from head to foot. In addition, in 1915 gas had been used as a weapon. In the autumn of 1916, permission was granted to deploy incendiary and explosive bullets against Zeppelins and balloons but this was restricted initially to use in Britain to shoot the gas chamber and not the crew. The pilots were required to carry written orders on their person when using this ammunition as a precaution; to protect them if the bullets were used near enemy territory where the airmen may have been taken prisoner. In his book, *Heaven High, Hell Deep*, Norman 'Jim' Silas Archibald talks at length about Operational Orders 38 and 39 requiring pilots to carry these papers when flying against balloons and airships and declaring that these regulations were rarely observed by the pilots.

Forty-four days after the approval for use of these bullets and 21 months after the first air raid on London, SL11 was destroyed. After the war, the Awards Committee took all aspects into consideration including the number of rounds ordered and they concluded that the Brock bullet was worth 31.35 per cent and the Pomeroy bullet 35 per cent. A Zeppelin was assigned an arbitrary value of £70,000.

After these British home defence successes against airships, the German air raids continued but they were increasingly undertaken by their bomber aircraft and Zeppelins were restricted to operations on very cloudy nights, which reduced their ability to locate their targets. As reported in *Flight* magazine, on 6th September 1917, Post-Admiral Reinhard Scheer, commander of the German High Sea Fleet, declared that Zeppelins were an excellent overseas weapon and hoped that the people of England will have further experience of them. 'But bad weather,' he added, 'is a handicap to Zeppelins, and I believe that the future belongs to aeroplanes.'

General 'Splash' Ashmore took command of the London Air Defence Area (LADA) in August 1917, a time when the German bombing campaign was being bolstered by their large long-range bombers, the Gothas and Giants. The defences were deployed in concentric zones around the city and information from the observation posts was passed to a central location and plotted on a map. These data relevant to each zone were then fed directly to that zone for them to direct their defensive forces of AA, searchlights and aircraft. They also included balloons where the tethering and additional wires formed barrages. However, the large German bombers operated at over 18,000 feet so the protective barrage would not have been that effective as even the largest balloons, used as they were in groups of three, could only reach to 11,000 feet supporting their weight of wires. However, these barrages were still deployed by General Ashmore preventing more accurate low-level attacks and they were much feared by enemy aircrew.

Ashmore became a leading figure in the air defence of the United Kingdom, founding what would eventually become the Royal Observer Corps. He was appointed to devise improved systems of detection, communication and control. The LADA was extended towards the coasts of Kent and Essex but this extended system was not fully working until the late summer of 1918 and the last air raid took place on London on 19th May. The lessons learnt were to prove valuable for the developments in the 1940s. Today we have surveillance, identification and interception protecting the UK airspace and, if required, the ground-based capabilities of 7 Air Defence Group (7 AD Gp).

When the 34-year-old Captain Philip Edward Broadley Fooks transferred from the Royal Garrison Artillery to the Anti-Aircraft Defences, Home Forces in June

1918, he suggested displaying the latest information graphically on a large horizontal map at central control near Horse Guards in Spring Gardens. This map was marked with a grid upon which different shaped and annotated pieces representing the airborne forces were colour coded to the clocks to distinguish fresh from older information and were manipulated with wooden rakes by operators guided by information read to them from the incoming reports by other operators. By WWII, the control room depicted in countless movies was essentially the same although now it was also fed with radar data. The markers still showed the size and direction of travel of the forces they represented and were colour coded to match coloured 5 minute clock sectors so that the difference between the latest 'green' and older 'red' data was distinguished at a glance and 'yellow' markers were used for information older than ten minutes that was being temporarily retained. Those directing the barrage balloons, anti-aircraft artillery, searchlights and aircraft defences did so while observing the developing situation shown on this map table. This was the system that existed at the end of 1918 and it was fed by information reported in a timely manner, principally over the dedicated telephone ABRS system. Captain Philip Fooks was in spirit 'one of the few' and also one of the much-maligned echelon of World War I back-room officers who fought the war behind the front lines and on the home front. Fooks had been a solicitor before joining up in World War I and ended his working life as a much-travelled director of an insurance company.

Early Warning is vital to all defence systems and in WWI the back-room boys of wireless Direction Finding (DF) would provide this while wireless communications required considerable improvement during the war to become effective for aerial work.

One of the first tentative steps occurred when John Ambrose Fleming of University College, London, a distinguished scientist in his mid fifties, wanted to accurately measure high frequency alternating currents. The best instrument available was a galvanometer but this device only responds to current flowing in one direction. He submitted his patent application on the 16th November 1904 for 'an appliance which permits the passage of electric current in only one direction and constitutes therefore an electric valve.' With his new 'appliance' in the circuit he obtained his reading on the galvanometer. This appliance was the first vacuum tube, the two electrode 'diode' that started the 'epoch' of electronics. In the new epoch of electronics that this began, this thermionic valve/tube age accelerated the development of radio and all that has followed and it lasted into the 1950s when we entered the 'solid state' 'semi-conductor' transistor age. From it would come an explosion of inventions and applications.

Another important radio engineer was Charles Samuel Franklin. He was born in London in 1879, the 13th child in his family. From this unpromising beginning, he started with the Wireless Telegraph and Signal Co. (the Marconi Company) in 1899 gaining experience in South Africa during the Boer War and invented important components of radio equipment prior to the war including the co-axial cable. Early in the war he went on Marconi business, sailing from Liverpool to New York on the *Lusitania*'s 201st Atlantic crossing, arriving on 24th April 1915.[4]

Reginald Aubrey Fessenden was another who made many contributions to wireless development, such as his highly sensitive 'liquid barretta' detector. He created receiver designs mixing the incoming signal with one produced in the receiver (a local oscillator signal) and named these 'heterodyne' systems. He recognised that it would not be possible to achieve the transmission of readily intelligible speech using any form of Spark Gap transmission and that voice communication would only be achieved if it was carried on continuous wave transmissions. He pursued solutions to many problems encountered in the creation of a continuous wave system. Along with Ernst Frederick Werner Alexanderson, who created an alternator with a suitable output to use as a high frequency continuous wave transmitter, they made 'one of the first quality audio' broadcast transmissions. Although Canadian by birth, Aubrey lived in the US and would have been only 20 miles from the Wright Brothers, first flights at Kitty Hawk, had he been home in Manteo North Carolina in December 1903. However, he was in London progressing his British patent for his 'liquid barretta'. As with many advances, Aubrey was not the only 'first' in the field of broadcasting. The Copenhagen-based engineer Valdemar Poulsen and Lee de Forest from New York made great progress around the same time. Poulsen was already famed for his magnetic wire recorder. In the process of his work, on 25th October 1906 de Forest patented his Triode valve and in 1907, by which time the valve was known as an Audion, he patented a refinement, naming his third electrode the 'grid'.

Two Italian engineers, Ettore Bellini and Alessandro Tosi, were based at 4 Rue du 29 Juillet near the Tuileries Garden in Paris in 1910 when they raised their patents. Their 'spark' was to devise a way of simplifying the equipment at Wireless Telegraphy Stations by arranging static aerials that combined to act as if they were an expensive and cumbersome (dirigible) steerable aerial. In 1912, they were associated with Marconi's when they developing their Bellini-Tosi based DF systems. This technology was not to be bettered until World War II when the High Frequency Direction Finding, HF-DF otherwise known as Huff-Duff systems were developed.

Henry Joseph Round, known to all as 'HJ', and George Maurice Wright[5] worked on 'valve' development and on the British network of DF stations. HJ was with the Marconi Company from 1902 and had patented a number of developments, including his form of the Triode valve. While working to refine the network of DF Stations, George Wright (a Marconi man from 1912) recognised they could also gather radio intercept intelligence and pin-point its source. This was the birth of Signals Intelligence (SIGINT). But the DF networks primary and crucial use remained the tracking of the enemies significant movable assets, particularly enemy surface vessels, submarines and those super-marine airships and aircraft. On the 30th May 1916 it was DF intelligence that alerted the British admiralty when the German fleet moved from Wilhelmshaven. What followed was the battle of Jutland.

Techniques that could create high (hard) vacua were patented in 1913 by Wolfgang Gaede from Freiburg in Germany and from 1916 by Irving Langmuir in Schenectady, New York State. Using these new vacuum techniques 'HJ' and other Marconi engineers produced a new range of higher performance and more reliable valves.[6]

Britain's 'back-room boys' were abreast of these new developments and their work on wireless communications was an important and fertile field of development. For a brief interval in 1910, Robert Bilcliffe Loraine became one of the first of these. He was a very successful, internationally renowned actor and an adventurous pilot. Although he was a civilian, he left his role in the West End to his understudy and joined the experiments on Salisbury Plain conducted by the London-based inventor Thomas Thorn Baker during the Army Manoeuvres in September. On the 26th, with the radio equipment installed in place of the passenger seat, he transmitted from his Bristol Boxkite aircraft, using his left hand on a Morse key while flying this frail machine for about a quarter of a mile. This was the first successful UK air to ground radio communication and it was received by the ground station specially set up at Lark Hill for the trial. The spark gap transmitter's aerial was about 65-feet long and was rigged from the aircraft's nose to its tail via the wing tip with the ground wire mounted similarly on the other side of the machine. At Larkhill a crystal detector was used in the receiver. This was 18 months before the RFC was created.

Marconi's Wireless Telegraph Company Limited started using the Brooklands site for their radio experiments in 1910 and before the war a Marconi engineer, James Darrington Bangay, designed another transmitter for airborne use. He produced a substantial book, *The Elementary Principles of Wireless Telegraphy*, which was published in 1914.[7]

From March 1913, all of the RFC's development work was under the command of Herbert Musgrave and, when Brooklands became an RFC base at the start of the war, the Marconi establishment and many of its staff at Brooklands were absorbed into the RFC's wireless research and training organisation. In the spring of 1915, Charles Edmond Prince took charge of the radio communication work. Prince was 41 and had worked for the Marconi company since 1907 where he had assisted 'HJ' Round developing those early electronic valves.

Prince's RFC unit was charged by Trenchard to produce, to a comprehensive and exacting specification, verbal (telephonic) two-way communication for aircraft to overcome the difficulty of using Morse code in the deafening, cramped cockpits.

Armed with the knowledge that they would have to use continuous wave designs, and with these latest valves, the unit's engineers (ranging from Robert Orme in his 50s to John Megarry Furnival and Edward Herbert Trump who were both born in 1892) strived to meet Trenchard's requirement for 'air to ground' and 'air to air' two-way voice communications, technically known as duplex telephony. Their Wireless Testing Park establishment was relocated from Brooklands to Joyce Green in August 1915 to eliminate the friction developing between the long-serving, regulation-bound Royal Engineers at Brooklands and the unit's more cavalier RFC experimental staff. The RFC radio training continued at Brooklands with the establishment of the Wireless School in November 1915. At the new site, Prince obtained the support of Hugh Caswall Tremenheere Dowding and they conspired to purloin the equipment Prince needed. Here at this Wireless Experimental Station on 20th September 1915 they were joined by Peter Pendleton Eckersley, another 23-year-old.[8] As the war progressed, increasing numbers of aircraft received more and more capable communications equipment. The unit moved again to Biggin Hill, arriving in early 1917 before this new site's official opening on St. Valentine's Day. By 1918, Trenchard's original aerial communications challenges were met.

Integrating these evolving wireless capabilities into meaningful and efficient systems was dangerous work on the front line. The first to use their wireless set in action observing for the artillery were 4 Squadron's Wireless Flight on 24th September 1914 during the first battle of the Aisne. These officers were Donald Swain Lewis and Baron (Bron) Trevenen James in their B.E.2as. They were at the forefront of the evolving close liaison between the RFC and Artillery, developing processes such as the 'grid square' map system. They were both killed while involved in their duties in aircraft bought down by ground fire. Baron's BE2a of 6 Squadron was hit on 13th July 1915 while engaged in Artillery Registration near Verlorenhoek. His aircraft caught fire at 6,000 ft and nose-dived. Lieutenant-Colonel Lewis was a much-valued wing commander when he was killed on 10th April 1916. The day before his fateful flight, Lewis had asked Trenchard if he minded him going up. Flying in a No. 1 Squadron Morane Parasol, he was killed along with his passenger Captain Arthur Witherby Gale of the 2nd Life Guards, the O.C. Trench Mortar Batteries, 3rd Div. Royal Field Artillery. They were flying over the northern end of the Messines ridge east of Wytschaete.

A large number of inventors worked on the problems of communicating vital information quickly to and from aircraft. Even Archibald Low, engaged as he was in all of the other tasks of his experimental works but never slow to spot a 'need', raised Patent 244,297 in August 1918 for a radio transmitted facsimile (fax) like system stating that the 'invention is of particular utility in the case of signalling from aeroplanes'.

Two years into the war, even the most sceptical old school in the army could not deny the importance of the aerial role in the battle on all fronts. This placed huge and increasing pressure upon the RFC's resources; a problem created by its own success. The primary motivation for developing the Aerial Target had been its potential use against Zeppelins but the airship threat was now contained. In this environment, where resources were so stretched, the continuation of the AT project must have been questioned. For it to continue as it did, it must have shown considerable potential. Indeed, this top-secret project engaged most of the top aircraft design teams (Sopwith, Folland, DeHavilland and others) to develop pilotless aircraft and their prototype aircraft were then fitted with sets of the Feltham Experimental Works, control systems.

The very success of air power in the war spurred on promising projects like the AT but it had a darker side. The insatiable demand for replacement aircrews placed enormous stains on those responsible for their training and a heavy, often fatal, toll on the recruits.

CHAPTER 8

Fatal Training

It is generally, frequently and rather sensationally stated that the life expectancy of a pilot posted to the front in World War I was 'just a few weeks'. What is not added to these statements is the caveat that the 'background' aerial mortality rates away from the front were significant and fatal accidents were almost a daily occurrence. In addition, there was the toll due to air raids that added to the carnage associated with aerial warfare. In such circumstances, there tends to develop within those most affected an inappropriate, almost insouciant bravado.

By the time war was declared, 47 more British subjects had died flying aircraft since the death of Charles Rolls in 1910. Three years later on the home front in Britain, details of coroners' inquests, normally reported in the press despite war time restrictions, contained daily accounts of aircraft fatalities.

The deaths of Capt. Patrick Hamilton and Lt. Wyness Stuart (The Graveley Accident) followed by those of Lt. Edward Hotchkiss and Lt. Claude Albemarle Bettington (The Oxford Accident) while flying to Army Manouevres in 1912 led to the RFC suspending flights and work on monoplanes. The subsequent monoplanes' report produced by the inevitable inquiry concluded that monoplanes were no more or less safe than multi-plane aircraft but it recommended that checks should be carried out on designs and major changes to all aircraft types. Of course there cannot be checks without a 'department' to specify and oversee the checks, so the Aeronautical Inspectorate Division (AID) was created in December 1913 with 28 staff. By the time of the Armistice in November 1918, it had a staff of 10,600.

The first RFC casualties of the war occurred on 12th August 1914 in the UK. The coroner's inquest tells the story of what happened:

> About a quarter past five o'clock Second-Lieutenant Robin Reginald Skene, of the Third Squadron, accompanied by Raymond Keith Barlow, a first air mechanic in the corps, ascended from Netheravon sheds in a Bristol monoplane which was ready for active service. That the aeroplane was not loaded to a dangerous extent is shown by the fact that several other machines left the school carrying similar weights without accident. The monoplane had not proceeded far on its journey when the pilot in taking a left-handed turn banked sharply. The result was that the machine lost speed and dived vertically to the ground. Lieutenant Skene was found under the

wrecked monoplane, while Barlow was pitched clear of it. Both died before medical aid could be obtained. The jury returned a verdict of accidental death.

The loss of aviators through injury and death in non-combat circumstances continued at a high rate throughout the war and those associated coroners' inquest reports in the press were depressingly frequent. Surviving recipients of the Victoria Cross show that the skilled, brave and experienced fared no better than the average. Rhodes-Moorhouse was the first and Warneford was the second V.C. awarded to the flying services. During World War I about 645 V.C.s were won of which only 19 were to members of the flying services. Of these, 8 died in their victorious actions or a subsequent enemy engagement, 7 survived, the last of whom died in 1988 but 4 died in flying accidents. One of these was Andrew (Anthony) Frederick Weatherby Beauchamp-Proctor, the 23-year-old air mechanic who was only five-feet two-inches tall. 'Prockie' became South Africa's leading ace credited with 54 aerial victories. His aircraft had to be modified; the seat was raised and blocks of wood were fastened on his rudder bars so he could operate them. He survived the war but was killed in a flying accident on 21st June 1921.

One reason for these high fatality rates is that few of those on board survived any significant failure on their aircraft. The newer and better machines tended to be deployed at the front line. The majority of aircraft on the home front were at either end of the infamous bathtub curve of reliability. The training aircraft tended to be obsolescent types with worn-out parts while new aircraft flying over Britain from the factories had been hastily readied for ferrying across to the fight and were untried machines with potentially fatal design or manufacturing flaws.

A tragic but somewhat bizarre accident in 1918 under the press headline 'The Looping Fatality at Brighton' was reported in *Flight* magazine on 18th July as follows:

> Ralph Sinde, a builders' foreman, was killed on 8th July by a sandbag, which fell from a machine which was looping over the town…. Police had been unable to get any trace of the pilot. The coroner said it did not seem to him that any military purpose could be served in 'looping' over Brighton. Something should be done to stop the practice unless it was absolutely necessary for military reasons.

With no enemy to fight in home skies unless there was a raid, with an audience on the ground, an over abundance of energy and new skills under their belt, those 'circus feats' of early flyers continued to inflate the death toll. Years later the famous phrase, 'There are old pilots and there are bold pilots, but there are no old, bold pilots' would become popular.

One of the experienced old school was Charles Gordon-Bell who according to Archie 'used to "loop" trembling observers within a few inches of the tarmac, once flew under the bridge at Brooklands, and on another occasion, after saying he could land in a hangar, only flew into one and out the other side – through the wall.' This crash had occurred on Friday 13th June, 1913. It resulted in the death of

Bell's passenger, Naval Lieutenant James Robert Branch Kennedy. The conclusion of the Accident Investigation Committee of the Royal Aero Club Report No. 14 was remarkably tolerant of Bell's behaviour in the atmosphere of the growing international tension, saying: 'The pilot, experienced and competent as he was, showed a grave error of judgement in flying as he did over and around the sheds at Brooklands… At the same time it should be pointed out that the practice of steeply-banked turns and close steering of aircraft may be highly valuable, provided this be done with due regard for the life and property of others.' Archie recalled that it may have been after an engagement recorded on 7th November 1915 when Bell landed in a tree at St. Omer that his commanding officer shouted, 'What do you think you are doing?' Bell replied, with his quaint stammer, 'I always l-l-l-land like that, sir'. Bell, who had flown one of the four B.E.2as of 'A' flight to France on the RFC's initial deployment in 1914, was another to die in an accident, flying in the prototype F.B.16E on 29th July 1918 in France.

The air raids over Britain during the war had a significant impact on the relatively few they directly affected but they probably gave those on the home front and those on the front lines a greater sense of unity and of being 'all in it together'. Of the 84 airships used in these raids, 30 were lost (in action and in accidents) and 62 German aircraft were lost. British casualties totalled over 1,400 killed and over 3,400 injured. In January 1919, the War Office Press Bureau issued a detailed report on German airship and aeroplane raids over Great Britain with the resulting casualty data for each raid. They did not include any of the German crew losses but that oxymoron 'friendly fire' in the form of spent shell fragments from the barrage and targeted AA firing must have killed and maimed some of these victims. These British losses are summarised below:

> The first airship raid was on 19th January 1915, on Norfolk. The last raid was 13th April 1918, on Lincolnshire, Lancashire and Warwickshire. Civilian casualties were 217 men, 171 women and 110 children killed, totalling 498. 587 men, 431 women and 218 children, totalling 1236, were injured. 58 soldiers and sailors were killed, with 121 injured. The first aircraft (Gotha and Giant) raid was 24th December 1914, on Dover. The last raid was 20th May 1918, on Kent, Essex and London. This was the largest raid by Gothas and the Riesenflugzeuge (Giants) which were larger than any of the German bombers used during the Second World War. Civilian casualties were 282 men, 195 women and 142 children killed, 629 in total. 741 men, 585 women and 324 children were injured, totalling 1650. 238 soldiers and sailors were killed, with 400 injured. There were no casualties from a final raid on Kent on 17th June.

To stem the carnage of the air war, aircrew may have been provided greater personal protection. Head protection helmets had been used and parachutes were available. Their use from aircraft had been demonstrated. 9th May 1914 was a chilly day and could have been even colder for William Newell who was about to make the first parachute jump from an aeroplane in Britain. Seated on one of the chassis skids of the Grahame-White biplane over Hendon the parachutist continued to postpone the jump until Frank Widenham Goodden, who was himself an experienced balloon parachutist, became impatient and, climbed out on the wings to kick his passenger off …. Luckily the landing was effected without a hitch.

During World War I, Everard Richard Calthrop was one supplier who continued to improve and promote his parachutes. They were deployed with compressed air forced into pockets in the canopy to ensure they opened. The authorities were sometimes portrayed callously denying the brave aircrews these life-saving devices when the truth is that the introduction of parachutes was a complex problem. These early airman needed to move about in their cockpits and were often standing up to aim, unjam or re-arm their guns or to operate their aerial cameras while parachutes were large, bulky and heavy and it was difficult to exit a fast-moving aircraft wearing one. Parachutes could not be issued to the few crew that could operate effectively wearing them without sanctioning their use for all crews and it would have been nigh on impossible to retro design existing machines to accommodate parachutes. However, the plight of an observer trapped in a machine with an incapacitated pilot must have been a horrifying and not uncommon occurrence. Archibald Low wrote his book on this subject called *Parachutes in Peace and War* in 1942.

Handheld fire extinguishers were fitted. These were used, as in the famous action of Sergeant Thomas 'Tom' Mottershead and his observer Lieutenant William Edward Gower on 7th January 1917 for which Mottershead received his posthumous Victoria Cross. The petrol tank of their aircraft was pierced when they were attacked at 9,000 ft and Gower was unable to subdue the flames with the extinguisher. Severely burned, Mottershead regained the British lines and Gower survived due to his pilots gallant action. Rank demanded that they were taken for treatment to separate commissioned and non-commissioned medical facilities and Gower had to ask a padre to locate Mottershead for him.

Many aeronautical pioneers, such as Frederick William Lanchester, addressed the problems of aircraft control and stability which, along with structural integrity and engine reliability, were major factors in aircraft safety. In 1903, George Hartley Bryan defined the wine-glass resonator effect used in solid-state motion sensors today. He also helped to crystalise the issues associated with aircraft stability, and in 1911, with his colleagues William Ellis Williams and Edgar Henry Harper at Bangor University in Wales, he published his tome *Stability in Aviation*. That same year Harper published *Aerial Locomotion*. Others on the continent pursued stable designs and so did John William Dunne, first at the balloon factory and then at Eastchurch on the Isle of Sheppey in Kent. Being full of partial differential equations, Bryan's book was not a bedtime read for the average aviator after a hard day's work in the hangar. But Edward Teshmaker Busk from Rudgwick in West Sussex was no average aviator. He deliberately flew through those dangerous instability modes using his custom-designed precision instruments to obtain the resistance derivatives necessary for Bryan's equations to be applied to his aircraft designs. His work influenced the design of the B.E.2c, the aircraft that became known as 'Stability Jane' and was in service throughout the war where its stability was a great asset when needed but a liability against an agile foe. Busk died on 5th November 1914 when his aircraft caught fire and Harper died at the Somme.

Two other pioneers were the Barnwell brothers from the Cathedral city of Canterbury in Kent who made the first powered flight in Scotland on 28th July 1909. Richard Harold Barnwell joined Vickers Limited in 1912 and his 'Barnwell Bullet' prototypes, produced without the permission of his employers, inspired designs by Reginald Kirshaw 'Rex' Pierson and George Henry Challenger. Harold was Vickers' chief test pilot and died on 25th August 1917 when he failed to recover from a spin at Joyce Green in Kent.

Frank Sowter Barnwell had a more successful career as a designer than his older brother. He co-designed the Bristol Scout before the war. This self-effacing chief designer of the Bristol Aeroplane Company was known as 'Daddy' and in later life 'the old man'. The company produced many iconic aircraft and at a time when Orville Wright was still fighting for his intellectual property and recognition, Frank was keen to share his knowledge. He presented his design methods in a paper he read to the public in the James Watt Laboratories at Glasgow University to their engineering society on the day Busk was killed. Early in 1915, C. G. Grey published Frank's paper serially in the *Aeroplane* periodical. Due to its popularity, Grey suggested to his friend Frank that the paper, along with another frequently requested item by William Higley Sayers on the continuing much-discussed topic of inherent stability, should be produced as a small book. This book went on sale under the title *Aeroplane Design and A Simple Explanation of Inherent Stability*. For the first time and in a convenient form this defined for public consumption a logical method for designing an aircraft. This useful book could have been considered helpful to the enemy but it was not censored and indeed, it sold so well that despite paper shortages it went to a number of reprints throughout the war.

The fatalities among military airmen engaged upon general duties and training on the home front continued at a flagitious rate as the war progressed. This tragic loss of talented young men persisted, despite the improvements in aircraft design. In its editorial on 12th April 1917 – 'Bloody April' – *Flight* magazine asked, 'Is our Training System Right?' It questioned why fatalities in training 'hardly fall short of our average of losses at the front'. The article goes on to assert that freshly trained pilots at the front were allocated the new high-performance aircraft while the experienced pilot kept their older aircraft and it states that this 'is the root cause of the large number of fatalities.'

In part, the increased fatality rate was because higher performance aircraft accidents were less survivable. There were, however, other reasons. On 26th February 1918, Sir Henry Norman submitted a report to Lord Rothermere, the president of the Air Council. Being much concerned, as he had always been, with the welfare of those in service and being in a privileged position to obtain the statistics from source, Sir Henry questioned the methods and policy of the RFC pilot training.

He wrote: 'The total number of fatalities in the Training division in 1917 was 391 for 5,946 pilots turned out; a rate of 6.57%.'

This resulted in a lengthy exchange of opinions concerning what was and was not included in the figures such as NCOs, pupils who failed, ferry pilots, instructors and other categories. There must have been a considerable number who were seriously injured in addition to these fatalities. The demand for pilots required training hours to be maximised, requiring flights by these inexperienced crews in more marginal conditions, at night and throughout the winter. This was justified by the argument that the successful and surviving pilots were more capable at the end of such training. Eventually, Sir Henry, probably realising that this was not an arrangement that his concerns were going to alter, graciously conceded.

Sir Norman's figure for 1917 of 391 RFC fatalities in training compared with a total of 1,195 RFC killed in action on the Western Front, so in this difficult year at least 1,586 RFC airmen died – for every 3 that died in France, 1 died in Britain. This rigorous and deadly training regime underscored the aggressive policy pursued in the field. The fight was taken to the enemy so that in 1917, for example, 1,381 aircrew were lost east of the lines (killed or became POWs) which is well over 3 times more than the 396 who were killed or died of their wounds after getting back on the Allied side of the lines. The figures for 1918 were even more horrendous.

Sir Henry was personally motivated to question the safety of flight training. His brother-in-law, MP Francis Walter Stafford McLaren, who had survived front-line action in Turkey, fought his bout of chronic illness and lost and regained his commission in the RFC, was then killed while on pilot training flying about a mile off the shore at Montrose on 30th August 1917. His machine nose-dived into the water and he died from internal injuries shortly after being brought ashore.

As with the other aspects of aviation, accident investigation became more organised. George Bertram Cockburn was, by training a research chemist but, by inclination, an aviation pioneer and he held the 5th Aero Club pilot's licence, awarded to him on 26th April 1910. He represented Great Britain in the first international air race at Rheims and co-founded the first aerodrome for the army at Larkhill. He also trained the first four pilots of what was to become the Fleet Air Arm. During World War I he worked as a government inspector of aeroplanes for the Royal Flying Corps at Farnborough and subsequently became head of the Accidents Branch of the Department of the Controller-General of Civil Aviation at the Air Ministry.

Francis McLaren was the fifteenth member of the House of Commons to die on active service in the war. 264 MPs in the House of Commons volunteered for service in the armed forces and the 'Recording Angel Memorial' in Westminster Hall commemorates the 22 MPs and 20 members of the Lords who died on active service during the Great War.

For the duration of the war there was an understanding between the political parties that by-elections went uncontested and the party holding the seat at the vacancy could put up a candidate who would not be opposed. This occurred in Spalding,

Lincolnshire after the death of Francis but only after two others from other parties had put themselves forward as potential candidates before withdrawing.

When the creation of an Independent Bomber Force was proposed, Sir Henry provided his assessment on 25th March 1918. In 23 pages that included details of the tasks envisaged for the bombers such as distances to be flown to reach the German cities and considerations of the available machines, engines and armaments, he concluded that this perilous game was not worth the candle – but if it was to be done it should use the FB27B Vicker's Vimy. His argument for this was that, when shot down, this lost 2 engines, 3 men and 2 guns whereas the Handley Page 'V' type lost 4 engines, 11 guns and 11 men (perhaps overstating the loss of guns and men to make his point!).

The IAF operated with continued, determined resolve and ruthless endeavour in the face of bitter losses, with Trenchard in command as the war drew towards its conclusion. As 1918 ebbed away, the war reached its final crescendo but, as we know, the echo did not completely fade but rose again just 20 years later with annexations and further invasions.

Design improvements and innovation made little impact on the dangers of flying when they were set against the ever increasing tide of aerial activity during the war but perhaps uniquely, the AT project offered the possibility of eliminating these dangers.

Meanwhile, the novice aircrews and the very few experienced pilots who endured the bombing and survived the military flight training now had to cross the sea and go to war.

CHAPTER 9

The Bravest Star

For many today it is difficult to understand why the majority of the population of Britain voluntarily entered into war work. For many of the less privileged, in days when many forms of employment were hazardous, war service offered more secure work at no increased level of risk to their pre-war jobs and with medical assistance in case of injury. For others, it was employment where there had been no regular work. Others may have imagined the comradeship and revelry, the chance to sit around with your mates and sing songs such as 'Hullo, my dearie,' or 'Some Girl Has Got to Darn His Socks'. But for many of the middle classes and more favoured in British society, it was a vastly more hazardous enterprise than they had experienced previously. For the 'young bucks' it offered the allure of adventure but for many, perhaps the majority, it was duty that called them; simply the right thing to do. There was to be a national learning process through the war; a growing understanding of the scale of horror wrought by static entrenched warfare and the privations caused by naval blockades. But still, for most, they would not experience 'the front' or be present where the bombs dropped and they would spend the war employed in support and supply roles.

Much has been written and rewritten describing the great flying aces of the war and their derring-do, of the momentous dog fights such as that of 23rd September 1917. These aces, by and large, could be described as 'those young bucks', courageous young men. A few like Brabazon were volunteers of more mature years out of the ranks of the existing civilian pilots and these were generally absorbed into the Royal Flying Corps' embryonic command structure alongside Henderson, Trenchard and the other career officers. But some flew in the front-line squadrons.

The war threw generations and classes together. The Hon. Eric Fox Pitt Lubbock was an 'old Etonion' whose youth shone through his short career. Recruits from public schools would expect to enter service with a commission but Eric was one who broke this mould. He was somewhat obsessed with his girlfriend Winifred Martin Smith, of whom his mother disapproved, and with his 'motors', as many a boy was in those days and still are today. He left his mother to whom he wrote regularly of his experiences and enlisted in September 1914 as a private with the

69th Mechanical Transport Division of 'Ally Sloper's Cavalry', the Army Service Corps. Eric served in the UK and in France until February 1915. Concerns were expressed by his family and peers regarding the reception he would get from the rough company he would encounter but these did not materialise. He was then commissioned as an officer with the 4th Divisional Supply Column and in August 1915 he transferred to the RFC.

After being trained as an observer Eric was assigned to No. 5 Squadron at Poperinghe. This tour included the action on 26th October 1915, which he described in *Flight*:

> We sighted a German about four miles off and attacked. We both opened fire about fifty yards. I fired again at about twenty-five, firing twenty-six rounds, and then guns jammed. We were diving, I standing almost on the front of the body. Then we turned level. I spent another five minutes at the guns and finally got both done. We saw another enemy coming in the distance…I put my stiff and aching hands in my mouth praying for sufficient life to come back to them; they were frozen. Then our engine stopped, and we were helpless, so we turned and glided homewards. Unable to reach the aerodrome we landed in a plough, a beautiful landing…The luckless Boche fell behind our front line trench. The pilot was shot through the stomach; the observer, a boy of seventeen, just grazed in the head. There was a camera with a Zeiss lens, which will be most valuable to us…a priceless pair of binoculars, magnifying eighteen times. I went to a town last night to have my hair cut. I walked with some 'Tommies.' 'Lummy,' said one to the others, 'did yer see that fight in the air this morning? German fell twenty yards behind our trench.'

This young 'observer' Eric and his pilot Robert Loraine were both awarded the Military Cross.

In early 1916 Eric, having obtained his wings, was on active service in France when he wrote home to his mother:

> My darling Mum, one is here confronted almost daily with the possibility of Death, and when one looks forward to the next few months this possibility becomes really a probability.
>
> As my object in life is to comfort and help you, so it is my last hope if I should be taken from you, that I may not cause you too great a grief.
>
> Also I know that if in my last hour, I am conscious, my chief consolation will be to feel that these thoughts may reach you.

On 11th March 1917 near Railway Wood, Ypres at 11:15 a.m. he was attacked by 2 Albatros D. IIIs flown by German ace Lieutenant Paul Strähle and the tall 23-year-old Lieutenant Josef Flink. Eric and his observer, Sub-Lieutenant John Thompson of the Royal Naval Volunteer Reserve, in their No. 45 Squadron Sopwith Strutter were killed.

Eric's pilot in the 1915 action was Major Robert Loraine, the commander of 'B' Flight. He was born on 14th January 1876 and went on the stage at the age of 13, destined for a life in the entertainment industry. He was in his late 30s at the start of the World War I but had already seen service in the Boer War and achieved international fame and fortune as an actor and a pioneer aviator. By the end of the war he was an air ace with a reputation as a heroic pilot. It is astounding that he is not remembered as one of the most exceptional 'celebrities' of the war.

Robert's father and mother were theatrical. Henry Bilcliffe Loraine was a comedian, his wife Mary Ellen Loraine (nee Baylis) known as Nell was the actress 'Edith Kingsley'. Robert's early years were not privileged. He nearly died of a childhood illness and he may well have been given an opiate like 'Syrup of Poppies' or 'Godfrey's Cordial' to 'aid his recovery'. His Aunt Bella had created a passion for books in young Robert and so when he was not reading his parents, weekly copy of *The Era*, a theatre newspaper, he immersed himself in popular literature. When he was about nine years old and busy reading a depressing book, he drank from a bottle clearly marked poison but at the time not shaped differently to indicate the danger. Later in life Robert's poor eyesight was an issue and it may have contributed to the accident or have been a consequence of the poisoning.

John Wightman of *The Playgoer and Society Illustrated* interviewed Robert for their 15th January 1912 'Man and Superman' edition. In the article Robert was described as a typical Englishman, tall, clean-made, with a fresh complexion. After describing his apprenticeship in the British theatre and his service in the Yeomanry in the war in South Africa, Robert traced his career on the American stage which began in 1901 and led to him taking George Bernard Shaw's 'Man and Superman' to New York in 1905 where it then toured all of the Eastern Cities.

Loraine was known to the world at that time as the Bobbie. His first public appearances as a pilot were under the alias Robert Jones.

FLIGHT PIONEERS.

MR. ROBERT LORAINE (MR. "JONES").

Robert Loraine as John Tanner (PlayGoers Society)

Robert Loraine as Robert Jones (Flight Global)

Just before his participation in the Morse Code experiment of 26th September 1910, Loraine was the first to fly through a rain storm when competing for the 'Sea Prize' on the 3rd day of the Bournemouth International Flying Week on Saturday 16th July and on landing became the first to land on the Isle of Wight. On 11th September 1910, he became the first man to fly across the Irish Sea but he wasn't credited with the achievement because he ditched and had to swim the last 200 ft to the shore. Coincidentally this was just before he was to appear in the 'The Man from the Sea' on stage in London.

In his aerial adventures Robert was assisted by his engineer Jules Charles Toussaint Védrines who was kept busy after each of the many crashes. Jules was exasperated at Robert's ability to smash aircraft, saying: 'Then away Loraine goes, quickly away, away and double quick down he crashes. After he crashes he still remains alive and walks back to the hangar.' Jules had his own pre-war flying achievements including flying the Deperdussin Monoplane in the RFC's 1912 Military Aeroplane Competition. Jules flew entry number 21 in the trial, an aircraft that was built by the British Deperdussin Aeroplane Company Limited and was subsequently purchased by the Royal Flying Corps after trial. Jules had an illustrious wartime flying career and as soon as hostilities ended he used his skill to earn a living. On 19th January 1919, he landed a Caudron G.3 on the roof of the 'Galeries Lafayette' department store in Paris, winning the 25,000 franc prize (£1,000) for the feat which had been offered before the war. On 21st April 1919, he was killed when one engine of his Caudron C.23 failed.

Of his flying, Robert said he was inspired when he saw Henry Farman flying his Voisin Brothers aircraft in July 1909 and that he was at Sangatte when Blériot took off for his successful flight across the Channel to Dover. Robert learnt to fly in April the following year at Blériot's base in Pau. The earliest record of the word 'joystick' when referring to the aircraft's controls occurred in his diary at this time. He crashed in a machine at Pau but on 21st June at Farman's establishment at Mourmelon-le-Grand he obtained his flying certificate.

If we go back to those first days of the war in France, 'in the field' we have seen that pilots like Duncan Pitcher were posted as observers. Charles George Gordon Bayly was a qualified pilot flying in the role as an observer in an AVRO 504 when he and his pilot Vincent Waterfall became early casualties of the war in the air. Robert had been similarly assigned as an observer despite having achieved such a level of celebrity as a civilian flyer, as we have seen. In Robert's case apparently, Boom Trenchard had taken a dim view of the damage to two aeroplanes Loraine had used in the required RFC training, and refused to endorse him as a pilot. Boom gave Sefton Brancker the job of informing 'Bobbie' Loraine. So he was assigned to No. 3 Squadron in France as an observer but, as Loraine was short-sighted and wore glasses when flying, there was some consternation that the Corps were being supplied with observers who couldn't see!

On 22nd November 1914, while on artillery observation duties with his pilot Lt. Denys Corbett Wilson, Robert suffered a serious wound when shrapnel from ground fire went up through his chest and exited at his collar bone severely damaging his right lung. Denys was not injured but Robert was close to death. At the base hospital in Boulogne he convinced the staff to transfer him and he was invalided home for treatment in England. Here, his old friend from the South Africa days, the eminent medical consultant James Purves-Stewart, supervised his treatment at Aldford House on Park Lane, London. In recovery Robert had lost a huge amount of weight and his hair had turned white although it did in time return to its natural brown.

Like Robert, the pioneering Irish pilot Denys had flown across the Irish Sea. Robert's attempt in 1910 had officially failed by some 300 yards. Nineteen months later, Denys made the first completed aircraft crossing of the Irish Sea on Monday 22nd April 1912. He had flown the 90-odd miles from Fishguard in Wales to Crane near Enniscorthy in County Wexford, Ireland in one hour and forty minutes.

However, Denys's triumph was tainted by regret as his close friend had disappeared on the previous Thursday in his attempt to fly to Ireland. Corbett Wilson and Damer Leslie Allen's adventure was all a bit spur of the moment and they had given little thought to safety. The newspapers were full of the latest details of RMS *Titanic*'s fate, so it is possible that they thought to lift the gloom of the nation with their exploits. Their two Blériot monoplanes set out on Wednesday 17th from Hendon in London to fly to their native Ireland across St. Georges Channel. This was not a race but an attempt to meet in Dublin and to celebrate their epic and record-breaking journey together. They didn't leave until after 3:30 in the afternoon. After spending the night in Chester, Allen took off just after 6 a.m. and an hour afterwards he passed over Holyhead, flew out to sea and was not seen or heard of again.

The dream had turned to nightmare for Damer Allen. Initially, communication delays from these more remote areas devoid of telephone or telegraph connections would have explained the lack of news but as the days passed Demer's disappearance would have been confirmed.

Denys's journey was also interrupted as he had lost his compass. He landed between 5 p.m and 6 p.m in a field close to Newchurch Farm, about fifteen miles north-west of Hereford. Despite the ongoing after effects of the miners strike on coal supplies and train timetables, Denys's mechanic, as planned, had travelled by rail to Chester to await news and was now 90 miles to the north of his pilot's forced landing. Mr A. Lewis Williams of the Manor House in Almeley assisted Denys and they decided to send telegrams to his mechanic and for a motor car to take Denys into Hereford. By 8 p.m a Mr Connelly was on his way through the darkening countryside to the village in a Wolseley car. Denys, still in his flying kit arrived at

Damer Allen (Flight Global)

(it is thought) The Green Dragon Hotel where the young lady in reception was suspicious of this visitor in his strange outfit talking about a friend (his mechanic) expected to arrive at three o'clock in the morning. Surprisingly, no room was found at this hotel but Denys did find lodgings at the Mitre Hotel on Broad Street. The next morning, when his mechanic was still en route, he found that he could buy petrol and oil locally. Having returned to Almeley to service his machine he was impatient to be on his way and seeing no reason to wait for his mechanic, he took off. At 4:30 that afternoon he was forced to land only about 10 miles further on at Colva in Radnorshire. His engine did not like the castor oil he had acquired as it was not of the correct grade. Denys was forced to wait for his mechanic to fix the problem.

Meantime, Allen, when he was stopped on his flight to Holyhead, had reported that 'it was very hazy and no matter what height I tried the wind was bad and the machine tossed about'. Early on Sunday morning Denys set off again but due to Allen's report he had decided to change his intended route via Chester and Holyhead and instead he headed for Fishguard. He landed in nearby Goodwick in the mid-morning. At 5:47 a.m. on the following day he took off for his record-breaking flight to Ireland.

This epic flight was over two years before Robert was wounded and a few months later Denys was shot down when his plane was hit by 'Archie' on 10th May 1915 and both Denys and his observer Lt. Isaac Newton Woodiwiss were killed. Confirmation of their deaths came from a German aircraft the following day which dropped a message over the British lines saying that a British Morane-Parasol machine had been struck by a shell from their artillery and both the pilot and observer had been killed instantly.

As part of his recuperation, Purves-Stewart insisted that Robert take a cruise, so he went off to South America. He returned on 6th March 1915 on the Royal Mail Packet Company 'Alcantar' from Buenos Aires to Liverpool.[1]

Robert, still classed as an observer, returned to France in April 1915 only to be recalled soon afterwards for pilot training. It is possible that his friend Duncan Pitcher at the Central Flying School arranged this to get Robert his wings. He returned to France in September 1915 as a pilot and joined No. 2 Squadron which was equipped with the B.E.2c and were based at Hesdigneul. The B.E.2c was a general-purpose workhorse frequently seen fitted with all manner of different equipments and with this variety of 'ornamentation' it gained the name 'the Christmas Tree aeroplane'. By the 11th Oct 1915 Robert had been transferred to No. 5 Squadron and was flying an FB5 at 8500 feet with his 'Geordie' observer, Cpl. George Fineran when he was in combat with a Fokker near Voormezele, a scrap that proved inconclusive. George was destined to get his wings as an NCO pilot a year later and he survived the war as an officer.

Robert was in action again on 8th February 1916 at 10:30 a.m. when at 9,000 feet over Polygon Wood, near Hoogein, he was in combat with an Aviatik while flying his DH2 of No. 5 Squadron. In March 1916, Loraine was promoted to Major and took command of No. 40 Squadron that was being formed with F.E. 8 fighters at Gosport, in England. They deployed to France in August 1916 but before leaving Robert sent Shaw a packet containing his Military Cross, keys, and Pilot's Flying Log Book for safe keeping and G. B. Shaw acknowledged the receipt of these.

Robert was considered by his squadron's junior members to be 'a hard task master' and this may well have arisen from his competitive nature, sharpened by the loss of George Henry Smart so early in the conflict. George had been born in India on 29th April 1883 and, like Robert, had been in the theatrical arts and he had served in South Africa. So the two had a number of common bonds and had formed a close and long friendship, shattered at the start of this long and terrible war.

That winter, which was one of the coldest for some years, Harold Harington Balfour recorded that his squadron was deployed on the other end of the field from Loraine's establishment. The new arrivals had little to sustain them as their cooking facilities and supplies had not arrived. Robert sent word immediately and invited them to No. 40 Squadron's mess. Balfour described 'the Actor Airman's' organisation. It was very theatrical, with customised bells used to signal different events such as the departure of a sortie or the sighting of enemy aircraft. On the occasion of the enemy aircraft bell ringing Harold recalled in his book *Wings Over Westminster* that

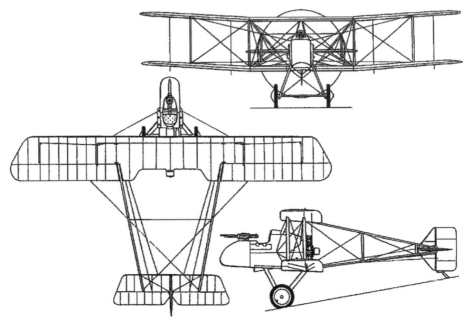

The Royal Aircraft Factory F.E.8, drawing produced by Darracq Motor Engineering at Townmead Road, Fulham and at Vickers at Brooklands

Loraine merely turned slightly to one of his flight commanders saying 'I think there may be an enemy around. Perhaps you had better see to it.' He then continued with his game of bridge.

Another example of Robert's style of management of No. 40 Squadron happened during dinner, as recounted in Harold's book *Wings Over Westminster*:

> All the alarms in the camp started ringing simultaneously. Fire had broken out in one of the sheds which held four of their aircraft. Fire pickets had doubled to the spot but nothing could be done except to form a semi-circle round the blazing hanger and let the fire burn itself out. It was a grand fire to see for the petrol tanks had gone up, doped wings were burning furiously likewise the wooden airframes, while machine gun ammunition went off with continuous pops. The hanger had a lean-to shed in which mechanics kept their tools. It had not yet caught fire and a little sergeant thought he could help by going to the lean-to and starting to throw out spanners, vices and screwdrivers. Hardly had he begun this rather futile task than Robert Loraine strode into the centre of the firelit ring of men, seized the little sergeant by the coat collar and pushed him aside. In a loud stage voice he cried out, 'Away! Away! Away!, my man! If this is anybody's place, it is mine.' Then in order to show his contempt for the incident, he stepped into the middle of the arena and there, in the full glare of the light, performed a perfectly natural function to the admiring eyes of the assembled pilots and mechanics.

Acts such as this (and an act it most certainly was) do more for morale than any speech.

In December 1916, David Lloyd-George succeeded Herbert Henry Asquith as Prime Minister and his government bought changes to the conduct of the war. To add credence to reporting from the front, a selection of influential detractors were invited to witness the war at first hand. Shaw was an obvious choice as his views on the war had blunted his popularity with the patriotic public. For unknown reasons, his 1915 play *O'Flaherty VC*, written to encourage recruitment in Ireland, was not thought to fit the bill and was not staged in Britain until after the war. General Haig invited Shaw to visit the front in early 1917 and after considering the offer, Shaw agreed. Suitably equipped with his trench boots, a khaki tunic and breeches he crossed over to France on 28th January 1917. Shaw's articles on his experience did not please anybody; they were not intended to but as they conveyed such a level of empathy with the common soldier at the front they were seen as honest and were published. After this Shaw's work became more accepted by society again.

During his visit to France Shaw had insisted on experiencing some of the areas under fire, commenting 'we had come to the theatre to see the play not to enjoy the interval.' Having achieved this he went to Trezennes to visit Loraine's squadron. Loraine was also using his theatrical experience to provide entertainment for his men, including staging short plays which were performed in a disused Red Cross hut. They put on both *The Inca of Perusalem* and *O'Flaherty VC* and Shaw got to see some of the squadron's dress rehearsals.

Loraine's squadron had some aerial successes before Shaw's visit but on 9th March nine F.E.8s were mauled by five Albatros D. III sesquiplane fighters of Manfred von Richthofen's Jagdstaffel 11. After this disaster, No. 40 Squadron was re-equipped with French Nieuports. Having commanded No. 40 Squadron for a year, Loraine's move was in the pipeline before this scrap with The Red Baron's Jasta 11 and he was promoted to Lieut. Col. to take command of 14 Wing – just in time for 'Bloody April'. Having been mentioned in despatches numerous times, on 3rd June 1917, Loraine was made a Companion of the Distinguished Service Order. The wing was part of IV Brigade RFC when it began operations on 10th July in preparation for Operation Hush on the Belgian coast. 'Hush' would have involved landings on the German held coast as an outflanking manoeuvre with the additional aim of disrupting German U-boat operations in the area. These 'Hush' landings did not happen but the RFC were fully occupied in the 4th Army's offensive which began on 31st July 1917, the start of the third battle of Ypres, the battle of Passchendaele. The war and particularly air operations were becoming increasingly complex. The RFC were required to undertake more and more new types of duties and security was ever more important. Squadrons were isolated when the need for security demanded it, with vague rumours about quarantine and the like being circulated to explain away these unusual arrangements.

In late 1917, Robert was exhausted by the constant strain that went with the daily deadly routine of air operations. In the late evenings he began to have visions of George Smart sitting quietly in the corner his office, conjured up by his active imagination perhaps as a cry for help to a comforting friend and confidant. At this time he was awarded his bar to his DSO for the tactical innovations he introduced while commanding 14 Wing, possibly relating to Operation *Hush*. His ill-health was diagnosed as the newly recognised condition, Neurasthenia. Loraine was moved to London and given command of 18 Training Wing and then, on 31st October he was appointed officer commanding 36 Training Wing based at Thruxton, in Duncan Pitcher's back yard. As we know, casualty rates among trainee pilots were extremely high and Robert's tough approach to the training did not endear him to the students. He sought efficiency over popularity, driving his young trainees hard that they might learn enough to survive more than a few days of their deadly business with front line squadrons. Back in England this posting did not relieve Robert from the stress of losing pilots and his illness did not abate. It must have appeared that there were about as many killed and injured in training in any week as there were on the Western Front and they were generally even a few weeks younger. Writing to their next of kin must have been an even more difficult task when denied the stock phases, white lies and platitudes of battle to allude to, such as 'brave and courageous acts against the enemy'.

He was accused of being drunk on duty, a charge that one officer described as a 'dirty trick'. A court martial acquitted Robert but he requested a posting back to the Western Front. Reverting to the rank of major, on 26th May 1918, he took command of what had been No. 11 Squadron RNAS. Now as part of the brand new Royal Air Force it had been renumbered as No. 211 Squadron; 1st April 1918 – April Fools Day – having been chosen as the birthday of both the RAF in 1918 and Fleet Air Arm in 1924. With its Airco DH9s it operated bombing and reconnaissance missions over Flanders. They were based in Petite-Synthe, Dunkirk and, even though it was the cricket season they occasionally played baseball with No. 85 Squadron RAF who were also based there and had a few American pilots, most notably the three musketeers, Springs, Callahan and Grider. Lawrence 'Larry' Kingsley Callahan and Elliott White Springs became aces in their short combat careers. Lawrence had left Chicago to join up, while Elliott joined from his home in South Carolina. At 9:15 a.m. on 18th June 1918, John McGavock Grider, who was from Arkansas was in his SE5a (occasionally referred to as the Spitfire of World War I) and was last seen in combat with an enemy aircraft over Menin. Posted as missing, sometime later the Germans dropped a note confirming his burial. Although, like so many, this was never located he is listed on the 'Tablets of the Missing' at Flanders Field American Cemetery at Waregem, Belgium.

At this time the ban on C.O.'s flying was rescinded, probably due the strain caused by the shortage of pilots. Robert would get to fly into action six more times but always as the observer/gunner. The war hung in the balance and Robert's mental state was still at tipping point. After the war he said that George Smart, his long dead close friend, reappeared as soon as he inspected his new command and would be there with him in the cold light of day, in front of the aircraft on these missions. Many carried their own particular demons and apparitions with them during this war and some were probably even encouraged, recruited or invented to further the ends of the Allied cause, such as 'The Angels of Mons'.

Despite his inner turmoil, Robert remained a hard task master in his command. When the wing commander gave the squadron a day to recuperate Loraine decided their time would be better spent practicing a fast retreat to a site ten miles away. After the recent attacks of the German 1918 offensives the need for such retreats was far from a remote possibility and Loraine's state of mind was not too delicately balanced that he needed to court the love of his troops. Just two months earlier, the army retreats had been so sudden that the RFC mechanics and fitters had no choice but to travel with and fight with the infantry. Fritz was far from being beaten and they had to be prepared. After their practice move, Elliott Springs wrote of Robert: 'Then he drove up magnificently in the squadron car and inspected them and gave the order to them to move back again and unpack. They were so mad they wanted to kill him' and Springs implied that they tried, as during a baseball game, 'Bobby was there one afternoon and kept in the limelight by getting hit by a foul ball.'[2]

On one mission, accompanied as always by the spectre of George Smart, Robert was the observer flying with the Canadian pilot Harold Mervyn Ireland. Even in July the cold at altitude made the work difficult, the sway of the aircraft exaggerated the wooziness of hypoxia and added to the sickening anxiety that was an inevitable consequence of flying into the enemies' midst. They had dropped their eight twenty-pound Cooper bombs (which with their 4 pounds of H. E. weighed 24 pounds each) from 16,000 feet at 7:20 p.m. when 'Three EA [enemy aircraft] came up in front but always kept far off in the vicinity of Ostend.' For Robert, with only one healthy lung and 'old' by comparison to the men under his command, to be flying and fighting at these heights must have been physically and mentally exhausting. They were not so lucky on a subsequent mission on 20th July 1918 when their aircraft was damaged during combat. Harold was not hurt and landed the plane at La Panne Beach north of Dunkirk but Robert was wounded yet again.

They were flying in a DH9. The design of the DH9 had replaced the 'traditional' nose radiator by raising the engine and fitting a vertical water tank with a radiator in the bottom of the fuselage. However, it must be said that any traditions in aircraft design at this juncture were not long established. This required the forward (pilots) cockpit to be positioned further back than in the earlier DH4's and so it was very close to the rear cockpit. With this arrangement crew communications in the DH9 were significantly improved by this design. The Siddeley Puma engine however, was notoriously unreliable.

Harold reported that Robert was at the Lewis gun mounted on its Scarff ring and he 'engaged the enemy EA as he turned behind us. The EA's first burst wounded Major Loraine in the leg and punctured the water pump above the cowling. EA continued to attack from behind and then broke off the engagement; but returned to the attack immediately. EA was again engaged by Major Loraine who finally sent EA down decidedly out of control. (We watched EA fall for about 2,000 feet).'

Ironically, they had landed on 'The Breakdown', La Panne beach. Ireland drove over to Queen Alexandria Hospital in Dunkirk to see Robert two days later and found him recovering from the three bullets which were extracted from his left leg and hip bone, which had been cracked. His suffering was horrible. 'Sent him up some Chlorodone [sic] later,' Harold noted.

The British flying services lost a total of 16,623 casualties in the war of which 37 per cent were killed and a further 19 per cent were missing and had either died or been take prisoner. The remaining 44 per cent were wounded and survived. Casualties were generally passed down the line from advanced dressing stations by ambulance wagon which, as the war progressed, would be more likely to be a heated motorised vehicle which was thought to be of great benefit to troops who had endured the wet, cold mud of the trenches or numbing cold of the cockpit. The priority at the clearing stations was to classify the wounded and identify those that were treatable. Treatment concentrated initially on haemorrhaging to stem the blood loss and then on cleaning the wound of foreign matter, clothing and excision of the dead tissue to prevent infection. The severely injured who were deemed to survive transporting were immediately sent (most often by train) to a base hospital. The casualty clearing station treated those that needed immediate surgery or those whose wounds were more superficial. Up to 1917, anaesthetists had their own equipment that had to transported when they moved site. Following the work of Geoffrey Marshall and the Bajan medical officer known as 'Cocky' but more formally as Henry Edmund Gaskin Boyle this all changed. The anaesthetists were given a new and more controllable instrument to use that was installed in the surgical units. The invention of this Boyle machine for administering anaesthetics was a huge improvement and reduced mortality rates. From 1917 onwards these machines became more available in the larger treatment centres.

Shaw wrote to Robert: 'Why the devil need they have hit you in the knee joint? The shin would have served their purpose just as well.'

Robert had not only lost his knee cap but a large part of his knee joint and amputation of his leg was being considered as this was the least bothersome option for the hard-pressed medical staff. Having heard of Robert's consternation at the prospect of losing his leg, Shaw wrote to him again, 'You have, God forgive you, bombed enough German homesteads to fill ten pages of the Recording Angel's debit column … It behooves (sic) you to start a credit by drying up the Atlantic for ever. I no longer think of you as an actor, except as a joke or a reminiscence:' Shaw wrote later, 'I have the clown in me; and the clown trips me up every time.' We can only hope that both men regretted that exchange, although it may have been more difficult to forgive if Robert had actually lost his leg.

In excruciating pain and severe mental anguish at the thought of losing his leg, Bobbie insisted on being transferred to England and on 7th August, a full 18 days after he was wounded, he was taken to Bryanston Square Hospital in London. Here he was referred by friends to that eminent surgeon with a royal clientele, Alfred Downing Fripp who rebuilt his knee.

The following day saw the massive initial assault by the Allies on the first day of the battle of Amien. This, the Third Battle of Picardy, would on reflection become known as the Hundred Days Offensive, the beginning of the end of the long bloody war.

Harold Ireland survived the war and in 1923 he bought his mother to Scotland were he settled as a farmer in Tullochvenus House, Lumphanan, Banchory in what he would have called Kincardineshire, not too far from Aberdeen and the old RFC base at Montrose.

Callahan and Springs also survived the war and Springs went on to write about his wartime experiences and his period of 'barnstorming'. He was eventually drawn back into his family's very large and successful cotton and textile business in the 1930s and you can still buy their Springmaid Sheets and Bedding.

Although written by Springs, the book *Warbirds: The Diary of an Unknown Aviator* is now attributed to John McGavock Grider, his colleague who died. The book was based in part on Grider's war diary and the authorship issue resulted in a court case. Many pilots carried mascots or good luck charms. Grider had a doll, reputedly given to him by Florence Leonora Stewart better known as the young musical stage star Billie Carlton. It is entirely possible Billie met John because, before transferring to France, the Americans were based in Oxford but they had rented accommodation in up-market Belgravia in London. There they did a great deal of socialising, drinking, letting off steam with 'original' parties and of course, womanising. While in Oxford, in keeping with the No. 85 Squadron's reputation, they joined in the chaos of the Mess, known for its drink fuelled games such as High Cockalorum and of course, still womanising. After a Victory Ball in late November 1918, Billie Carlton died from a drug overdose. This led to the first big drugs scandal in Britain.

They say a good pilot is one whose log book shows the same number of landings as take-offs. Robert must have been a good pilot but by a different yardstick than this old adage! He was reported to be 'a ham-handed pilot who maltreated his engine, but was always as brave as a lion.' He was certainly a lucky flyer, walking, swimming or at times being carried away from prang after prang and scrap after scrap and scrape after scrape. He had held the highest rank of any 'civilian' officer in the RAF during the war. GBS's offish remarks sent to Robert in the hours of his anguish and pain in the hospital in Dunkirk were not only hurtful but totally inaccurate. Robert's theatrical career, while never to reach the heights of those pre war years, was far from over. The war left him with grave injuries to his right lung and left leg and with a sorely troubled mind. In this condition most men would have longed for a quieter existence and settled back in a domestic, homely setting but Robert Loraine had a rich and colourful life and was not one to settle for less.

His fame has not endured and his exploits have not been immortalised in celluloid as they have been for others of his ilk. He was born in New Brighton, Liscard, Cheshire, England and made his first stage appearance in the English provinces in 1889. He married the American actress Julie Opp on 7th November 1897. In 1902 they divorced (well he divorced her because as we have seen, it was virtually impossible for a women to instigate the process). That same year she married the British actor William Faversham.

In 1905, Robert became acquainted with his fellow Fabians George Bernard and Charlotte Shaw. The Shaws and Robert became lifelong friends. Charlotte Frances Payne-Townshend's political views were well known before she met and married GBS. In August 1907 while on holiday with the Shaws in Llanbedr, Wales, Loraine and Shaw nearly drowned when swimming in the sea. Robert had far more than nine lives.

Other notable Fabians in Robert's social sphere were Sydney and Martha Beatrice Webb. Martha, Baroness Passfield coined the term 'collective bargaining' but after the war she failed in her dealings with H. G. Wells who championed a more radical line for the Fabians, although at the time he was immersed in producing his epic influential and highly successful work 'The Whole Story of Man'.

In 1905, when Robert introduced Shaw's play 'Man and Superman' to Broadway, he would have known the actress Margaret Halstan and may well have shared the stage with her. Halstan was the stage name of Clara Maud Morgan; the wife of the lawyer, John Hartman Morgan. It is known that in productions of Shaws 'Arms and the Man', Robert played Bluntschli in 1907 and again in 1919 while Margaret played Raina in 1911. Auriol Lee also worked with Robert, acting and directing and Robert would certainly have known Sefton Brancker and John Morgan.

After the war, Robert went back to acting and theatrical management, returning to Hollywood. He crossed the wide Atlantic a great many times and as far as is known, always by sea. Travelling between the Americas and Europe by air prior to the 1920s was achieved by very few people; fewer than have been into space. The first non stop airship flight across the Atlantic was achieved by Britain's R34 some two weeks after that first aircraft transatlantic crossing we noted earlier that was achieved in the modified Vickers Vimy aircraft with its two Rolls-Royce Eagle engines flown by the two British pilots Alcock and Brown from the US to Ireland on 15th June 1919. However, R34's flight was the first East to West crossing of the ocean by air; the Vimy having crossed West to East. The flight of R34 was also the first crossing to carry fare paying passengers and, as it made the return flight, R34 was the first to complete the two-way crossing. Major George Herbert Scott of the Royal Air Force captained the R34 airship on these flights with his passengers and crew.

R34 left RAF East Fortune, near Edinburgh, Scotland with 30 people on board flying to Mineola, New York and arriving on 2nd July 1919. The crossing was completed in 108 hours and 12 minutes and the 'landing' involved Major John Edward Maddock Pritchard parachuting from the airship to supervise the ground crews and thus he become the first person to enter the USA by air from Europe. Sadly, Major Pritchard was killed in the crash of R38 in 1921 and Major Scott was with Sir William Sefton Brancker in the fatal crash of the R101 in October 1930.

One might wonder why an airship was not the first to cross an ocean but there are many complications involved in the management of gas supplies on an airship on a voyage which extends over twenty-four hours or more.

A flight across the South Atlantic was accomplished in 1922 but many were lost in Atlantic crossing attempts. A loss that occurred shortly after Lindbergh's famous flight in 1927 was that of Princess Anne of Löwenstein-Wertheim-Freudenberg, Lieutenant-Colonel Frederick Frank Reilly Minchin and Captain Leslie Hamilton. They started their East to West record attempt from Upavon Aerodrome, on Wednesday 31st August, at 7:15 a.m. in the St. Raphael, a Fokker monoplane fitted with a Bristol 'Jupiter' engine of 500 h.p. The last sighting of the aircraft was by a ship in mid Atlantic that evening.

So Robert had sailed once more. In California, he took a trip with Edward Knoblock involving a mule ride into the Grand Canyon. Possibly finding it difficult to accept routine after so many years of war, Robert then took a much longer vacation to Hawaii and onward to China, shaving his head during a two week stay in a Buddhist monastery and visiting the Great Wall. Despite the civil unrest in the country he went to Shanghai and Nanking. He had met the exiled Dr. Sun Yat-Sen in 1910 when attempts to win the De Forest Cross-Channel Distance competition was underway. Dr. Sun was then living at 4 Warwick Court, Holborn, London WC1 and was frequently at Dr James Cantlie's London home or at his country house, The Old Kennels at Cottered in Hertfordshire. James was a pioneer of the concept of applying 'first aid' to casualties and he had been Sun's old tutor from Hong Kong. In 1896 he was to make gallant efforts for over a week to rescue Sun from his kidnappers at the Chinese Legation when Sun first visited London. This action, which was widely reported in the press, had saved Sun from forced rendition to Imperial China where he would have probably faced torture and death but it made him internationally famous and enhanced his position. After the Wuchang Uprising of 10th October 1911 (celebrated as Double Ten Day), in early 1912 Dr. Sun Yat-Sen become the first Provisional President of the Republic of China and he become known as 'The Father of Modern China'. On 5th January, when Sefton Brancker was getting ready for the Calcutta Durbar pageant, Dr. Sun issued the 'Manifesto from the Republic of China to All Friendly Nations' ending the isolationist policies of the Manchu Emperors 'to rejoin China with the international community' and he offered his support in allowing women the right to vote in the new Republic, supporting the suffragist Lin Zongsu.

Renewing his acquaintance in China at the time involved Robert in a covert meeting as Sun was managing a fragile set of alliances as the head of the Kuomintang, pitted against the powers in Beijing. The security measures included being blindfolded and taken for a fifteen-hour trip in a palanquin. Robert and Sun were both well travelled and had a number of mutual friends around the world so it would have been a very welcome meeting for them both. Robert's background in the Fabian Society would also have been of interest to Sun. They were not to meet again as Sun died on 12th March 1925 of cancer. He was a Christian and had a suitable elaborate funeral ceremony in Peking. His death marked the beginning of an even more turbulent period in China's history. Dr. Sun Yat-Sen is still honoured in both Chinese territories and in many other countries and his words are still repeated in the national anthem of the People's Republic of China.

Robert continued his epic trip by way of a seven weeks hack through the forests and rivers in Sarawak on the island of Borneo, he visited India to see the Taj Mahal by moonlight and went to the 2,500-year-old Shwedagon Pagoda in Yangon, Burma (now Myanmar).

On 12th May 1921, he left Bombay on a steamer bound for England. Sir Thomas and Lady Mary Strangman and their daughter Winifred Lydia were on-board. Thomas was the Adjutant General of Bombay, who would, in Ahmedabad in 1922, be the first to prosecute Mahātmā Mohandas Karamchand Gandhi.

Winifred was born on 25th October 1898 in Johannesburg, South Africa and to this point had lived in India most of her life. Her most poignant experience during the war was the death of her cousin, the RNAS Sub-Lt. Reginald Warneford VC of German airship LZ 37 fame. Winifred was a great beauty and on the long voyage through tropical waters there was plenty of time for Robert to' admire the scenery'. They arrived in Plymouth, England on 3rd June 1921 and disembarked from the Peninsula and Orient Steam Navigation Co. Ltd.'s S.S. *Naldera*. Robert started to introduce Winifred to his wide circle of friends and associates and he formed the opinion, despite the fact that he was over twenty years her senior, that they were engaged. Winifred may have ploughed a somewhat narrower channel in India but now that she was in London she was not short of suitors and did not share Robert's reading of their relationship. At this time Robert's resources were stretched and he owed money after his extensive travels but this was not unusual in his profession and this situation had not come to Winifred's notice. Despite her protests that she had her heart set on another, in the back of a taxi at the end of their 'negotiations' he made her an offer she did not refuse. If she married him and after a year regretted it, he would let her go and pay her an allowance. She decided that £2,000 per year would do for her and her hearts delight, her intended 'subaltern' who by then had been told that his regiment objected to him marrying. This was an extraordinary proposal but it was now the Roaring 20s after all.

Robert and Winifred married on 14th July 1921 at St. George's, Hanover Square with a reception at the Ritz Hotel. Because Julie Opp had died in April, Robert listed his condition as 'widower'. It is interesting to note the presence of the Chinese representatives of Dr. Sun Yat-Sen government.

The first year of this marriage was turbulent and to some extent spent apart but despite this by their first anniversary Winifred said a final goodbye to her subaltern and awaited the arrival of the first of their three daughters, Alice or more formally, Roberte Winifred Alice.

The marriage survived and although Robert spent a great deal of the 20s and early 30s in the US, his most prosperous years were over. In 1935 he returned to England on the *Normandie* from New York. She docked at Plymouth on 14th October and this proved to be the last of his many sailings across the Atlantic. Two days before Christmas he died. Fortunately for posterity he appears in roles such as 'Ratcliff' in the 1934 Spencer Bonaventure Tracy film *Marie Galant*.

In 1938 Winifred Loraine published her biography of Robert. Their daughter Joan Beatrice Loraine who was born on 17th April 1924 was a teacher who had worked in Rome, Ankara and Uganda before settling down in Somerset. There she gained her reputation as a gardener developing Greencombe Gardens, West Porlock and setting up the Loraine Trust. In 1990 in Ursoaia, Romania she started her relief work which she continued for 14 years. She remembered her father's answer when as a young girl she had asked what he would do if he met a lion in the jungle. His advice had been 'stand tall and look him in the eye'. She was also in the film industry – with a very short career as the voice of the hedgehog in an Aardman Animations' *Creature Comforts* production. Sadly, she died on 19th February 2016.

Amongst all of his other achievements Robert Loraine was an aerial pioneer and innovator, from naming the joystick, the experiments in radio transmission to his contribution to the development of military aviation tactics during the war.

CHAPTER 10

The Industry of Invention

Sir Henry Norman was the Munitions Inventions Department's permanent attaché to the French Ministry of Inventions and by May 1917 he was sufficiently concerned to write to the prime minister about the ineffective oversight of research and development. In this correspondence he listed the BIR (Board of Invention and Research), HMS *Vernon*, the Signals Experimental Establishment at Woolwich, the aviation departments in London, at Eastchurch, at Brooklands, at Farnborough and at Feltham, the NPL (National Physical Laboratory), and the technical commands at GHQ (in France) saying that due to the lack of overall control these establishments may be working simultaneously on the same problem and nobody would know. We should note Sir Henry's inclusion of A. M. Low's establishment in Feltham in his list.

No draconian centralised control of invention and development was enforced and for the RFC the level of innovative development work at squadron level was not to be stifled. However, to be adopted and provided across the services, any new contrivance had to gain approval.

Although the Munitions Inventions Department of the Ministry of Munition never achieved Sir Henry's desire for total co-ordination of the research and development efforts in World War I, a brief survey of some of its work and scope provides an insight into the vast amount of background effort that was required to win the first modern 'technological' war and it reveals some of the back-room boys and girls of World War I.

During the war, Sir Henry's correspondence and contacts were worldwide. He worked for the MID from his homes in Surrey, London and Paris, and was highly qualified to undertake this work. He had travelled extensively over many years as a journalist and politician. He was technically well read and had practical engineering experience. In 1908, along with Thomas Bertram Reader of Hindhead, he patented a system for the automatic switching of public lighting using selenium cells. He was appointed assistant postmaster-general in 1910 although a general election curtailed his term of office within days. He was very active in the development of radio and in 1914 he designed a radio set, the details of which are still available.

With his journalistic background and close involvement in the development of the Imperial Wireless Chain (IWC), he must have taken great interest in 1912 in what became known as the 'Marconi Scandal', an event that would rumble on through 1913 and taint the careers of some political figures, most notably David Lloyd-George. Just like the French Dreyfus affair (in which he had been involved) and the Douglas-Pennant affair, titbits from the Marconi scandal would feed pages of the press for many years. Misguided accusations, summary dismissal of public servants and whiffs of insider-trading are not good news for those in high office.

In addition to assessing inventions, the MID monitored developments in other countries: Allied, neutral and enemy. They collected reports from neutral countries, particularly any related to developments in Germany. In many cases 'needs' were assessed by undertaking what we would now class as 'operational analysis', a field of research that took a leap forward during World War I. Frederick Lanchester's work is but one example, with his analysis of the changing nature of war and the effects of weapons capability on the outcome of conflicts. Such analysis was pertinent to conflicts involving attrition. In his 1916 publication, *Aircraft in Warfare,* he states that 'Germany backed the wrong horse' developing dirigibles as a weapon and that for Britain the maximum possible rate of production of aircraft must be maintained even as new designs are being developed. In this book, he tested his n-square law, applying its principles to his analysis of historical battles.

Sir Henry was in a position to assist with insights and suggestions at a high level in the political, military, scientific and 'media' spheres. For example, on 27th April 1916, Sir Henry wrote privately from Paris to Lloyd George who was then the minister of munitions, thanking him for his letter of the 2nd and then describing the French political crisis and the situation at Verdun. In this letter, he urged the need for big guns and for expediting the procedure for dealing with inventions. He also asserted that the supply question is more important than Ireland. And Sir Henry had had experience of Ireland, as this article in the *New Zealand Herald* on 13th October 1917 attests:

> It being his duty to keep the Munitions Inventions Department in touch with any new French military invention, Major Sir Henry Norman, who has been decorated with the Cross of Officer of the Legion of Honour; makes frequent visits to the French and British fronts. Sir Henry is one of the members for Blackburn, and has travelled extensively and met with many adventures. On one occasion, while in Ireland, he was present at a wholesale eviction, and saw a burly agent of the evictors strike a young girl. Mr. Norman: as he was then, immediately knocked the fellow, down, and in remembrance the people subscribed to give him a large golden Cross suitably inscribed.

The World War I use of aircraft offered a whole new dimension for invention, similar to that offered in the 1950s and 60s by the dawn of the space age. One aspect of this was the development of aerial photography, another was that of weaponry; how to locate and bring down your opponent. Some of this we have seen already with the development of ordnance capable of destroying airships and balloons but there were many other advances needed to counter the enemy.

War always creates technological leaps as the 'means' and 'needs' for invention increase. But this in itself would not produce anything without an increase in those 'sparks' of inspiration. One mechanism for a rise in inventiveness is caused by dragging talented people into different fields of study. One such example of re-application was Archibald Vivian Hill.

At Cambridge, Archibald studied mathematics but after graduating in 1909 he started his research work in physiology. His career in the study of muscle function would be interrupted by both world wars but after World War I he shared the 1922 Nobel Prize for Physiology and Medicine. In 1916, he was a captain in the army and was transferred from the infantry to the Ministry of Munitions to work on anti-aircraft gunnery. Here he devised a location system by simultaneously viewing the images of an object in two graduated mirrors set at a known distance apart. This system was documented in a patent in 1921 raised by Hill with Sir Horace Darwin, Reginald Foster Pitt Maton, the R.N. Experimental Department, Shoeburyness and the Cambridge and Paul Instrument Company Ltd.

PATENT SPECIFICATION

Application Date: Mar. 17, 1921.   No. 8373/21.

178,678

Complete Accepted: Apr. 27, 1922.

COMPLETE SPECIFICATION.

Improved Method and Apparatus for Position Finding.

We, Archibald Vivian Hill, Sc.D., F.R.S., of "Arcot", 45, The Downs, Altrincham, in the County of Chester, Sir Horace Darwin, K.B.E., F.R.S., of 5 "The Orchard", Cambridge, in the County of Cambridge, and Reginald afe easily calculated, the plane surfaces being reflecting or transparent with their relative positions known in all respects and the apparent positions of the object being viewed through aperture eyepieces 50 arranged at a known position with regard

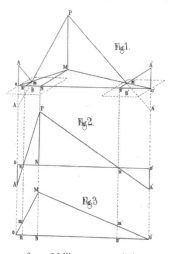

The diagram from Hill's post-war A.A. system patent

A group of mathematicians that became known as Hill's Brigands developed these techniques with anti-aircraft gunners and carried out artillery trials to determine aircraft positions, tracks and velocities with respect to the position of anti-aircraft shell bursts. This work also enabled the velocity (speed and direction) of the wind at various heights to be measured from the drift of the smoke from these shell bursts. These investigations of variables such as performance at different altitudes and the effect of barrel rifling on shell fusing led to other improvements. All of this work contributed to the dawn of operations' research and a more systematic approach to air defence. This continued with the contributions of Patrick Maynard Stuart Blackett and Albert Percival (Jimmy) Rowe and many others in World War II.

Other examples of re-application can be found in the recruitment policy in the field of cryptology, engaging civilian scholars of all varieties in the code breaking. Yet another example was Dr. Keith Lucas who had a distinguished academic career in the physiological sciences. Getting lost was a mortal threat to aviators so Lucas devoted his service duties during the hostilities to perfecting and providing the RFC with its MkII compass. Catastrophically, he decided he needed to fly to further this war work and died in a mid-air collision on 5th October 1916 over Salisbury Plain along with the pilot of the other aircraft – illustrating the dangers faced by some of the back-room boys and adding two more to the numbers of aerial 'training' fatalities.

Britain looked to Professor Andrew Gray and his sons, John and James Gordon, for their knowledge of gyroscopes. James Gordon Gray raised many patents on the subject, some with his older brother John. He was awarded £2900 by the Royal Commission on Awards to Inventors for his work on gyro-stabilised platforms for use in aeroplane navigation and bomb aiming.[1]

As previously noted, Hertha Ayrton had studied fluid flows in her work on the formation of sand ripples on the beach. In the war, this inspired her to work on a design for a trench fan that could be used efficiently to dispel the lingering gases after a chemical attack, as she explains in this extract from her 1915 patent:

> In a paper which I read before the Royal Society on the 6th of May 1915, and which will be found in their proceedings for the current year I demonstrated somewhat contrary to the accepted theory, that certain special local currents were set up by the presence of an obstacle in oscillating water.

> It occurred to me that such local currents could be set up by making the obstacle oscillate instead of the water, and this led me to think that by oscillating an obstacle in air at any desired spot it might be possible to create local currents of fresh air, which would keep any foul or objectionable air or gasses (sic) from reaching the point of operation. Further, a continuance of the action will in some cases drive the foul air back beyond its point of origin.

> I find that by imparting quite small impulses to the air at a given spot, it is possible to set large masses of air in motion at some distance from that spot. The impulses may be given by means of a small blade, fan or similar moveable body beating against the ground or some flat surface near to the ground.

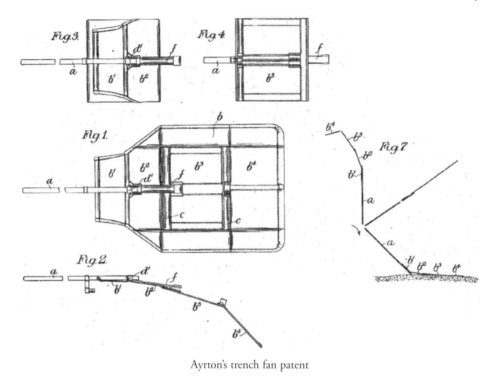

Ayrton's trench fan patent

From mid 1916, these handheld manual flapper fans were supplied in large numbers to the trenches on the Western Front. She went on to devise an electrically driven fan. Not all of the World War I back-room boys were boys!

To some extent Archibald Low's inventive mind was 'diverted' by the war and applied to the Aerial Target, although Archie flitted from project to project so much through his life that this almost formed part of his normal pattern.

In mid 1918, Sir Henry was still sifting through information. He made these handwritten notes on the current aircraft developments. The notes suggest he thought that the F.B.16D should be ordered:

D.H.10 being redesigned – so bad. 700 on order £10 m

DH9 5000 on order £10 m

J type HP only prototype (10/6/18 fell apart in air – 1 died, another went through a slate roof – both arms and legs broken & skull fractured, 5 were burnt) 190 ordered £3.5 m.

F.B.27 Good 350 ordered for delivery in Jan 1919 night bombers and changed to fit air bags for anti submarine patrols.

F.B.16D single seater scout superior to SE5. Only one built. 21–5–18 flown by Capt McCudden fastest in world low level 167 mph, at 10,000 ft 149 MPH, at 20,000 ft 108 MPH, to 10,000 ft in 7.5 mins, to 20,000 ft in 23 min – Not one has been ordered.

Regarding these notes, HP was Handley Page, FB was a Vickers aircraft designation and air bags were fitted under the wings of some RNAS machines to keep them afloat if they ditched. The RFC and RAF used miles per hour and only changed to knots at the end of WWII. As with ground warfare, in aerial combat getting above the enemy was paramount. Even in WWII it took the Spitfire about 7 minutes to climb to 20,000 feet, hence the need for early warning and the 'scramble', that most appropriate 'climb quickly' word that was applied to getting airborne immediately. John Anthony Logan 'Jack' Currie, a WWII bomber pilot, said that it was difficult to reach 20,000 feet before getting to the Ruhr from his Lincolnshire base in his bomb-laden Lancaster. 'Jimmy' McCudden said he was very interested in the F.B.16D with its 150 h.p. Hispano V8 engine. 'Rex' Pierson of Vickers designed the F.B.16 but it did not go into service.

The scale and intensity of the aerial battleground gathered pace as the war progressed and the tactics and strategies of the combat included more than the one-to-one battles and the general melee of the dog fight. On 17th March 1918, in a pre-planned inventive tactic, the RFC goaded the German forces at Bisigny with a small flight whilst keeping their main force ready to pounce with the sun behind them once the German aircraft took off. On the 18th, they tried the same tactic but the Germans were more prepared than the previous day and they had managed to muster around 50 aircraft. A prolonged dog fight ensued, during which John (Jack) Anthony McCudden, the younger brother of most famous James, was killed. Soon after this scrap, the expected German 1918 spring offensive was launched.

Many put their energy into the problem of surprise attacks. Henry Norman was monitoring the work in France on aircraft acoustic early warning systems, obtaining photographs of French detection troops using their portable detector. In the inter-war years, the development of a chain of fixed 'early warning' acoustic detectors in the south of England was linked into the elaborate rapid communication and control system to utilize the detected data while it was still relevant. Feeding updated plotting tables similar to Philip Fooks' plotting table, a system was ready and waiting when radar replaced acoustics as the detection source.

Henry singled out the use of metallic disintegrating links in place of webbing belts for the Vickers gun as a very significant invention of the World War I. The RFC was the first to put frangible-linked belts into regular service use and they were then used in many machine gun types. The lighter Lewis gun used a drum-loaded system but the Vickers gun used belt ammunition, sustaining longer engagement and eliminating the need to reload for most operations, as new belts could be spliced to the belt in use to provide a continuous feed. In the aircraft physical environment, with weight considerations and little option in most situations but to return to base if the belt feed jammed, a reliable system to feed the machine gun was critical.

William de Courcy Prideaux was the designer of these links. He was born in Somerset in 1863. Both of his parents were from established West Country families.

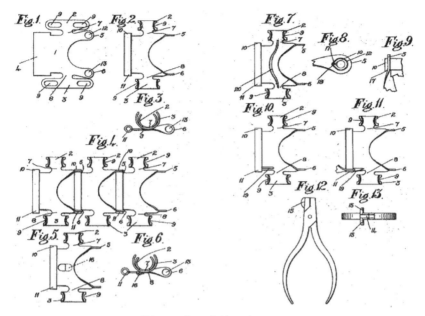

Diagram from Prideaux's patent

At the turn of the century, he and his younger brother Charles were both qualified dental surgeons and they ran a dental practice in Dorchester. He had started his inventions career in his late 20s and in 1893 he was granted the letters patent for a clip to hold the bullets for a revolver so that all the chambers could be filled with one action. He went on to patent a number of items, some of which were connected with his medical trade.

In the autumn of 1901, he married Mary Ludlow in Wellington, Somerset and just after Christmas in 1904 they had their first daughter, Gulielma (after William). Just before the war, the Webley Pistol. 455 Prideaux Quick Loader was marketed and William raised his full patent for this based upon his 1893 submission. By the start of the war, the Prideaux family home and dental practice was between the sea and the river Wey in the centre of the little coastal town of Weymouth in Dorset. Weymouth was adjacent to Nothe Fort and the deep water harbour and crucial naval dockyard of Portland, an area with significant military connections. It may well have been that some of William's military patients complained of aching teeth and jammed guns. In the autumn of 1915, one of these officer patients was the famous RFC flying ace Lanoe Hawker, the third pilot to receive the Victoria Cross, who was on seven days' leave having just returned from France. Known as 'Jolly H' (or more formally Jolly Old Harry) he was visiting family in the town and was intrigued when William showed him the Quick Loader. This meeting inspired William's invention of the metal-linked ammunition belts. His patent for this invention states:

> This invention relates to metal links having clips for carrying cartridges and of which links a number are joined together to form an ammunition belt for use with machine-guns, the object being to construct each link for ammunition belts of machine guns in such a manner that there shall be perfect freedom of movement between each link forming the belt, the links can be jointed together without the use of separate axle pins or like appliances and with perfect safety that each link and consequently also the belt shall be lighter in weight than those now in use, that the links may be readily attached to or detached from one another and that irrespective any usual strain put upon the belt the links are prevented from leaving one another.

After his spell of leave in Weymouth, on 28th September, 'Jolly H', the one-time Royal Engineer, was ordered to take over the command of the 5th Wing's No. 24 Squadron which was stationed at Hounslow, Middlesex. Being initially based in England for this command, he worked to develop the Prideaux disintegrating link machine-gun belt feed for use in the RFC aircraft and finally this new belt system was approved for general use by the Allied services in the autumn of 1917 and was then produced in great quantities. William's first patent application for the links is dated 9th November 1915.

It is possible that the action by the 100th Company of the Machine Gun Corps at High Wood on 24th August 1916 used an earlier version of disintegrating link belts. In this action, ten Vickers guns gave barrage (elevated arced) fire of about a million rounds in 12 hours. Towards the end of the engagement they were running out of cooling water and resorted to using urine to keep the guns firing.

Lanoe Hawker also addressed the problem of flight clothing and had his design of boot made by Harrods. Christened the 'Charfor' boot, these fur-lined, thigh-high boots gained approval and when they went into production and became standard issue, they were universally known as 'fug boots'. Hawker's quest to make his squadron's gunnery more effective resulted in a training aid in which trainees sat in a 'rocking fuselage', aiming at a target on a wire. This was later adopted across the RFC. He also set up an image of a German aircraft on the airfield for returning sorties to use up remaining ammunition – the image being named 'Boche'.

Hawker, with air mechanic W. L. French, developed the 'double drum' for the Lewis machine gun. This increased the capacity of the ammunition drum for the gun from 47 to 97 rounds. The larger drum came into service in the second half of 1916, addressing complaints about the lack of fire power, like the comment of NCO pilot F./Sgt. Thomas Frederick Boyd Carlisle M. M. who reported that on 30th April 1916, in the early morning light and at 12,000 feet above Comines-Warneton, he engaged an Aviatik and then a second one, 40 minutes later. He was with No. 1 Squadron flying a Nieuport 16. He said that he would have had more success if the drums contained more than 47 rounds and also that he suspected the Hun knew when a drum was empty and they then started firing at him.

No. 11 Squadron was also 'tinkering' with its machines. The Australian Sergeant R. G. Foster devised a mounting that allowed a Lewis gun to be run down in front of the pilot to the drum change and un-jamming position or deployed to firing positions upwards and forwards over the upper wing, being operated when the trigger was out of reach by a Bowden cable. On 18th October 1916, it was announced that Foster was awarded the Meritorious Service Medal in recognition of his valuable services during the war.

Bowden cables had come into common use around the turn of the century in 1900 and were mainly used on the brakes of a new form of personal transport, the 'safety bicycle', when their popularity supplanted the old-time 'ordinaries' (penny-farthings). Even the modern bicycle had not been 'invented' when these young aircrew were born. Although there are other contenders for the honour, in the list of Cambridge University Alumni, the entry for Ernest Monnington Bowden states that he was the inventor of the 'Bowden Wire'. His patent is dated 1896.

In addition to the efforts to perfect systems for forward-firing, synchronised fixed guns, many other methods were investigated for gun mounts. One of the most successful was developed by the RNAS NCO Frederick William Scarff. After the war, and now commissioned, Major Scarff was awarded £1,000 by the Royal Commission on Awards to Inventors 'in respect of communication to the US government of inventions, designs, etc in relation to aircraft and aircraft accessories, specifically the Scarff ring mounting.' Bungee shock cord had been in use on aircraft undercarriages and Scarff used it to counter the weight of the gun on its mount, improving the aim of the gunner and reducing fatigue. Scarff also worked with Lieutenant Victor Dibowski, an officer of the Imperial Russian Navy who was part of a Russian mission to Britain. They developed Dibowski's concept on what became the Scarff-Dibowski synchronisation gear. This was a mechanically linked synchroniser system and these did not work well in the 'dynamic' flexible airframes as they could not achieve the extreme accuracy in all conditions to reliably fire through the propeller.

Both the British and French aircraft and ground forces used Vickers Guns with Prideaux's metal belt ammunition. After World War I, William De Courcy-Prideaux was awarded £2,000 by the Royal Commission on Awards to Inventors for the disintegrating belt link. Obviously unaware of this award, Lanoe's younger brother Tyrrel Mann Hawker M. C. said that Prideaux 'was unable to obtain payment for his invention, and died a ruined and disillusioned man.' By the time of William's death on 8th June 1923 at Herrison near Dorchester, this West Country Englishman was a French knight; a Chevalier de L'Etoile Noire and he left an estate of £4563 8s 5d to his wife Mary. He was cremated at Woking on June 13th and on 15th June, at St. George's, Fordington, near Dorchester, in an unusual procedure at this time, William's cremated ashes were placed in the crypt wall. The crypt listing No. 155 for William De Courcey Prideaux of Weymouth includes 'Fellow of The Society of Antiquaries, Chevalier de l'Étoile Noire'. If life were fair, William would be famous.

It had been bitter cold throughout the November of 1915 and the cold intensified towards the latter half of the month. It was so cold that in parts of northern England people were skating on the rivers. Then the rains came in December. On 6th

December 1915, Sir Henry forwarded a letter from London on the Gidino proposal for a bouncing bomb. Guiseppe Gidino filed a patent of 10th January 1916 for his invention when he was working at The Creed and Co Telegraph Works, East Croydon.[2] The suggested bomb had two charges. The first blasted the main bomb upwards on impact so that the main charge exploded above ground.

Having spent long periods at school in Heidelberg and university in Leipzig, Sir Henry was ideally qualified to pen some of the propaganda leaflets distributed behind the German lines. Being acutely aware that airmen suspected of distributing leaflets might not be protected by the prevailing conventions, he also wrote to the secretary of state for air, asking: 'Action by Germans against flyers distributing propaganda – any inventions for automatic distribution of leaflets?' Despite the success of powered flight in many roles, the balloon still had its uses and by 1918 they were drifting over the lines laden with bundles of the leaflets released as the fuses tethering them timed out.

Further uses of the balloon were the barrage aprons erected as a defence against the German bombers. In 1916, Edgar Booth, a solicitor in his late 60s who lived in Halifax, Yorkshire, sent a 29-page illustrated proposal for such aerial traps to Captain William Henry Dennis Clark who was the comptroller of Munitions Inventions. On 29th November 1917, Dr. Frederick William Chamier, a consulting engineer who had patented an inertia-activated safety arming device for projectile shells in 1916, submitted the patent application for his balloon apron idea. He was based in the elegant buildings at 59 Jermyn Street, London.

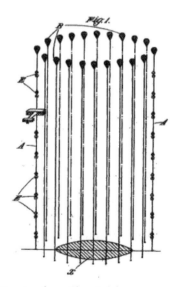

Drawing from Chamier's barrage patent

Protective aprons were used towards the end of the war. An apron consisted of three of the largest balloons that could only reach to heights of 11,000 feet, connected together by 500-foot horizontal cables which carried vertical hanging cables every 25 yards. These aprons forced the large German bombers to operate at greater heights, reducing their bombing accuracy and giving the anti-aircraft batteries a much narrower range of target altitudes to concentrate their fire on. Twenty-one aprons were planned to the east of London but only 10 of these were erected.

Facilities for the procurement, support and operation of surveillance balloons were well established and their use increased despite the fact that the RFC were now also relied upon for 'spotting and aerial photography'. Most of the large balloons used by the Allies were made in France. These were Caquot balloons designed by Albert Irénée Caquot[3] and with their uses extended to supporting these barrage aprons, they became very familiar sights in the Allies' cities in both World Wars. They had a volume of about 70,000 cubic feet and were stable even in strong winds.

Sir Henry noted a proposal for a helicopter which was accompanied by perfor-mance claims that, if true, were remarkable for their time. These were that it would raise to 3000 feet, travel at 40 mph and have a 5-hour duration carrying a substantial payload of bombs. The idea 'never got off the ground'. However, Louis Brennan, of torpedo and monorail fame, joined the Munitions Inventions Department in 1916 and filed his patent for a pilot-carrying helicopter on 19th May. The control was enabled by 'feathering of the lifting propeller blades'.

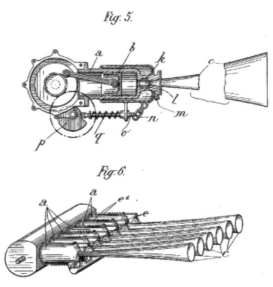

Lorin's WWI jet engine patent

A somewhat more serious 'spark' was the Great War's jet engine. On 14th May 1908, Camille Jules René Lorin submitted his patent application for a ram jet. After further work, at the start of World War I his engine was demonstrated and he suggested it be used to power radio-guided missiles capable of reaching Berlin. It was another concept that was ahead of its time, faltering immediately on the difficulties of its implementation. Only the 'concept' reached Berlin and in the inter-war years they turned a version of it into a weapon, the V1 'doodlebug'. In the 1930s, Dr Eugen Sänger and his assistant, an engineer, mathematician and physicist, Irene Reinhild Agnes Elisabeth Bredt, worked on their rocket-powered lifting body known as Silbervogel (Silverbird). This was a German project to design an orbital bomber capable of reaching America. This 'Amerika Bomber' was an alternative to their A10 ballistic missile. When the Silverbird project was abandoned and the war demanded more defensive products, Sänger worked on the ram jet for the proposed Škoda-Kauba Sk P.14 interceptor aircraft. By the end of World War II, Lieutenant-Colonel Grigori Aleksandrovich Tokaev (anglicised as Tokaty) was a lecturer in jet and rocket propulsion at the Zhukovsky Air Force academy near Moscow and was the chair of the Soviet State Commission on missile development. Dr Sänger and Irene Bredt were under 'the protection' of the French in Berlin. Grigori was ordered to Berlin to persuade Dr Sänger to go to Russia. He was informed that if persuasion failed, force would be used. Outspoken and opposed to many of Stalin's policies, he had no option but to defect to Britain in late 1947 with his wife and young daughter. Grigori Tokaty (British code name 'Excise') was thought to have ensured that the French did not lose their two German scientists. In the 1950s, Eugen and Irene were married and Professor Tokaty went on to his academic career and family life in England.

Arthur Cyril Webb Aldis, a Birmingham-based manufacturing optician of Sare Hole Road, Sparkhill and Lt-Col Charles James Burke DSO, the commandant of the Central Flying School at Upavon in Wiltshire raised the patent on 11th April 1916 for an aero-signalling lamp. The lamp was lightweight and capable of being aimed adequately by aircrew wearing goggles. The trigger lever tilted a lens mirror to provide the beam to the receiver but when the trigger was relaxed, a spring caused the mirror to tilt back, providing an abrupt occultation of the beam as viewed by the receiving observer while the lamp remained continuously lit via a cable from the aircraft's electrical power source. Attention to weight can be noted in the patent as it specifies such things as 'a light body' and 'a hollow handle'. The patent also incorporates means to correctly position the filament focus bulb with respect to the lens mirror.

Between 1908 and 1953, Arthur Aldis raised a significant number of patents. Some of these were in conjunction with his older brother Hugh Lancelot Aldis. One in 1909 concerned 'Improvements relating to Apparatus for Photographic Surveying'. Prior to World War I, some of these patents were raised in conjunction with the company 'The Improved Periscope Limited' and concerned periscopes and other such surveillance devices. Much later in the 1950s, he raised patents with his youngest son Arthur John Aldis whose last patent was in 1969.

In 1912, Charles Burke had put his flying experience and wit to use, creating an extensive list of 'Maxims' for the flying school. He was killed by shell fire on Monday 9th April 1917 on the first day of the battle of Arras.

Inventors such as these and many more like them fed the MID selection and evaluation machine from the autumn of 1915 onwards. After the war the MID records were used, with other evidence, to evaluate any rewards for these 'intellectual property'.

Sir Henry's office was very productive, firing off suggestions and queries and reports from Sweden extracted from the *Svenska Dagblad* including the use in Germany of electric air-raid sirens. Another SvD report detailed the Aerial Postal Service that started on 14th March 1918 between cities in Germany that indicated at this point, just seven months from their eventual defeat, that German was far from vitiated – it was not a spent force.

Just like the optical glass that Brabazon lacked for his cameras and caused the difficulties supplying field glasses and range finders, some other raw materials were in short supply. One was shellac, most famously the material used for 78 rpm records. It was used in World War I in munitions production, for insulating electric wires and for forming emery wheels. For the Germans, rubber was an essential but particularly difficult product to obtain. Over 24,000 tonnes of the inferior methyl rubber were produced in Germany between 1914 and 1918. Agents in neutral countries could assist and in 1915, in exchange for 25,000 German binoculars needed by the Allies, a suitable quantity of British natural rubber was diverted to Germany (despite rules on trading with the enemy). The new material stainless steel was the result of work in 1913 by Harry Brearley in Sheffield. This Yorkshire town set in the valley of the river Sheaf was a cauldron of steel production in Britain and since Henry Bessemer's day, with a little help from Sidney Gilchrist Thomas, it offered a vision of Dante's inferno every night when viewed from the surrounding hills as the 'converters' blew. This stainless form of steel sparked new avenues for the industry, making the town a byname in cutlery. It also opened new opportunities in engine manufacture, medical instruments and many other fields and the increased waste provided large quantities of phosphate fertiliser. Unfortunately, these processes also greatly assisted Germany's production of steel.

High explosives and other essential products relied upon supplies of basic material and there were many such materials required in Britain in World War I. But the period leading up to World War I was also the dawn of the 'Age of Plastics'. In 1856, in Birmingham, Alexander Parkes, the inventor of the Parkes process for desilvering lead, produced a nitrocellulose he named parkesine which added to the range of mouldable materials such as Charles Goodyear's vulcanised rubber.

N° 1921   A.D. 1908

Samples furnished under Section 3 (s, s. 5).

Date of Application, 28th Jan., 1908—Accepted, 7th Jan., 1909

COMPLETE SPECIFICATION.

"Insoluble Condensation Products of Phenols and Formaldehyde".

I, LEO HENDRIK BAEKELAND, of "Snug Rock", Harmony Park, Yonkers Township, Westchester County, State of New York, United States of America, Chemist, do hereby declare the nature of this invention and in what manner the same is to be performed to be particularly described and ascertained in
5 and by the following statement:

The action of phenols on aldehydes and more particularly formaldehyde is a much more complicated process than seems at first. Without entering into theoretical speculations, I may state broadly that, according to proportions, temperature, condensing agents and methods of preparation, products may
10 be obtained differing in physical and chemical properties and of which the possible industrial applications are widely divergent. Some may be liquid

The patent for Baekeland's compound

Although it was the first thermoplastic, parkesine was not a great success due to cost and durability issues. Flexible products were still made from whale bone and other natural material. In 1907, the Belgian chemist Leo Henricus Arthur Baekeland had perfected the method for the production of a usable form of phenol formaldehyde compound and for this he has been called 'The Father of the Plastics Industry'. In the late 1890s and then living in the US, he invented the first photographic paper 'Veloxin'. The proceeds from Veloxin enabled him to marry and purchase a property in Yonkers, New York known as 'Snug Rock'. Here, with his wife Céline Swarts, he had three children, George, Nina, and Jenny and, through his meticulous approach to the process of experimentation, he perfected the manufacture of the compound he named bakelite. Leo Baekeland patented his material and by the start of the war bakelite was being used for a growing variety of products.

Leo was honoured by many of the Allied countries for his work and its effect upon the war effort and Céline for her work in Belgium complementing the work of 'The Commission for Relief in Belgium'.

Within the MID there was some concern when monitoring detected that Germany had under development a synthetic substitute material for vulcanite, and maybe rubber, made by Traun & Söhne of Hamburg, renowned before the war as a natural rubber manufacturing company. Named futuran, this material was subsequently found by Sir Henry's contacts to be a compound of phenol and formaldehyde and therefore another form of bakelite.

The Traun company had a branch on Long Island which was not far from the origins of bakelite in Yonkers. Futuran had probably been named to honour the memory of the founder's son, Friedrich Adolf 'Fritz' Traun, who had died in tragic circumstances. Maybe as a consequence of this MID investigation, on 29th August 1918, for trading with the enemy, the company Winter and Almenraeder was ordered to be wound up. According to *The London Gazette* (18th April 1919), they were 'importers of Vulcanite &c., successors of H. Traun and Sons, 25, Goswell Road, London, Manufacturers of Ebonite.'

The monitoring of patents was an essential occupation. Indeed the application for British patents by citizens of the Central Powers was possible via the intermediary of a neutral country. For example, Dr. Fritz Pollak of Vienna applied for his British patent on the manufacture of hollow shapes from phenol and formaldehyde in 1915.

Gaining and maintaining technical advantage over the enemy was paramount and the air services, as the new 'eyes' of the battlefield, were in this arms race. Major Tom Vincent Smith, M.C. was another RFC officer foremost in the introduction of 'wireless' and its protocols in the RFC. He was born in London in 1872, and received his technical education at the Regent Street Polytechnic, then at Northampton Institute (where Frederick Handley Page in 1911 and Professor Grigori Tokaty in the 1960s lectured in aeronautics) and Birkbeck College.

At the beginning of the war he joined the RFC and in France in February 1915 he was one of the first to be commissioned for specialist duties as a squadron technical wireless officer, with Brabazon holding a similar post on the photographic speciality. In May 1915, the 1st Wing were fitted with wireless, and these were particularly effective during the battle of Aubers Ridge although in the aftermath of this battle the first notes of 'the munitions crisis' were sounded and the 'Shell Scandal' that provoked the creation of the Ministry of Munitions went into full cry in the media. During the battle of Loos, the 1st, 2nd and 3rd Wings were deployed, their radio transmitting targeting information being used to minimise wastage of the precious munitions. Boom Trenchard was in overall control with Splash Ashmore, John Maitland Salmond, and Sefton Brancker commanding their respective wings. This battle saw the first use of poison gas by the British and tunnelling was undertaken to lay mines under the German lines. As the battle progressed, the RFC flew low over the lines, dropping 100 lb bombs on priority targets in what became the first extensive use of tactical bombing. On 15th October 1915, Sir John French noted the effective use of the new radio methods in directing artillery fire.

Promoted to officer-in-charge of wireless at No. 1 Aircraft Depot, Smith established formal training for wireless personnel, and devised tuning methods which allowed aircraft to work in closer proximity with others. In March 1916 he was posted to the RFC GHQ. Here, he standardised aeroplane wireless procedures used on the entire front. At the battle of the Somme there were over 500 wireless stations, although one report put it at 1000 but this level was only achieved at the end of the war in November 1918. Procedural refinements improved crucial factors; for example, flight patterns for sorties ensured that aircraft wireless reporting was undertaken when the orientation of the aircraft to the ground station optimised reception.

Innovation in bombing came when Vickers responded to the requirement for a night bomber capable of attacking targets in Germany. Their chief designer 'Rex' Pierson had been with Vickers since 1908, in Erith where Archie Low had grown up. Rex designed a twin-engine biplane bomber, the Vickers F. B.27 'Vimy' and won a contract to build three prototypes on 14th August 1917.[4] Such was the urgency, it was flying on 30th November 1917 and went into production. It was named after the battle of Vimy Ridge.

In the autumn of 1918, concentration shifted sufficiently from the war to focus on the 1913 *Daily Mail* prize of £10,000 for 'the aviator who shall first cross the Atlantic in an aeroplane in flight from any point in the United States of America, Canada or Newfoundland and any point in Great Britain or Ireland in 72 continuous hours'. In August 1918, Henry Norman got involved in the detailed planning for a proposed transatlantic flight using an F.B.27 Vickers Vimy. This planning included the route to be flown and of course, the hangar facilities and the provision of fuel needed for preparation of the aircraft in Newfoundland.

Alcock and his navigator Brown took the prize. After less than 16 hours in the air, their Vimy landed in what, unfortunately, turned out to be a bog at 8:40 a.m. on 15th June 1919 in County Galway, Ireland, not far from their intended destination. Just 11 years after French aviators and the Wright Brothers had publicly demonstrated manned powered flight in 1908, man had completed a trans-oceanic flight.

As flight durations and aircraft range increased, navigation became an even greater challenge. Aircraft flew too high and often above cloud cover so Bradshawing could not be relied upon. Dead reckoning became an essential skill and over featureless terrain such as deserts and oceans it could only be supplemented with celestial navigational 'fixes'. However, the nautical sextant was useless when there was no horizon and when used at altitude. After the war, Lionel Barton Booth at the British Royal Aircraft Establishment developed a bubble sextant and by 1924 it reached a standard suitable for use. Other countries also developed useable instruments but they all took many years of development to reach a high level of accuracy and ease of use.

On 31st January 1918, Sir Henry requested the loan of Segrave, an officer who due to his injuries was no longer flying. Henry O'Neal de Hane Segrave was, by all accounts, one to make light of dramatic events in his life. He had had an eventful war up to this point, shot in a hand-to-hand trench encounter with the Hun on 17th May 1915 and close to death, he survived and recovered. He joined the RFC and got his pilot's certificate on 19th November 1915. He was injured again in France in a prang on 6th July 1916 when his FE8 crashed on take off on a practice flight.

Six months after he 'piloted' the AT in the trials, on 4th October 1917 he married Miss Doris Mary Stocker, the well-known actress. Having worked for Sir Henry through much of 1918, Segrave was sent to the US in the autumn as part of Brig. Gen. Charles Frederick Lee's British aviation mission to Washington to help with the development of military aviation in the US.

Segrave kept Sir Norman informed about the work of the mission and the progress in the US on aviation matters. In August he sent a précis of the senatorial inquiry into US air work: '601 DH4's had embarked for France. 67 were at the Front by July 1918. First engagement was 7th August 1918.'

The Delco plant incorporated the Dayton-Wright Airplane Company that manufactured, under licence from Airco in England, the de Havilland DH-4 bomber of British design but fitted with American Liberty engines. This was the only American-built airplane to see action in World War I. These were deployed with the 135th Observation Squadron. The first contact engagement of these aircraft occurred on 16th August when a photographic patrol was shot up by an Albatros D which hit the engine and the DH-4 was forced to glide back and land in friendly territory. American pilots had been flying with the British and the French as volunteers and, from March 1916, in the Lafayette Escadrille.

The subject of Segrave's report was one of the American enquiries into why such enormous expenditure on the air effort resulted in such a small number of machines put into service. The unachievable promise in the press had been to 'darken the skies over Germany'. In the end, less than 200 American-built aircraft

Squadron insignia of the Lafayette Escadrille

were deployed in Europe, and they were all British-designed DH4s. Having said that, the American forces in Europe flew locally built aircraft and many more of the American-produced aircraft were 'on their way' but there just was not enough time for the US to create an aircraft industry from scratch in 1917 and deliver aircraft in significant quantities by war's end, no matter how much money had been made available. The spark had been struck in the US in 1903 but without the need or the means, no significant American aircraft manufacturing industry had emerged. Sadly, the British aviation mission was marred by another fatal accident when the ace, Captain James Fitz-Morris M. C. was killed giving an exhibition of flying in Cincinnati, the second city they were visiting.

The nature of the MID, supported as it was by seconded experts and volunteer scientist, made it predisposed to rapid demobilisation. Segrave was distressed by those 'let go' in the unseemly 'race for peace' after the armistice and especially the speed at which the authorities dispensed with the services of Sir Henry Norman. But he had returned from the US with his actress wife, a British bulldog, a large American motor and his new passion … racing motors.

Archie said that Sir Henry also assisted him with his case for gaining an award for his wartime endeavours. On 15th November 1917, an exchange took place in the House of Commons. Major Sir Henry Norman asked the chancellor of the exchequer if he would state, in the case of a technical temporary officer of one of the services who may have made important war inventions for which he has been required to take out secret patents and assign these to the government, what is the financial position of such an officer in respect of these patents, and in what manner and on what basis he is remunerated for his inventions? In reply Sir Worthington Laming Evans merely described the existing provisions appertaining to any requests but included 'regard will be paid to any facilities which the inventor may have enjoyed by reason of his official position.' Archie subsequently turned this clause on its head and applied for payment for the use made of his premises.

Flight magazine, 4th May 1916, produced an article highlighting the lack of support and standing of inventors saying:

> The public pay rich fees to men who invent revues and music hall jokes, but the inventive engineer has a poor time of it. Our whole system of education is anti-technical. Our newspapers put politics, sport, society gossip, fashion puffs, and theatrical rubbish in front of science and technical affairs, and it is really a marvel that we have held our own so well against Germany, where so much has been done to foster invention and industry.

There were exceptions. One such was Admiral Percy Scott, whose work on improvements to naval gunnery well before the war continued and was carried out in co-operation with the Vickers Company, which left him a wealthy man when he died. Although an expert in gunnery, he was also a thorn in the side of many for his outspoken opinions concerning the conservatism of the naval authorities. This attitude and entrepreneurial enterprise were probably reasons he was often the cause for concern despite his contributions to the development of the Lonon Air Defence Area and to coding machines.

In later years, post World War II, Sir Christopher Sydney Cockerell's experience trying to promote his Hovercraft invention was often used as a demonstration of the British establishment's classically inspired approach to industrial innovation. There were numerous instances through the decades of the past century that reinforced the suspicion that rather than admit their incompetence and inability to understand what they are being told and seeing demonstrated, 'the British mandarins' stifle new concepts to death under red tape or make gifts of them to other nations.

After many had failed trying, Cockerill solved the problem of retaining the cushioning air under hovering vehicles by injecting a high pressure curtain around the periphery of the vehicles platform. He demonstrated the military potential of such vehicles to the government. The reaction was inaction; there was to be no development of the concept by the government and a ban (for security reasons) on Cockerell pursuing the work. Over the course of the year following this decision, Cockerell's financial situation became critical. Only when other countries became interested was Hovercraft Development Ltd. formed and work was started. All of the benefits were retained for the Crown, who took over his patents. Years later, after resorting to the courts, the British government were paid by the US for the privileged information, but none of this was passed on the Cockerell.

Over his career designing and patenting radio and radar aids for aerial navigation from the mid-1930s through World War II, Cockerell filed hundreds of patents. One of these (claimed in June 1939) was with the German Reichspatentamt. He ended his career setting up Wavepower Ltd. and berating the British system that 'produces engineers who are quite unsuitable for positions of influence, and managers who can do no better than stagger through our highly technological age.'

The ethical and moral implications of some new weapons and military activities of World War I caused a great deal of debate. The use of exploding small calibre ordnance and the distribution of propaganda leaflets from aircraft were examples but more obvious ones were the introduction of submarine warfare and of course, chemical offensive weapons with the first use of gas. Indeed, Archie had much to say on invention and the role of science in war. In the chapter 'Swords into Ploughshares' of his book *Modern Armaments* published in 1939, he makes the case that war is historically the one cause that unites a nation and the resulting single-minded endeavour creates in the longer term more that is beneficial to mankind than is evil. He laments this state of the affairs of mankind but acknowledges that survival through warfare 'is the only' cause that demands the complete focus of a whole population and that it cannot be created by some artificial proclamation. During World War II he wrote his book *Benefits of War,* concluding that one of the greatest benefits is that the spiritual and psychological aspects of peace are most appreciated in the immediate aftermath of war.

Illustration 1

The World's first Drone – surviving WWI parts in the I.W.M. stores

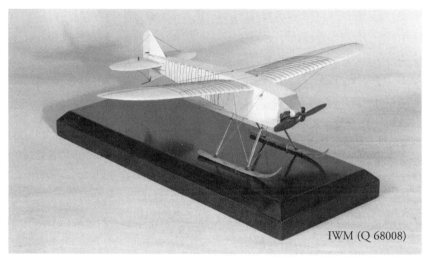

IWM (Q 68008)

This is the model commissioned by Prof. A. M. Low of the first radio-controlled monoplane, the Aerial Target design that was used in the successful trial flights of 21st March 1917 at Upavon. These experimental radio-controlled monoplanes were designed by de Havilland and were powered by their flat twin opposed 35 h.p. engines that were designed by Granville Bradshaw. Note the aerial wires on the wings and fuselage.

IWM (Q 68005)

A prototype control system test unit for the Distance Control Boats.
Label reads 'Laboratory R.F.C. Feltham, Middlesex' and
the control selections are PORT, STARBOARD, 1/2 SPEED, EXPLODE

Illustration 2

Selective Receiver

Coherer   Coherer Relay   Main Relay   The Pecker Gear

IWM (Q 68006)

PATENT SPECIFICATION   **244,258**

Application Date : Jan. 9, 1918. No. 541 / 18.

Accepted : Dec. 10, 1918 (but withheld from publication under section 30 of Patents & Designs Acts 1907 & 1919).

Authorised to be Published : Nov. 17, 1925. Date of Publication : Jan. 14, 1926.

COMPLETE SPECIFICATION.

Improved Aerial Projectile.

I, ARCHIBALD MONTGOMERY LOW, Captain in His Majesty's Army, of Royal Flying Corps, Experimental Works, Feltham, Middlesex, do hereby declare compartment, receptacle or reservoir such as *e* formed in, upon, or by the body of 45 the aeroplane a charge of any suitable high explosive or other explosive charge

The selective receiver that flew in the 1917 Aerial Target and the title banner and drawings from its patent.

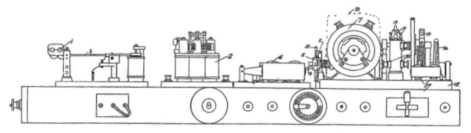

Patent drawing front view – compare with picture above

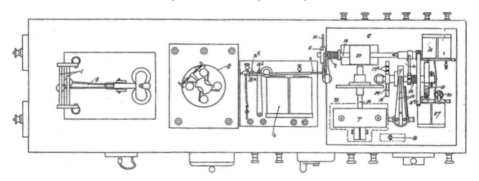

Patent drawing plan view

Illustration 3

The Selective Receiver Rear View

IWM (Q 68007)

Key Hole Slots in Lid
for easy access

An earlier version of the receiver

IWM (Q 67989)

Low said that the Feltham Works developed many types of relays and imaginative innovations such as their smoke aerial. The vast majority of their components had to be designed and built by their unit, and we know that some of the production involved considerable quantities of these items. Three components are shown below mounted on their presentation stands for the IWM Exhibition in the 1950s. The label reads 'Laboratory R.F.C. Feltham'.

IWM (Q 68012)

Illustration 4
The 1917 AT Ground Control Unit

IWM (Q 68010)

IWM (Q 68011)

Illustration 5

'Steering the Aerial Target'

Climb, Dive and Turn – The AT's Elevator and Rudder controls

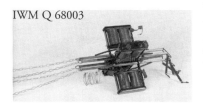

IWM Q 68003

The cable runs from the AT's Elevator and Rudder control surfaces were attached to the bars of the 'actuator' unit. When activated by the relevant signal from the ground controller, this actuator's electro-magnets, which were arranged around a drive screw, forced their armature rod onto these bars engaging a stud into a drive screw which moved the bar. Circular tracks at each end of the drive screw prevent over run if the control demand was held ON. The drive screw was driven by the AT's aero-engine.

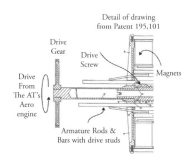

Detail of drawing from Patent 195,101

This 'Actuator' in the Imperial War Museum is identical to the apparatus described in its related Patent 195,101. It is referred to as 'actuating gear' in the AT Patent 244,258 which also shows where it was positioned in the AT.

For other control functions, additional magnets and armature rods with their drive bars could be positioned around the drive screw but the 1917 de Havilland AT only had these four that were used to move its elevator and rudder.

Further examples of the 'Actuator' operating the elevator are shown in these adjacent diagrams.

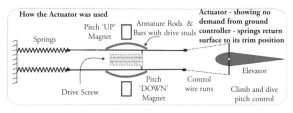

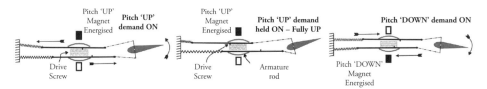

Note: Engaged drive studs travel towards circular track nearest to the springs.

Illustration 6

IWM (Q 67984)

Poole   Low   Bowen

The Feltham Secret Experimental Works.
The older officers in the back row may be
Mantell and Whitton.

Poole at the transmitter selector – note
the second set of controls.

IWM (Q 67988)

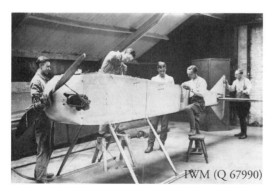

IWM (Q 67990)

Fitting the control system into an Aerial
Target.

Illustration 7

In later years, Prof. Archie Low busy in his laboratory, with the garden foliage encroaching over the doorway. In a different image taken in his lab in 1923, fully four years after the 1917 AT Flight, Archie Low has his arm resting on a version of the AT Controller with six selection levers and its motor driven selection disks clearly visible. This image is in the Emil Otto Hoppé Estate Collection.

Archie Low in his converted Bédélia cyclecar 1912

Archie Low with H.R.H. Prince Philip, The Duke of Edinburgh at the Isle of Man T.T. races

Illustration 8
Some of the patents for the AT

PATENT SPECIFICATION

Application Date: June 22, 1917. No. 8976/17. **195,101**

Accepted: Nov. 11, 1919 (but withheld from Publication under Section 30 of Patents and Designs Acts, 1907 and 1919).
Authorised to be Published: March 5, 1923. Date of Publication: April 19, 1923.

COMPLETE SPECIFICATION.

Improvements in Electrical Controlling Apparatus.

I, ARCHIBALD MONTGOMERY LOW, Captain in His Majesty's Army, of Royal Flying Corps Experimental Works, Feltham, Middlesex, do hereby declare the nature of this invention and in what — magnets being secured to the outer ends of the arms. The armatures 7 of the magnets are adapted to slide between the arms 4 and carry studs or the like 8 in which are pivoted rods 9 which pass 50

PATENT SPECIFICATION

Application Date: June 22, 1917. No. 8979/17. **191,402**

Accepted: Jan. 15, 1919 (but withheld from Publication under Section 30 of Patents and Designs Acts, 1907 and 1919).
Authorised to be Published: Dec. 13, 1922. Date of Publication: Feb. 8, 1923.

COMPLETE SPECIFICATION.

Improvements in Signalling Apparatus.

I, ARCHIBALD MONTGOMERY LOW, Captain in His Majesty's Army, of Royal Flying Corps Experimental Works, Feltham, Middlesex, do hereby declare — receiving apparatus is operative at a time and consequently signals may be sent to the corresponding receiving station without being picked up at any one of the 50 other stations.

PATENT SPECIFICATION

Application Date: Jan. 9, 1918. No. 540/18. **191,406**

Accepted: Jan. 26, 1918 (but withheld from Publication under Section 30 of Patents and Designs Acts, 1907 and 1910).
Authorised to be Published: Dec. 13, 1922. Date of Publication: Feb. 8, 1923.

COMPLETE SPECIFICATION.

Improvements in Wireless Telegraphic Apparatus.

I, ARCHIBALD MONTGOMERY LOW, Captain in His Majesty's Army, of Royal Flying Corps Experimental Works, Feltham, Middlesex, do hereby declare — other suitable insulating means with a metallic or other suitable box or casing suspended from or supported by but insulated from a support. The box or casing is provided with an elbow pipe from 50

PATENT SPECIFICATION

Application Date: July 25, 1918. No. 12,344/18. **191,410**

(Patent of Addition to No. 191,407: Jan. 22, 1918.)

Accepted: Aug. 13, 1918 (but withheld from Publication under Section 30 of Patents and Designs Acts, 1907 and 1919).
Authorised to be Published: Dec. 13, 1922. Date of Publication: Feb. 8, 1923.

COMPLETE SPECIFICATION.

Improvements in Electrically Driven Gyroscopes.

I, ARCHIBALD MONTGOMERY LOW, Captain in His Majesty's Army, of Air Force Experimental Works, Feltham, Middlesex, do hereby — of apparatus hereinafter described and illustrated.
The accompanying drawings illustrate two modes of carrying out the invention.

PATENT SPECIFICATION

Application Date: Jan. 9, 1918. No. 542/18. **191,756**

Accepted: Jan. 26, 1918 (but withheld from Publication under Section 30 of Patents and Designs Acts, 1907 and 1919).
Authorised to be Published: Dec. 13, 1922. Date of Publication: Feb. 15, 1923.

COMPLETE SPECIFICATION.

Improvements in Electro Magnetic Relays.

I, ARCHIBALD MONTGOMERY LOW, Captain in His Majesty's Army, of Royal Flying Corps Experimental Works, Feltham, Middlesex, do hereby declare — employed and the current which actuates the relay is used to excite the relay magnets, or it may be applied to relays in which permanent magnets are used, the

---

PATENT SPECIFICATION

Application Date: June 22, 1917. No. 8976/17. **195,101**

Accepted: Nov. 11, 1919 (but withheld from Publication under Section 30 of Patents and Designs Acts, 1907 and 1919).
Authorised to be Published: March 5, 1923. Date of Publication: April 19, 1923.

COMPLETE SPECIFICATION.

Improvements in Electrical Controlling Apparatus.

I, ARCHIBALD MONTGOMERY LOW, Captain in His Majesty's Army, of Royal Flying Corps Experimental Works, Feltham, Middlesex, do hereby declare — magnets being secured to the outer ends of the arms. The armatures 7 of the magnets are adapted to slide between the arms 4 and carry studs or the like 8 in which are pivoted rods 9 which pass 50

PATENT SPECIFICATION

Application Date: April 10, 1918. No. 6110/18. **195,991**

Accepted: May 14, 1918 (but withheld from Publication under Section 30 of Patents and Designs Acts, 1907 and 1919).
Authorised to be Published: March 5, 1923. Date of Publication: May 10, 1923.

COMPLETE SPECIFICATION.

Improved Apparatus for Launching Aerial Projectiles or the like.

I, ARCHIBALD MONTGOMERY LOW, Captain in His Majesty's Army, of Royal Flying Corps Experimental Works, Feltham, Middlesex, do hereby declare — Figure 3 is a part sectional elevation on a larger scale showing a detail.
In carrying my invention into effect in convenient manner I prefer to arrange 50

PATENT SPECIFICATION

Application Date: Jan. 19, 1918. No. 1110/18. **195,102**

Accepted: May 26, 1919 (but withheld from Publication under Section 30 of Patents and Designs, Acts 1907 and 1919).
Authorised to be Published: March 5, 1923. Date of Publication: April 19, 1923.

COMPLETE SPECIFICATION.

Improvements in High Frequency Transformers.

I, ARCHIBALD MONTGOMERY LOW, Captain in His Majesty's Army, of Royal Flying Corps Experimental Works, Feltham, Middlesex, do hereby declare the nature of this invention and in what — is that of two separate coils under the same inductance which having different choke values, but being connected 50 together, can have different voltages and consequently current factors lagging an

---

PATENT SPECIFICATION

Application Date: Aug. 10, 1917. No. 11,496/17. **191,404**

Accepted: Dec. 20, 1917 (but withheld from Publication under Section 30 of Patents and Designs Acts 1907 and 1919)
Authorised to be Published: Dec. 13, 1922. Date of Publication: Feb. 8, 1923.

COMPLETE SPECIFICATION.

Improvements in Coherers for Detecting Electric Radiation.

I, ARCHIBALD MONTGOMERY LOW, Captain in His Majesty's Army, of Royal Flying Corps Experimental Works, Feltham, Middlesex, do hereby declare — stream or in an atmosphere of silver dioxide.
The particles or filings may be employed in any suitable form of coherer, 40

PATENT SPECIFICATION

Application Date: Jan. 22, 1918. No. 1267/18. **191,407**

Accepted: May 14, 1918 (but withheld from Publication under Section 30 of Patents and Designs Acts 1907 and 1919).
Authorised to be Published: Dec. 13, 1922. Date of Publication: Feb. 8, 1923.

COMPLETE SPECIFICATION.

Improvements in Electrically Driven Gyroscopes.

I, ARCHIBALD MONTGOMERY LOW, Captain in His Majesty's Army, of Royal Flying Corps Experimental Works, Feltham, Middlesex, do hereby declare the nature of this invention and in what — ing the scheme of connections and a portion of the gyroscope in side elevation. 50
In carrying my invention into effect in the manner illustrated I form my improved gyroscope with a gyroscope

---

PATENT SPECIFICATION

Application Date: June 22, 1917. No. 8961/17. **191,753**

Accepted: Jan. 15, 1919 (but withheld from Publication under Section 30 of Patents and Designs Acts 1907 and 1919).
Authorised to be Published: Dec. 13, 1922. Date of Publication: Feb. 15, 1923.

COMPLETE SPECIFICATION.

Improvements in Electro-magnetic Relays.

I, ARCHIBALD MONTGOMERY LOW, Captain in His Majesty's Army, of Royal Flying Corps Experimental Works, Feltham, Middlesex, do hereby declare — in the upper and lower plates of the cage 8. This spindle has secured to it a block 10, the four arms 11 of the armature being seated in the face of this block and

---

PATENT SPECIFICATION

Application Date: June 8, 1917. No. 8187/17. **195,100**

Accepted: Jan. 11, 1921 (but withheld from Publication under Section 30 of Patents and Designs Acts, 1907 and 1919).
Authorised to be Published: March 5, 1923. Date of Publication: April 19, 1923.

COMPLETE SPECIFICATION.

Improved Apparatus for Selectively Sending Pre-arranged Electric Signals.

I, ARCHIBALD MONTGOMERY LOW, Captain in His Majesty's Army, of Royal Flying Corps Experimental Works, Feltham, Middlesex, do hereby declare — before the disc has made a complete revolution thus bringing the disc to rest. 45
If now the above mentioned handle or the like be released the disc continues to

---

PATENT SPECIFICATION

Application Date: Jan. 19, 1918. No. 1110/18. **195,102**

Accepted: May 26, 1919 (but withheld from Publication under Section 30 of Patents and Designs, Acts 1907 and 1919).
Authorised to be Published: March 5, 1923. Date of Publication: April 19, 1923.

COMPLETE SPECIFICATION.

Improvements in High Frequency Transformers.

I, ARCHIBALD MONTGOMERY LOW, Captain in His Majesty's Army, of Royal Flying Corps Experimental Works, Feltham, Middlesex, do hereby declare the — is that of two separate coils under the same inductance which having different choke values, but being connected 50 together, can have different voltages and consequently current factors lagging an

---

PATENT SPECIFICATION

Application Date: Jan. 9, 1918. No. 541/18. **244,258**

Accepted: Dec. 10, 1918 (but withheld from publication under section 30 of Patents & Designs Acts 1907 & 1919).
Authorised to be Published: Nov. 17, 1925. Date of Publication: Jan. 14, 1926.

COMPLETE SPECIFICATION.

Improved Aerial Projectile.

I, ARCHIBALD MONTGOMERY LOW, Captain in His Majesty's Army, of Royal Flying Corps Experimental Works, Feltham, Middlesex, do hereby declare — compartment, receptacle or reservoir such as is formed in, upon, or by the body of 45 the aeroplane a charge of any suitable high explosive or other explosive charge

CHAPTER 11

Archie's Marching Orders

When World War I started, all of the home comforts now derived from electrical supplies and other services were missing from the lives of the British public. Most of the British Army's new recruits who joined the rank and file were young men experiencing their first steps away from their 'home turf' where traditionally they would have followed in their forefathers' footsteps. In general, those entering as officers had been moulded more by the educational establishments they had been afforded rather than their home environments. Archie Low was working in the musty, dingy Edwardian offices of his uncle's shipping-cum-engineering company in the City of London and his education placed him firmly in this officer class.

In these early months of the war, many like Archie Low who were in business and had knowledge they thought was potentially useful to the war effort wanted to 'do their bit' in a role where their particular skills would be of most benefit. The forces needed 'boffins' – much later to be called back-room boys. The informal, word-of-mouth, old boy network had served the military well and proved useful. This worked on the principle of 'someone I know at the club knows someone who might have just the chap for …' which today has been sanitised and re-christened as 'networking'.

The professionals and business men who had their eyes on the prize sought service that allowed them plenty of opportunity to 'mind the shop'. After all, the public perception that the war would be over in months rather than years didn't dissipate until the spring of 1915 and while 'one had to do their bit', their business interests had to be sustained in the meantime. To sweeten the deal, while serving they would receive a reasonable wage employed as officers as their status warranted. Pay for a private was at least six times less than a junior officer although the latter had some initial expenses to find for his uniform and other sundry items. Out of his six shillings a day (about £21) a lieutenant would pay about 6d. (£1.75 at today's prices) for a pint of beer and 3d. for a pack of 20 cigarettes. However, under laws to curb the consumption of alcohol that were introduced in the spring of 1915, one was not allowed to buy a round of drinks for others in the restricted hours when pubs were now allowed to serve the diluted version of his favourite tipple.

The war was not over quickly and officers were one and a half times more likely than their men to become casualties if they were assigned to the forward trenches. Despite this, it became necessary for orders to be issued to stop senior officers joining their men as so many were being lost, including in the end about 200 generals.

When it came to joining the army, the logical scientist, Archie, was no different to the rest of the patriotic eligible population. As a cadet he remembered that he was only interviewed once by an officer he took to be the padre. On telling this man that he was 'the only Christian in the show' Low was informed that he was indeed addressing a military chaplain but that he was a rabbi. Once enlisted, he discovered that failure during initial training was referred to as 'taking the felt', as it meant returning to the bowler hat of civilian life. But Archie did not fail and later, when he found the rabbi in deep despair because the Passover cakes would not arrive in time, he contacted Harry Gordon Selfridge Jr. for help and young Gordon's batch of cakes arrived on the next train from London. Archie said that this was the highlight in an otherwise dismal introduction to his military service. During that wet and dreary 1915 spring, the scandalous U-boat sinking of the passenger liner *Lusitania* and the five-train disaster at Quintinshill added to the confusing and worrying news from France.

Archie had taken every opportunity to publicly demonstrate his capabilities but he must still have been pleasantly surprised when, against all of the perceived capacity of the services to always find a round hole for every square peg, he received a request for his assistance. The War Office had identified Low's Televista as a possible means of enhancing range finders and the Royal Ordnance College in Woolwich wrote to Low, who was appointed as Honorary Assistant Professor and set to work with their commandant to develop the idea. After making some progress on this project, he got another summons.

He was 'invited' to the huts on the roof of the War Offices opposite Horse Guards Arch on Whitehall. These huts housed the headquarters of the Royal Flying Corps. Archie describes his meeting there and how he opted to join the RFC. On 2nd June 1915, Archie was commissioned as a second lieutenant after meeting Pelham Francis Warner, the famous cricketer. 'Plum' Warner had captained the team that bought the Ashes back to England in 1904 but Archie only realised later that Plum, who had been born in Trinidad, was a friend of his mother's side of his family. Archie recalled that Plum's only real interest in the interview was to enquire as to the school he had attended as, in this society, the right school mattered. All was well on that front for, after all, Archie had had Monty as a classmate. Low ordered his uniform at the Army and Navy Co-operative Society Ltd but due to the huge demand they could not supply the essential officer's sword, so he had to use his grandfather's old sabre.

Archie was now tasked with creating and developing a means of radio control for an unmanned aircraft. His account of the naming by General Henderson of the Aerial Target in 1915 is questionable as we have already seen that the RAF were producing designs for an AT in 1914 although, of course, Henderson may still have been involved in naming them at that time. The general had been director of military intelligence in the Second Boer War so misinformation was his forte. The AT was christened to fool the enemy into thinking that these planes were to test anti-aircraft capabilities. With the later development of the Queen Bee, this rouse turned into an accurate description.

For a number of years, Archie had been modifying and repairing his cars, designing his two-stroke engine, building his Televista system and promoting and selling his company's 'cup' plugs so he was acquainted with a number of engineers. The AT project started in a fairly low-key manner. Low convinced one of his acquaintances, the tall and rather elegant Henry Jeffrey Poole who owned a specialised and successful garage business, to help him assemble a collection of salvaged and scrounged aircraft parts into a complete aircraft. Into this they could put their control system for test and demonstration purposes. Henry's workshop became their first base. Being about 15 years older than Archie and a man of property, Henry's participation in this venture demonstrates the high level of regard he had for Archie. They assembled the 1916 'Heath Robinson' Aerial Target from these salvaged parts. (William Heath Robinson's name was just entering the English language but is an apt description for this AT).[1]

Henry's previous career was as a professor of music, but by the time he met Archie, he had acquired an interest in motor engineering and was the proprietor of his specialist Motor Works on Back Common Road (aka Chiswick Common Road) in West London. Henry's Colville Motor Works attracted talented engineers. Back in 1904, when the business may well have been sited in Colville Road about a mile away from Chiswick Common Road, the Irish engineer Louis Mantell started working there. He had been educated at the Methodist College in Belfast, and then studied medicine at Queen's University College. Louis became a well-known carburation specialist who later wrote a great many articles and the book, *A Manual of Motor Mechanics*, copies of which still circulate today. This book was adopted in World War I by the War Office as a standard textbook for the Mechanical and Transport Schools of the RFC and the Royal Army Service Corps (RASC). Louis left Colville's in 1908 but from 1916 to 1919 Louis served as an experimental officer with the RFC in Low's unit.

Another motor engineer and inventor who was 'in the area' was Ernest Windsor Bowen, a 33-year-old Welshman. Back in 1905 this young man had a business interest in 'The South Wales Transport Company' in Cardiff before selling up and moving to London. Ernie used the Grahame-White Aviation Company address at 1 Albermarle St. to register as a member of the Institute of Automobile Engineers although he lived with his wife Emily and daughter Patricia Jane in Bedford Park, Ealing. This desirable area is claimed to be the world's first garden suburb and their eight-room residence was large enough for them to have a live-in maid. By the time he met Archie Low and Henry Poole, Ernie was an established inventor and had filed a number of patents relating mainly to engine valves.

Colville Motors' advert

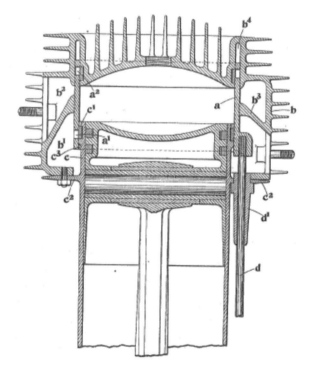

A drawing of one of Bowen's patents

Zeppelin raid recruitment poster (Library of Congress, Prints & Photographs Division, WWI Posters LC-USZC4-10972)

Low talked affectionately, and perhaps with a little touch of envy, about Bowen, this good looking 'great engineer' who was full of mischief. One memorable phone call of complaint recalled by Low was from a commandant who had observed 'an officer' talking too cheerily to one of his nurses. This incident was assumed to have involved Bowen. The commandant's description of one of Low's officers in his fur-collared 'British Warm' made Low check his own coat hanging on the door and caused him to, although entirely innocent, share a fleeting moment of collective guilt.

General Caddell (at this time the Deputy Assistant Director of Military Aeronautics) was now Low's boss in the Aerial Target enterprise. By now sufficient progress had been made with the AT control system, even though it was demonstrated in such an inferior airframe, that Low was allowed (or most probably ordered) to recruit a team and find a workshop for this RFC Experimental Works. His selection of officers and men was complicated as they would have to be agreeable to joining the RFC or transferring if they were already in the services and all of this would take time. He was also younger than most of the experienced engineers he would want on his design team. However, Low's AT project offered potential recruits a service posting 'at home', using their particular skills to aid the war effort when the social pressure to join up was at fever pitch.

It would be many more months before conscription was introduced and by then Henry would have been beyond the call up age anyway, so his motivation to join up was probably not as pressing as for the younger men. However, with the pressure

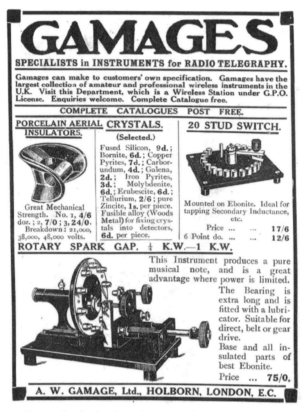

Gamages' radio brochure (courtesy of Aviation Ancestry)

to serve in the war combined with the social need to be in uniform and being in the same business of motors and engine design, Henry and Ernie would have been delighted to find that Archie's scheme for this interesting and completely novel, locally based development work was now to be officially established.

In late 1915 some form of conscription seemed inevitable as even with Kitchener's initiatives and the public pressure sometimes subtly but increasingly overtly applied to those not in uniform, recruitment was flagging. So, when Henry and Ernie joined the RFC, the Colville garage became the first home of the AT control system and saw the completion of this first aircraft, made out of 'scrap' and salvaged equipment. Henry and Ernest were both gazetted as second lieutenants RFC Special Reserve officers on 22nd December 1915.

The project was now formally established within the RFC as an Experimental Works to be run by three mature, highly qualified, ambitious, experienced and most importantly, well-respected consulting engineers. Captain Archie Low aged 27 was its commanding officer, Lieutenant Henry Poole aged 41 was second in command and Lieutenant Ernie Bowen was aged 34. Louis Mantell also became part of the team.

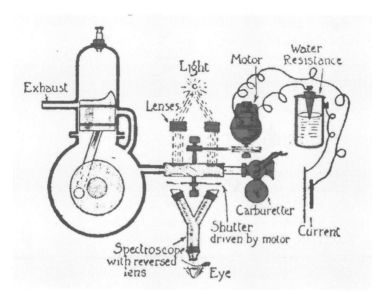

The cinematographic method in Archie's book (*The Two-Stroke Engine*, Temple Press, 1916)

What Low needed now was a radio engineer and he knew just where his chief radio engineer could be located. In those days, private experimenters were supplied by the specialist radio departments of some of the larger stores. Low had used the Gamages department store where he had obtained radio and specialist electrical parts for his Televista system from George William Mahoney Whitton. George joined the team and later in 1917 was to gain his commission.

If any one of these other four engineers had doubts about the feasibility of what Low was proposing they would have been unlikely to be associated with it, as their livelihood relied on their reputations and they had families to support. In addition, many of the country's top aeronautical design teams devoted precious time and resources producing the airframes and engines for the ATs at a time when their skills were at a premium in the technological race playing out on the front lines.

In time, Low's core of engineers acquired a team of skilled workers, instrument makers and mechanics, a detail of military guards and even a civilian police security presence as their status as a secret establishment warranted. They relied upon their contacts to fulfil their specialist design and material supply needs.

Meanwhile, Archie didn't ignore his pre-war business. He had been working on his first major publication and found enough time to get it into print by 1916. It was a substantial book on engine design, *The Two Stroke Engine: A manual of the coming form of the internal combustion engine*. The book draws upon the systematic and professional approach to engine design developed by Archie during his time at his Uncle Ted's establishment. For example, his cinematographic method for observing the petrol oil mixture in a glass inlet manifold is described in the book.

As well as internal combustion power plants, he had been working on gas turbine engines and in this book he tells us:

> Gas Turbine. Two- and four-stroke engines are reciprocating engines. … The same applies to the ordinary type of steam-engine…. the steam turbine was introduced, in which the power exerted is progressive and continuous. Attempts have been made to introduce a successful petrol turbine in which the explosions would have the same effect as the expansion of steam in a turbine.

Perhaps he would have been the first to develop a jet engine if he had continued with this work long enough for suitable materials to be developed that could withstand the heat and stress of a useful jet engine. However, here the trick would be to use some of the turbine's energy to drive a compressor and this 'spark' did not appear until 1921 in France. Meanwhile the war still had to be fought.

At the start of hostilities, the Brooklands track had been taken over by the RFC. The prewar Brooklands flying community within the racing track's Byfleet banking in its south-westerly end, bordering onto the infamous malodorous sewage farm, was a long walk from Weybridge where most of the workers were housed. They called the trek from the motoring paddock to the flying village 'the desert march'. The sense of community in 'the village', as the Brooklands Aviation Ground was known, owed a great deal to that homely melting pot that was the Blue Bird restaurant. The village became a busy community with its flying schools, a healthy representation of the famous names in aircraft design and manufacture and back in 1910 for a while, Thomas Sopwith's pet bear 'Poley'. As a cub it succeeded from time to time in its attempts to escape its keeper to search other people's sheds for tins of condensed milk. For decades, this sweet thick whitener was the most common ingredient to add to a mug of tea and was therefore not hard to find in the corners of the various flight sheds. Cans were punctured with two holes in the lid on either side, one hole to vent the tin for easy, steady pouring from the other. For Poley this was just right for drinking and for the young local lad employed as the cub's keeper, this delicacy was the only lure to get Poley down from the rafters of the sheds where he would usually hide. In 1913, after he had moved to Kingston, Sopwith had another bear 'Oonie' and this used to eat the wings when the sago starch was applied as a dope. Cecil Howard Pixton told stories of more conventional pets such as 'Seti' from Egypt and 'Whisky' who went flying, two of the dogs that were around at the village, and Hilda Hewlett, known for most of her life as 'Billy', had her Great Dane 'Kroshka'. Howard Pixton shot to fame when he flew Sopwith's Tabloid aircraft to win the second annual Jacques Schneider Trophy in 1914.

Initially, there had only been a farm house and a barn at the site of the flying village and even at the end of 1910, a year after the first flight shed had been erected, the only useable flying ground was about 100 yards (91 metres) wide and stretched from the corner of the sewage farm to shed No. 9 just beyond the Blue Bird in shed No. 7. One of the biggest aerial events took place on 22nd July 1911 when crowds of around 50,000 were at Brooklands to see the start of the first Circuit of Britain Air Race. Jean Louis Conneau, flying under the pseudonym André Beaumont, landed back at Brooklands five days later to claim the prize. Through 1911 the flying site was cleared and levelled by filling in the ditches and the deep ponds where material had been excavated to create the banking. Hedges were removed and more sheds were built so there were about forty by the end of 1911. Even the river was diverted to extend the airfield and one old hand recalled that 'practically every inch of the present aerodrome has been dug and levelled by hand.'

Towards the end of 1911 the maturing aviation development scene was looking to the future and assessing its potential as an 'industry'. The customer base for Britain's embryonic aircraft production facilities was tiny and comprised of, with few exceptions, the most gallant of the wealthy young men of the upper class. This market was now satiated. The producers looked to government and the military as the only other significant market. A group including A. V. Roe and Handley Page met Jack Seely. The outcome did not produce the encouragement these entrepreneurs hoped for and the repercussion of this response would colour the attitude of some outspoken aviation advocates over the following years. It was part of the reason Seely's reply concerning aircraft numbers in the 1913 Army Estimates Debate was not believed and why subsequently Sefton Brancker was tasked with rapidly acquiring anything with wings to make up the numbers. The 'industry' grew slowly with meagre demand from the military and a growing reliance on orders from the expanding number of flying schools. There was undoubtedly as much business in repairing pranged machines as there was in new builds. The scene changed and as the sun went down at Brooklands in the evening more went to the 'Health Club' to play billiards than to the Blue Bird to eat and chat or to stay at work until the daylight gave out.

By 1913, the aviation ground was quite extensive, sitting at the end of a short road that led away from the low inside edge of the Byfleet banking with its line of original sheds that ranged along the curve by the foot bridge. This little track ran across the inner field of the site and entered the flying village by the garden with its wind gauge mast, the privy outhouse and the cottage. The track turned to the left as it entered 'Bird Cage Walk' which ran off down through the middle of the village towards the sewage farm. On the left there were nine hangars and at the end a smaller shed. On the right, past the garden, the main block of buildings incorporating the little 'hospital' and the original farm house yard which accommodated the engine room, the forge, the carpenters shop and the 'Ladies'. This was accessed from the back door of the Blue Bird restaurant. Past these, the side lane on the right was called Swallow Walk and it provided access to the front line of hangars looking out over the flying ground. Beyond Swallow Walk there were three more sheds on the right of Bird Cage Walk. Looking back at the village from the flying ground there were buildings on the right between the sewage farm and Swallow Walk. Then a line of seven hangars, the last three being the 'Blue Bird' and finally the two hangars backing on to the garden. On the end of the left hand hangar was the only telephone in its little booth. Standing out in front of the village, from 1911 onwards, was the ticket office – the world's first air terminal check-in where the adventurous visitor might purchase a short recreational flight. This was the famous Brooklands Aviation Ground that accommodated, before the war, the exploits of 'those magnificent men in their flying machines'.

At the British Automobile Racing Club (BARC) meeting on the site on the very windy 3rd August 1914, the crowds were preoccupied with the expected declaration of war and keeping a watchful eye out for the delivery of the latest issue of the newspapers on sale in the paddock. They were very aware of the number of troop trains running down the line adjacent to the track, by now it would seem under the control of the Railway Executive Committee. This would prove to be the last large public meeting before the whole site was closed to civilian use.

No.1 Squadron of the RFC had moved into the site from Farnborough four months before the start of the war to train on their new machines, converting from airships as these had been transferred to the RNAS under the re-organisations. The entire Brooklands site became the RFC's Aircraft Acceptance Park and a major training school on 14th August.

However, the war didn't end the roaring around the Brooklands track as some individual speed trials were allowed and the RFC used the track for testing and accepting motorcycles for military use. Significant numbers of 'bikes' were ordered for the RFC and would prove themselves useful, speeding the intelligence from returning aircraft to 'their customers' in the artillery and central commands.

The Brooklands site was within easy reach of London and under RFC control it became a significant centre where large numbers of aircraft were manufactured during the war. More significantly, from a security perspective it was a trials and testing site for new models and novel features delivered to the grounds from many other aircraft production factories. The high level of activity and sensitivity of the work at Brooklands warranted protection and after reports of foreign spies, security on the site tightened. In the early hours of 16th August 1914, Private Robertson of the Royal West Surrey Regiment was guarding the aviation sheds when he challenged a man three times and then fired. The man immediately returned the fire, wounding Robertson severely in the arm. The aerodrome was searched without success, although a man was seen to disappear in the woods as the motor car conveying Robertson was on its way to hospital. Archie noted that when they were there in 1917 they were guarded by the army and the police and that Ernest Bowen was nearly shot one night by one over zealous sentry when he wandered back around the hangars from a 'domestic' visit.

A sizable section of the populous at this time quickly became paranoid and xenophobic. As we have seen with Archie's two 'frights' involving foreign agents, accounts may have been rather too widely and wildly reported. However, it was a time to be nervous as the Germans stormed through Belgium and on towards Paris. At Netheravon one night, about 7th August, the guards all turned out to scour the country in the vicinity to look for supposed spies who were reported to be prowling about with the intention of blowing up the sheds, but they did not find anyone. Night-time searches of the countryside after sighting of 'invaders' crawling over the hillside were often resolved by a local with the explanation 'de'ms be sheep'!

There weren't just spies, saboteurs and criminals to discourage. Where there is a barrier hiding such fascinating sights and dangerous souvenirs, boys will see it as a challenge to gain entry. There was a spate of cases of boys sliding down the track behind the aeroplane sheds into the Brooklands site in November 1916. Fourteen were bought before the Woking magistrates, charged with being on War Department land without a permit. The three eldest were fined 5s. each and the rest were told not to do it again.

Before the war, Archie would have been less familiar with the aircraft area of the Brooklands site, being drawn as he was by interest and business to the vehicles in the paddock, the pits and on the track. A year after the closure of the site for military use, part of the track was still being used for RFC acceptance testing of their motorbikes. Enthusiasts, including many in the forces, still hankered after the challenge of racing so, despite the damage to the track that had occurred from the military activity and with the co-operation of BARC and other organisations, an 'All Khaki Race meeting' was arranged for 7th August 1915. There were a large number of spectators at the meeting, predominantly dressed in khaki but also a lot in their convalescent blues (the light-blue and red-tie uniform worn by the injured). These will have been mainly from the Ethel Locke King Brooklands House military hospital. This event was followed shortly afterwards by a second meeting on 4th September. Finally, on 23rd October the Royal Aircraft Factory held a race meeting at Brooklands. Despite the rain they held races from the flying village round to the members, bridge and the finishing straight. It is possible that some races for side-cars may have included cycle-cars and that there may have been one race for touring cars. After the races there was a spectacular hair-raising aerial display by 'one of the latest army aeroplanes' that skimmed the finishing straight so low that it damaged the timing telegraph wire, stopping the clock in the paddock at 2:20 p.m. The aircraft was almost certainly an F.E.8 as this had only completed its first test flight on 15th October. The pilot on both of these occasions was Frank Goodden who had 'helped' William Newell make his record parachute jump in 1914.[2] Following this, there were adverse comments in the aviation press that precious aircraft and pilots were put at risk by such 'circus feats' and that the latest military hardware should not be 'exhibited to the assorted gatherings that are found at motor race meetings.'

This was probably the 'shoe string' attempt cobbled together from scavenged parts that was tested in March 1916 without any chance of making a successful flight at Upavon (Michael Draper)

The five officials at this October meeting included the RAF Superintendent Mervyn O'Gorman and Archibald Montgomery Low.

Racing at Brooklands was now over for the duration but others, recognising the need for some relief from the grind of war, were providing diverting activities. For example, at the Vickers aeroplane works on the site, the canteen could be transformed into a picture theatre or stage and reverted to a canteen in just 10 minutes.

In June 1916, Low's team carried out some of their first formal experiments, taking their AT to Brooklands and then to Upavon for trials. Sir Henry's status and technical radio knowledge would have made him an appropriate choice for this assessment, after which the RFC AT project would have also become an MID project.

In 1916, the deadly consequences of the war came crashing into the private lives of Amy and Archie's family with the news that Amy's brother, Thomas, had been killed in action on 3rd September. Amongst all the reports of the carnage at the time, people gained a level of immunity or isolation from its effects, until, that is, the casualty was a loved family member or close friend. In this case it was Amy's younger brother. Thomas had gone to Australia for work and enlisted in the Australian forces, assigned into the 9th Battalion of the 11th Reinforcement at Coopers Creek, Mullumbimby. This battalion, along with the rest of the eager young 'diggers' embarked for Egypt from Brisbane on the HMAT A48 *Seang Bee* on 21st October 1915. In Egypt, the 49th Battalion was formed on 27th February 1916 as part of the 'doubling' of the Australian Imperial Force. It went into the front line trenches on 21st June just nine days after its arrival in France and in time for the start of the Somme Offensive. In August 1916 it was engaged in the battle at Mouquet Farm and Thomas was killed in the assault that was mounted there on 3rd September, a day when the 49th suffered some of its heaviest casualties.

Archie's pre-war business had progressed financially and his annual income of about £1,500 enabled him to acquire his various premises. After the Upavon trials, Low's unit needed to expand and it is likely that it moved in stages to Feltham, taking this location into their formal name: 'The Royal Flying Corps: Experimental Works, Feltham, Middlesex'. On 12th November 1916 they occupied requisitioned premises in the old Ivory Works near Bedfont Lane, just 1 mile from Low's high street facility. These buildings were commandeered from the Davis Paraffin Carburettor Company and the Duval Composition Company. Here, through the winter of 1916, Archie complained that things kept breaking down and they spent as much time repairing the facilities as they spent on their primary tasks but it may just have been that he found fault because he preferred to work at his own property in the high street.

In early 1917, the officers of the unit were joined by another of mature years, the 36-year-old Bertie Charles Adamson. Archie recalled that they had all sorts of interruptions, even a visit to his unit by Eugen Sandow (aka Friedrich Wilhelm Müller), the body builder who was employed in the army to bolster recruiting and physical fitness. Archie was not impressed!

Throughout his life, Archie kept notepads to jot down any fleeting concept before it was forgotten. In emergencies, when an idea unexpectedly occurred, he would resort to soap-written memos on a mirror or ideas scratched in the sand, these being then transcribed onto less ethereal media. In later life, the notices in his office and labs would still declare 'keep out', 'danger' and the standing instruction 'No Piece Of Paper, However Old Or Dirty, Must Be Thrown Away'.

The use of an airship for the more basic trials of the control system could have been useful but it would not have helped with the critical problem of launching. Balloons were used in the testing by the AT team but they seem to have been tethered and used for work on transmission and reception optimisation. Low referred to 'experiments by transmitting to and from balloons and ancient aircraft flying at Hounslow'. When he was looking for a military position in 1939, Low included his management of a 'Balloon facility' at the Experimental Works as a 'qualification' in his applications.

Earlier attempts at radio control had used small model dirigible balloons or boats to give demonstrations. Low's team, while obviously aware of some of these, would not have gained much of use from these designs as little detail was published. However, some of these are worth acknowledging. Probably one of the earliest and most famous was Nikola Tesla who demonstrated his model boat at Madison Square Gardens in 1898. Louis Heathcote Walter's patent was also raised in 1898. Louis' family was German but he was born in England and became an electrical engineer. At the time of his patent he was a 27-year-old Cambridge graduate from Trinity College who was employed as an assistant to Hiram Maxim in his private laboratory.

This patent describes a control system designed to eliminate most of the spurious signals arising from any radio interference, or in the parlance of the 1890s' patent:

> This invention relates to the utilization of Hertzian and similar radiations, its object being to so effect the transmission and reception of such radiations that they may be utilized without fear of the operation of the receiving apparatus by the occurrence of unintentional or unauthorized radiations.

His patent suggests that it might also be used to detect unauthorised signals. There is no evidence that Louis ever attempted to develop his system but he did chose the firing of submarine mines as the example for its use in the patent, an application that Low did actually produce and was used in World War I.

Many of these inventions used rotors in the transmitter and the receiver and a method to synchronise these rotors, in similar fashions to that employed in Low's Televista system. They also emphasised the measures taken to achieve their immunity to spurious radio signals or maliciously contrived electrical noise. Although the radiation environment was comparatively quiet then, there were no controls either physically or legally to prevent radio interference and so it was necessary to ensure these relatively wide band receivers only reacted to 'genuine' signals.

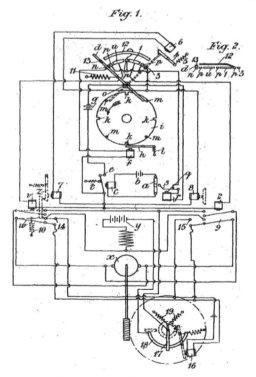

Diagram from Flettner's patent

The Institute of Electrical and Electronics Engineers (IEEE) recognises the Spanish inventor Leonardo Torres Quevedo for his work on remote control. He lived in Madrid and in 1901 he designed a control system. He called this system 'The Telekine' and applied it initially to test airship designs safely, without having to ascend in them. The method used the of pulse code from the receiver's coherer to drive a form of stepper motor switch, the number of pulses determining the total rotation of the switch and thereby the control that was activated. He made models to demonstrate his control system but it did not sell. Leonardo became more famous for his airships or in the terminology of one of his patents 'Fusiform Aerostats'. One of his airship designs, built by the Astra Company in Paris, was bought for the Royal Navy and entered service in 1913.

Anton Flettner's significant contribution to aeronautical development is well known but almost completely missed are his contributions to remote control. In 1906, he was a schoolmaster in Pfaffenwiesbach near Bad Homburg vor der Höhe. Together with the electrical cable-making firm of Felten and Guilleume-Lahmeeyerwerke Actiengesellschaft in Frankfurt, he patented a method of remote control using synchronous rotary time switches which used a coherer for wireless detection, the only real choice at this early date. By this means he achieved a 'cylindrical succession' of control transmissions.

Anton had the spark but he lacked both the money and the third side of the triangle, a market place in order to advance the technology in 1906. However, the patent does suggest some novel potential uses. It is in Tokaty's book on fluid mechanics that we find reference to Anton Flettner's radio control system being used to control a land vehicle that was demonstrated in Berlin in 1915.

In May 1910, many publications, including the *New York Times,* reported: 'The torpedo airship is the latest. An Englishman, Thomas Earnest Raymond Phillips is its inventor. He claims to be able, sitting at a transmitter in London, to send a dirigible balloon through the air at any height and almost any distance. He can load his balloon with dynamite bombs, he claims, and without leaving his office can send it over a city and wipe the city out.' *Flight* magazine also reported:

A Dirigible in a Music Hall.
There is no accounting for popular taste in the matter of public entertainment, but we must confess one would scarcely expect to witness the spectacle of a fairly big model dirigible sailing about the auditorium of the London Hippodrome, where at the moment it constitutes one of the star turns. The dirigible in question is fitted up with wireless control, and the operator, Mr. Raymond Phillips, makes it travel where he will, more or less, by the diligent rapping of an electric key on the stage. There is much crackling of electrical discharge, followed by the setting in motion of one or other of the various propellers with which the car of the dirigible is equipped. Two propellers on a pivoted cross-beam control the direction, while other two mounted on vertical shafts control the altitude. The little electric motors that drive the propellers obtain their energy from a small battery of cells, which are switched into action by a device that is sensitive to the wireless electric waves.

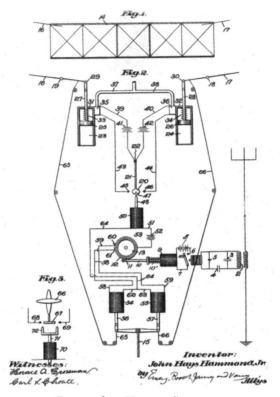

Drawing from Hammond's patent

Raymond Philips was living in Sefton Park in Liverpool when he raised his patent. The receiver in the airship had a coherer detector and the signal moved a single control a predetermined amount on each detection. Claude Grahame-White was enthralled and spent time with Raymond to learn more and even controlled the airship himself.

Work on airship control was also undertaken in the US. *Flight* magazine in January 1909 announced 'Wireless Airships. An inventor in America, Mr. Mark O. Anthony, is said to be able to control airships from land by the aid of wireless telegraphy, and is, it is said, organising a demonstration with a view to bringing the matter before the public.' Professor Anthony's (and his associate Leo Stephen's) wireless airship was a small powered blimp that was reported to have flown under remote control by wireless telegraphy in 1912.

Another American, John Hays Hammond Jr., known as 'Jack' to most of his contemporaries, under the guidance in his formative years of both Thomas Alva Edison and Alexander Graham Bell, was clearly interested in radio-control. Most of his pre-1920s radio control achievements were directed at boats but he certainly considered in some detail a method of aircraft remote control in his patent application of 7th March 1914. He realised that it was desirable and even essential to incorporate an on-board stabilisation mechanism so that the external operator control was only necessary for course changes; 'as for the purpose of compensating for deviations from a straight course due to phenomena previously referred to or other causes, and thereby greatly minimize the possibility of an enemy determining the wave lengths used in the control of the craft and thereupon interfering with the control thereof'. Jack had the spark and he certainly had the money from his family mining interests in Africa but he didn't have a market place.

The Franklin Institute awarded Jack the title 'Father of Radio Control' when they gave him their Elliott Cresson Medal for life achievement in 1959. He applied for his patent in 1914 but it was not published until 12th January 1926 so it could not have been seen by the RFC team. However, it may be that he was involved with Professor Bell in 1916 when a report was circulated claiming a radio-controlled aeroplane ascended to a height of 200 ft. from the ground, turning a complete circle, and alighting within a few feet of the starting point.

There were others, some of whom are probably lost to our records, who attempted the remote control of model ships and airships, switching on electric motors powered from on-board batteries to drive them forward and to the left and right. Airships had motors directed up and down, and even solenoid-powered bomb bay doors releasing paper 'munitions' for added effect. However, these systems were generally incapable of subtle control as they were not incremental. The sparks were flying but the need and the means were not there to fuel further development.

Low's team applied themselves to the much more difficult task of controlling full-sized, heavier-than-air machines, which involved the problem of launching them with enough speed to fly and to respond to movement of their control surfaces. Before moving from their Feltham base in the Ivory Works to Upavon for the March 1917 flight trials, Low's team moved the Aerial Target work back to Brooklands where they had worked on the 1916 version. They occupied the hangar that backed onto the garden and toilet block, the hangar next to the old Blue Bird was now closed, having been supplanted by a canteen. Archie identified their hangar as the one into which Charles Bell pranged. Here they integrated their control system with the de Havilland airframe and Bradshaw's engine.

So in the low-lying flood plain on the banks of the River Wey, in the militarised remains of the Brooklands flying village in that bitter spring of 1917, adjacent to

The layout of the aerial wire on the aircraft surfaces

the famous sewage farm, Low's team toiled in their damp, cold, poorly lit shelter, busily fitting their control system into the de Havilland Aerial Target airframe and coupling the gearbox and actuator to the engine. We know what they had to install and can imagine some of the problems they probably encountered.

Even though the fuselage was only a maximum of two-feet wide, rigging the control runs from the engine driven actuator to the empennage for the elevators and the rudder would have been bread and butter to the RFC airman after three years of repairing battle damaged machines in even worse conditions close to the front line or in the larger repair and reconstruction depots. However, wiring up complex electrical apparatus and festooning the airframe with aerial wires would have been a new skill acquired at Feltham. The aerials on the sides of the fuselage were laid in a square wave pattern. At least the finish was uncomplicated, just clear dope.

Part of being in a family is speaking the same dialect. In the army signalman's letter code which was used by the RFC, 'Ack' is 'A' and 'Emma' is M, hence Anti-Aircraft is AA is Ack-Ack and AM is Ack Emma. Air mechanics were also Ack Emmas. In signalese this would have made an AT an Ack-Toc.

Life and work for all the 'manual labour' classes were strenuous. There were few hand-powered tools available for the engineers, craftsmen, blacksmiths and mechanics but there was electric lighting. Most lifting jobs entailed levers, blocks and tackles strung up on 'A' frames or a suitable rafter. A power winch would only be used if the task warranted the expense. Floors of the hangars were mostly dirt or oil-soaked wood planking. Stoves provided some warmth but people often had to find a brazier to thaw out. Orderlies were needed for all of the domestic duties; making tea, tending the fires, replacing candles or trimming wicks in oil lamps.

A contemporary description of the hangars at Brooklands states, 'The original sheds had no windows, so we had to take the shutters down for light, and during the cold winter we had an old bucket with a coke fire to warm the handles of the tools. It was an awful time: mud floor, leaky roof, cold, long hours and floods. However, the coke fire cheered us a lot, because the smoke made us think it was warm.'

When the time for the trials came, the kit was packed and the transport was readied for the AT's long journey to Upavon.

Fate was with the AT team because a week or so after they left, on 28th March 1917, the old Blue Bird and adjacent hangars burnt down. Lamenting the loss, Howard Pixton remembered 'how one smoked, and ran brazing lamps, and even engines and used plain oil lamps in the old sheds at Brooklands, regardless of open cans of petrol and even pans full of petrol for the washing of parts, it seems a miracle that the whole place was not burned out years ago. And now the poor old "Blue Bird" disappears in flames under a strictly regulated military control. So passes the scene of what were the happiest days in the lives of many of the old hands of aviation!'

While aircraft manufacture at Brooklands was destined to rise from these ashes, those early pioneering days of aviation faded like the embers of the pyre that had been the Blue Bird, except in the imagined 'memories' that we relive when we read their stories. It is an incredible consequence of Locke King's decision to build a racetrack at Brooklands that this leafy London commuter area of 'the stockbroker's belt' around Weybridge and Kingston-upon-Thames became a huge centre of Britain's aircraft industry. At the end of World War I this area of Surrey accommodated the world's largest concentration of aircraft design, development and manufacturing facilities. Brooklands hosted 28 years of automotive activity before and after World War I but it was the site of over 80 continuous years of aviation endeavour from the trials and tribulations of A. V. Roe's experiments to the production of major elements of Concorde's structure.

After their work on the AT project at the end of the war, Poole, Bowen, Whitton, Mantell and Adamson all went their different ways.

George Whitton went on to a career in the British Broadcasting Corporation (BBC). Louis Mantell wrote articles for many years, particularly for the 'Light Car' magazine. He died on 2nd January 1949, at the age of 71 in Bangor, County Down, Northern Ireland. Bertie Adamson died on active service in World War II as a squadron leader on 20th April 1940.

On 14th February 1921, Henry raised a patent for a machine that rolled the edges of tin plate that was then used for making all manner of containers. In 1924, the Poole family moved to 1 Warwick Dene, Ealing, a very substantial property. By 1927 Henry seems to have been 'doing very well' when he arrived back in Southampton travelling 1st Class on the Royal Mail Steam Packet Company's 'Arlanza' from Buenos Aires.

Henry's connections with Northern Ireland seem to have contributed to his demise on an autumnal visit during the 'Great Slump'. In Belfast, on Monday 3rd October 1932, 30,000 Catholic and Protestant workers led by bands and singing appropriate music hall songs such as 'Yes! We have no bananas' marched to the Custom House to protest against the arrangements for 'Outdoor Relief', a system of unemployment benefit available only to unemployed married men who were classed as fit for work and regarded as requiring 'exceptional distress relief'. Single men, the disabled and sick, and women who could not find work were left with only the charity of the workhouse, by then called Public Assistance Institutions, to sustain them. A few days later on 16th November the new Parliament buildings at Stormont were opened by Edward, Prince of Wales (later King Edward VIII). On the 18th, Henry, aged 59, died in Belfast. He had with him the substantial sum of £228 15s. There were limited options for access to funds when travelling and these options would have been even more restricted during the banking crisis and depression of the early 1930s. This may explain why Henry was carrying such a large amount of cash. His estate of more than £6000 went to his widow Edith and his son Gerald. Much later and in a different context that had no financial connotations, Archie Low, lamenting the passing of his one-time colleague, simply said 'poor Poole'.

Bowen also did well after the war, right through into World War II by which time he had moved to Malvern Wells in Worcestershire and was still inventing and raising patents.

Low's team at the RFC Experimental Works, Feltham did not design the Aerial Targets, as they were not aeronautical engineers or aircraft designers. However, they were just as innovative; they were the World War I back-room boys who created the launching and control systems for these craft. Their systems were also used in the Royal Navy experimental boats and led to the British drone and guided weapons in the decades that followed.

For the Aerial Target invention, World War I was the mother as it created the necessity; the need to counter the threat posed by German airships. The Royal Flying Corps provided the means manifest in the RAF 1914 technical drawing of the AT. But the spark came with the control system created by our maverick inventor, Dr. Archie Low, out of his work on Televista. However big the need or the means, without the right spark there is no progress. In other words, there is no progress beyond conception if it is not supported by production and use; and none of the latter without the former. The three elements are required but for the AT the need waned for a while when the German airships became vulnerable to the clever explosive bullets. But then a naval need arose.

On 15th May 1915, the First Sea Lord, Admiral Lord John Arbuthnot 'Jackie' Fisher resigned his post following a long running and acrimonious 'debate' over the progress of the Gallipoli operations. He had championed the provision of shallow draft capital ships, three of which were available for proposed outflanking Baltic operations by the home fleet, against Wilhelmshaven and the Kaiser Wilhelm Kanal (now named the Kiel Canal). The proposal was 'to Copenhagen' the German Baltic Fleet much as was done in 1807 to the Danish fleet. Fisher had favoured this Northern flank plan rather than the attacks on the Ottoman Empire in Turkey. The need for a 'New Front' stemmed in large part from frustration. Embroiled now in this massive land war on the Western Front that the CID had not planned for, grand outflanking operations in the Baltic or in Turkey linking with the Russians were seen by the navy and some in government as the only two ways the costly naval assets could play a significant and decisive role in the proceedings. In short, Britain had been obliged by the Entente to participate in this huge land war on the continent with its asset comprised of lots of boats and sailors, an army of professional soldiers numbering less than one quarter those of France and a tiny air arm.

The ability to fire shells at a much greater rate than the country could make them and the failures in Turkey caused the government and military 'reorganisations' included the removal of Winston Churchill as First Lord of the Admiralty and the formation of the Ministry of Munitions under David Lloyd George. This also provided an opportunity to improve the control of resources used to assess and investigate inventions. The fragmented, duplicated and wasted resources spent on development could now be co-ordinated. In short, it was becoming evident to all that the new technologies of the late Victorian and Edwardian period and the increased impetus given to scientific advancement resulting from the demands of the war had made the control and encouragement of 'invention' a weapon of war in its own right. Lloyd George stated in the House of Commons in the evening of 28th July 1915: 'So far as naval inventions are concerned, the First Lord of the Admiralty has already set up a Naval Inventions Board.... I had just completed arrangements to constitute an Inventions Branch of the Ministry of Munitions....' He added: 'I think, to save disappointment, I should say that it ought to be clearly understood that only a very small minority of inventions are of practical value, especially under the stringent conditions of modern warfare.'

CHAPTER 12

How to Make a Great War Drone

In the Edwardian era, when schoolchildren dodged the wheels of the Hansom and the Clarence, the genesis of today's drones occurred in the dingy, dusty offices of 'Low Accessories & Ignition Co.' near the Bank of England in London.

A few years later during World War I, when aircraft design was still in its infancy and making a light and reliable aircraft engine with a useful amount of power was a very rare achievement, a number of inventors (whose feet were probably never really on firm ground) dreamed of controlling an aircraft without risking life and limb by actually travelling on it. In this early part of the 20th century, the difficult but conceivable task of replacing the pilot with a built-in automatic system that would control an aircraft and keep it on a straight and level flight was an aim that some were striving to achieve. But to actually make an unmanned plane that could be piloted and manoeuvred by control signals from the ground was pure science fiction. However, the ambition of the Royal Flying Corps was to produce such a machine.

Following my inspection of the model AT and its control equipments held in the Imperial War Museum stores, with the help of the explanations in the patents, I am able to explain how this first drone was controlled. In Bloom's book, Low said of the AT: 'It was a pilotless plane, with means for steering, controlling the engine, and exploding the warhead by a system of locks, which could be set anew every morning so that the enemy could not interfere'.

A number of different aircraft were designed and built to use Low's control system and what follows describes how one of these aircraft designs, the de Havilland AT, was launched and controlled. Breaking down the challenges of such an enterprise into discrete tasks we can create a list of 'technological enablers'. The Feltham team's solution to each of these challenges is detailed in their patents, which, along with the images of the hardware in the Imperial War Museum, illustrate the sophistication of this Aerial Target programme.

This list of challenges Low's team faced is greatly assisted by the patents that they filed. As with all patents, after the preamble identifying the originator, they declare that they address a novel device, a unique feature or several such features. These novel aspects are then addressed 'as to the manner in which they can be realised'. There are patents relating to all aspects of the AT and these are still available. These patents are such a close match to the exhibits in the IWM that they must refer directly to these equipments.

Patents are by definition a protective document for intellectual property and not a blueprint from which a device can be built. They generally encompass as many different possible means for achieving the stated purpose as is allowable and they are only as specific as they need to be; the aim being to make them as generally applicable as the patenting authorities will allow. However, the copious supply of supporting patents produced by Low's team for the AT are unusually detailed and revealing.

The objective here is to review the main aspects of the AT's control system, to provide an insight into how it worked and to show that it went beyond just controlling a remotely piloted vehicle, as serious consideration was given to the launching, use and operation of the system as a weapon to be deployed in war conditions.

The AT Concept

PATENT SPECIFICATION

244,258

Application Date: Jan. 9, 1918. No. 541 / 18.

Accepted : Dec. 10, 1918 (but withheld from publication under section 30 of Patents & Designs Acts 1907 & 1919).

Authorised to be Published : Nov. 17, 1925. Date of Publication : Jan. 14, 1926.

COMPLETE SPECIFICATION.

Improved Aerial Projectile.

I, ARCHIBALD MONTGOMERY LOW, Captain in His Majesty's Army, of Royal Flying Corps, Experimental Works, Feltham, Middlesex, do hereby declare
5 the nature of this invention and in what manner the same is to be performed, to be particularly described and ascertained

compartment, receptacle or reservoir such as e formed in, upon, or by the body of 45 the aeroplane a charge of any suitable high explosive or other explosive charge or an incendiary charge or combined explosive and incendiary charge, the nature of the charge depending upon the 50

Heading of the AT patent

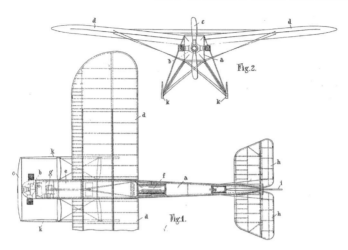

Drawing of the AT from the patent. The radio receiever and controller are positioned at 'f' and the actuator 'g' is driven by the engine 'b' to move the rudder 'i' and elevators 'h'

The AT described in Patent 244,258 was designed to carry 'a charge of explosive and/or incendiary material suitably positioned in the body of the aeroplane' and was 'operated and controlled by wireless'.

The specification goes on:

> After the projectile has been launched, it will be self-propelling and shall be controlled wirelessly during flight. It will be provided with a wireless receiver and fitted with means for producing a smoke aerial formed by the exhaust from the internal combustion engine. The aeroplane will be provided with skids for launching and the charge carried by the projectile will be exploded or ignited by wireless or by percussion when the projectile hits the ground or any other extraneous object.

The Airframes and Engines

There has been a great deal of interest in who built these prototypes, involving as they do some of the most famous pioneering British aircraft designers. However, what these machines all had in common was the control system that made them different to manned aircraft.

Here we will concentrate on the de Havilland ATs that were flown in March 1917 at Upavon. Low's team from Feltham seem to have been much more involved with this prototype as they not only supplied the control system but other ground equipment and Low was at the controls during the trial.

The various detailed aspects of the design that are explained below are the subject of other patents and these are listed in Appendix 2. Images of the these items that are stored in the IWM archives and a selection of images of the patent headings are included in the Illustrations section.

Launching

It was not intended that the AT land on its skis with much chance of survival. It was considered from the outset to be a weapon and in this sense all flights would end with a bang or a prang. However, they all had to take off. Consideration had to be given to the mobility of this weapon system and providing a mobile launching system was a great assistance in supporting the flight trials and also demonstrated that ATs could be deployed from an unprepared site on the battlefield. To achieve this, the AT's ground control transmitting equipment and powered launch ramp were installed in a 5-ton lorry which provided the electrical power and drove a pneumatic pump to charge up the launch system. This control and launch system only seems to have been employed for the de Havilland trials.

Aerodynamic force from the elevators and rudder was weak at low speeds. Hence, control at low speeds was a great problem so it was necessary to constrain the AT during the acceleration phase of take off by launching it from rails. For these Upavon trials, a pneumatic system slowly charged a cylinder to high pressure from a compressor driven by an auxiliary gearbox on the service lorry's engine. This compressed air was then used just prior to launch to drive a piston which unwound a drive cable from a drum that rapidly spun a flywheel up to a high speed before the cylinder completely discharged. At this point, with the flywheel racing and the AT's engine held at half power, the release of the 'half power' control lever could be co-ordinated with the engagement of the launch cable drum to the spinning flywheel, winding in the cable and pulling the AT's mounting carriage up the ramp

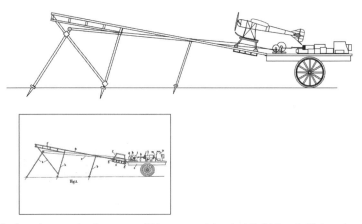

Diagram of a launch ramp in the patent. This was used by Archibald Low's Unit to launch the De Havilland Aerial Targets at the successful Upavon trials in March 1917. All of the other Aerial Target design teams, such as the Royal Aircraft Factory designs, used Low's control system but attempted to launched their aircraft solely under their own power on long tracks laid on the ground. Similar powered ramps were subsequently used for the Larynx, Queen Bee and many others projects.

with the engine racing up to full power. Thus the world's first aircraft pneumatic catapult launcher was invented. This system provided the required acceleration to reach flying speed when launching from the short rails set on an upward incline that Feltham provided for the de Havilland AT.

There is evidence that all of the other trials except those for the de Havilland AT attempted to launch from rails laid on the ground and only using the aircraft's own power. The Larynx programme in the 1920s used a cordite-powered ramp and the Queen Bee of the 1930s employed a pneumatically powered launch ramp remarkably similar to Low's of 1917.

The Control Equipments

The equipment in the IWM has been manufactured to a very high standard and, as we are told in the labels made for the IWM Exhibition, 'they are the original control gear which made the first radio-guided flight under selective control on 21st. March 1917.' The actuator control bars still have their attachments on the end for the control wires. The units are robust and have the appearance of 'production' items of a mature design. They are not prototypes.

There are a considerable number of patents for the different aspects of the design of the AT; launching as we have seen above but there are also patents for components such as aerials and relays. Although the applications for these patents were made in 1917, the documents were not published until 1923, delayed for security reasons.

Actuation

Most engineers would immediately focus on this aspect of the problem as a significant power source is required to move an aircraft's control surfaces in order to fly the plane – usually of course it takes 'one-man power'. With the technology available in 1915, electrical, hydraulic and pneumatic systems would fail at the first consideration as they would be too heavy for such a modest and moderately sized airframe and engine.

Fortunately, a four-function actuator from the Experimental Works exists in the Imperial War Museum collection. The actuator has a single lead screw that was turned in one direction continuously by a reduction gearbox drive connected to the aircraft's engine. Control wires from the pitch and turn surfaces were engaged with this lead screw when the appropriate control signal from the ground-based pilot was received by the AT. In response to a demand, the relevant electromagnet arrayed around the lead screw engaged a pin on the sprung bar into the lead screw and the bar would then be pulled along the channel of the screw as it turned until the demand to the electromagnet was removed and the pin disengaged from the lead screw. The screw channel ran into a circular grove at either end so that if the control signal and pin engagement was maintained until the control reached its limit, the pin merely stayed at this limit of travel in the circular groove. One pair of outputs of the actuator moved the appropriate control wires to the elevators in response to the up or down commands, another pair the wires were used for the left or right commands. The half-power and explode demands, being 'discrete' functions (not incremental) were implemented by simpler solenoid coil electromagnets. The throttle sprung to full power and pulled to half power by its solenoid unless and until it was released to spring back to full power. The explode munitions function was even easier to implement – once selected … Bang … (de-detonate being illogical).

The control bars have attachment points at both ends with substantial springs attached to one end. This implies that each set of control runs were connected either as continuous loops around locally anchored guide pulleys or more likely as shown in Illustration 5.

The relevant patent for the actuator also says:

> If desired in order to allow of intermittent rotation of the screw, the shaft may be driven through a friction clutch of the like. … Although the apparatus has been described as containing four electo-magnets it can obviously be adapted to employ a larger or smaller number … the number of magnets employed being equal to the number of different controls it is desired to obtain.

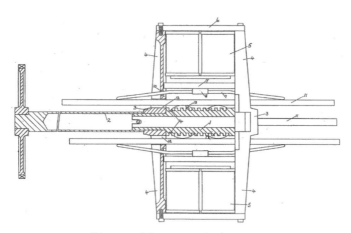

Diagram of the actuator in the patent

Stability

Aircraft were being designed with various stability characteristics but even the most stable would require active control to maintain straight and level flight for any prolonged period.

Now that we understand how the control surfaces of the AT were moved, what inputs were used to drive them? For short-term stability, on-board gyroscopic stabilisation was included in the guidance control system. The following label text was included in the IWM exhibition: 'For high speeds of control an electrically operated gyroscope was designed.'

Three patents are still available that relate to the inclusion of gyroscopes:

Patent 244,302 described two different methods of coupling the gyroscope into the guidance control mechanism of the weapon.

Patent 191,407 described the use of alternatively selectable windings incorporated within the electrically driven guidance gyroscope that could be used to precess the gyroscope for the purposes of steering the weapon by affecting the rotational speed to accomplish the guidance.

Patent 191,410 described the use of electromagnets incorporated within the guidance gyroscope that were used to precess the gyroscope for the purposes of steering the weapon. Two methods were described. The first acted upon the gimbal and the second affected the rotational speed acting as a brake to accomplish the guidance. This patent refers back to Patent 191,407.

Control

Control of the weapon required fast transfer of the ground commands to the aircraft. Effective control requires a number of different inputs made by the human controller to be received by the aircraft quickly enough to move the appropriate aircraft controls for the craft to move as intended and remain stable. This basic problem had been addressed in the implementation of Televista which had required a similar fast and repeated transfer of the changing image elements from the 'camera' to the 'screen'. Archie Low's work on Televista was the 'spark' that triggered the AT project as it provided convincing evidence that a remotely controlled unmanned aircraft was possible. The essence of the system was a form of synchronised transmission or cyclic transmission. Both the transmitter on the ground and the receiver in the AT ran on a rapid cycle, round and round, starting each cycle together. A pulse sent at a specific point in the 'pilots' transmitter cycle would be received at the same point in the AT receiver cycle. Technically this was a form of Pulse Position Modulation (PPM). Where the pulse occurred in the cycle determined the specific action required.

The Operators Control Unit – The Selective Transmitter

This device was used by the operator (pilot) to select the particular control signals to be sent to the aircraft and it contains the mechanism that kept them selected and then de-selected them in a pre-arranged sequence, The Feltham team designed the selective transmitter with six operator input levers, one for each of the six

Time

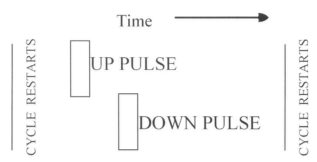

CYCLE RESTARTS

UP PULSE

DOWN PULSE

CYCLE RESTARTS

Diagram of pulses – normal cycle (simplified and only showing up and down pulses)

control signals; up, down, left, right, half-speed and explode, and each of these was implemented by pulses at a different points in the cycle.

When no pulse was sent, no action resulted except that the control for half-speed was returned to its normal full-speed position by spring action. The actuator had to follow the pilot's input immediately to achieve control of the aircraft.

These patents show that each control function (up, down etc.) corresponded to a dedicated disc which is attached to the motor-driven shaft by a slipping clutch with contacts at the appropriate angles (which equated to a specific time in the cycle) for that function. A brake on the associated disc was released when that function lever was pressed, allowing the clutch to spin the selected disc.

Of course it was not quite as simple as the diagram implies. Patent 195,100 describes the sequence of pulses created by the arrangement of contacts on the six cams controlled by the transmitter's operators keys. Mapped out as a pattern in time for one frame of transmission it shows that the first cam produced one pulse per rotation plus a cancelling long pulse, the second cam two pulses plus the cancelling

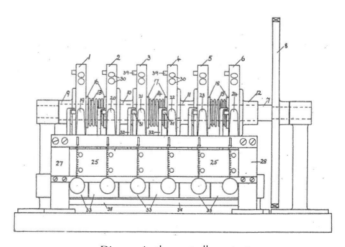

Diagram in the controller patent

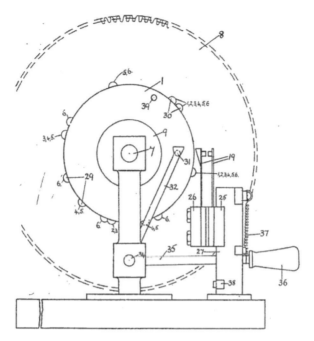

Diagram in the controller patent

(annulling) pulse and so on. But the multiple contacts producing the pulses were not evenly spread around the cams.

The motor driving the scanner in the Televista system ran at 3000 rpm and Low said the control system worked in fractions of a second. Although it was a challenging requirement, the system was capable of controlling the AT.

The Selective Receiver

In a 1944 letter, Low described this as a box with a glass lid, slung on rubber supports measuring about 2 ft 3 in by 9 in (0.69 by 0.23 m) and containing all the relays, receiver and the key system which prevented interference. In Patent 244,203, Archie states: 'The apparatus which I will now proceed to describe is one of a very large number that have been constructed by me, and has been successful in prolonged experimental trials.' Indeed, this patent has some statements and explanations not normally included in such formal, 'dry' documents. The choice of wavelength and the measures to control electronic noise and interference are detailed. The coherer and its circuit were designed to be unresponsive to all but the genuine signals and interfering signals of too long or too short a period would not be effective in selecting control outputs. We are told that this design yielded a relatively robust receiver that only weighed 7 lbs.

Patent 244,203 states that they were 'adapted to work at fairly high speed. I may take the case of four successive wireless impulses, each enduring for say 1/12th of a second, and separated by spaces each of the same duration.'

However, we are told in the patent that for security reasons, other and varied timings would be more appropriate. The patent describes the longer cancelling, releasing or annulling signal that is required. It suggests this 'work out' signal should be 1½ seconds long. This would give 6 control functions a cycle time of 2½ seconds comprising 6 pulses and 6 spaces plus the 'work out' pulse. This would imply that the system ran at 24 full control cycles per minute. The 'pecker' gear ensured that unless each signal was composed of an exact number of pulses exactly spaced the final contact could not be made.

The patent also suggest data recording and we might surmise that this is for subsequent 'post flight' analysis as no other purpose springs to mind. It states: 'A record of the signals may be made, if desired, by any well known means.' This could be the first example of flight data recording.

As already noted, Patent 244,203 is unusually informative in that it provides an outline of other design options and an explanation of why they chose their particular solutions for the AT controls. Archibald Low states:

> My apparatus may be operated by means of signals sent over a wire, but it is primarily intended for use by radio-telegraphy. It has been frequently proposed that different signals might be made at a distance by means of wireless radiation, by tuning receivers associated with these different circuits to different wave lengths so that any one circuit can only be operated by sending on a particular wavelength. It has also been suggested that such signals should be used in combination to prevent interference, but these systems have two great disadvantages. In the first place the signals transmitted must be more or less continuous, and they are therefore easy to pick up, measure and block and they interfere with other wireless stations. Secondly, it is not possible to get such delicate tuning as to operate many different contacts with any certainty, and without using very heavy, costly and delicate apparatus.
>
> In the present invention by means of a combination of so called tuning, synchronism and key signals it is possible to obtain the wireless operation of a number of instruments without any reasonable possibility of interference, and by means of a simple, small and light apparatus.

Of course, today these objections to a multi-channel system do not apply but in 1917 they were relevant. The design team's options were limited as the choice of radio equipment was not extensive at that time. Essentially it was Hobson's choice, an easy decision for the team as they were forced to use reliable and robust equipment and that ruled out the newer temperamental crystal receiver sets and Fleming's fragile 'electrical valve' technology.[1] Low's team used a spark gap transmitter with a coherer to detect the signals at the receiver. A great deal of painstaking work went into the radio transfer of the control data and the patents say: 'An incoming impulse to be effective must be of sufficient strength and duration to cause the special coherer employed to become conductive.'

The team will have had access to sophisticated measurement instruments but their accuracy and resolution would have limited their use for assessing the relative signal strength of the very small outputs of different coherer designs. Many of the design decisions would have relied upon a great degree of subjectivity. However, an inkling of the huge efforts that were made to obtain the best performance possible from the hardware can be gained from some of the patents. The work undertaken on coherer design is a case in point. The related patent on coherers says:

> It has hitherto been proposed to employ particles of sulphurated silver in the construction of such coherers, and it has also been proposed to employ a mixture of particles of silver nickel and copper.
>
> The present invention consists in a coherer of the kind referred to comprising a mixture of silver and nickel particles wholly or in part coated with the sulphides of the respective metals by heating the same in an atmosphere of sulphur dioxide.
>
> In carrying my invention into effect I take metallic filings or particles comprising a mixture of silver and nickel filings, and these particles I coat wholly or in part with the sulphides of the respective metals by heating the particles in a stream or in an atmosphere of silver dioxide.

A great deal of time and effort was also expended on refining the operation of relays. Work ranged from relays switching high currents for short periods to highly sensitive relays that were not susceptible to interruption or sticking.

SWITCH GEAR.

128,119, November 21st. 1918 Electric Relays, A. M. Low, Major, R.A.F., Royal Air Force Experimental Works,, Feltham., Middlesex

The invention consists in an electric relay of the spring armature type, provided with means for adjusting the magnet relatively to the armature, and in which the armature spring is surrounded by a coil of a few turns of comparatively heavy wire, through which a current is passed, this coil having the effect of oscillating or disturbing the particles in the armature and thus preventing any sticking of the latter in operation. The poles A of the electro-magnet are connected by means of a suitable yoke B which can be moved within the limits allowed by the slot C, by means of an adjusting screw D, the magnet being held in any required position by the clamping screw E. The armature F is mounted upon a spring arm rigidly fixed at one end, and provided at its free end with the usual contact points G. In order to facilitate the adjustment of the sensitivity

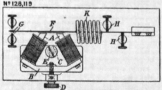

Nᵒ 128,119

of the relay, adjusting screws are provided mounted in fixed pillars H upon opposite sides of the spring arm and preferably adjacent to the fixed end. As the construction described provide for the production of an extremely sensitive relay, difficulties may be experienced in operation due to a tendency on the part of the armature to stick, and this tendency is eliminated by providing round the spring arm at as convenient point in its length a coil K of relatively few turns of comparatively heavy wire, through which coil an electric current of suitable strength is passed, the coil being either arranged in series with the coil of the electro-magnet or in a separate circuit as desired. The current passing through the coil may be of an intermittent character, or it may be such as to produce slight polarity opposite to that impressed on the armature by the poles A of the electro-magnet. – June 19th, 1919.

An article published in *The Engineer*, regarding Patent 128,119

As an example of this work the Patent 128,119 for a non-sticking relay was the subject of an article published in *The Engineer* on 25th June 1919.

Low was also experimenting with transformers and raised a patent application for a high-frequency transformer on 19th January 1918. He would have been aware of the early potential of magnetic amplifiers and the work and patents of Ernst Alexanderson, particularly those relating to control systems. The magnetic amplifier was superseded firstly by valve and then semiconductor technology for most applications but each time it has still been found to be the 'solid state' robust solution for use in the most extreme and harsh environments.

Communication

Reception was a particularly difficult problem. The AT had to receive an adequate signal at all distances and orientations. If you have ever tried to carry a small analogue radio around to listen to your favourite programme this problem will be most apparent to you. Signal reception had to be maximised and interference minimised without even the luxury of amplifiers in the system. The receiver had to reliably respond to genuine impulses while being unresponsive to noise and unwanted signals.

A great deal of effort went into layout of the wireless aerials. No doubt it was on an assessment experimental flight of these aerials that Low 'forgot to wind in a long trailing-aerial, which gaily tore down most of the telephone wires in the neighbourhood.' As already noted, the unit at Feltham had a tethered balloon facility where such trials could be undertaken.

The use of smoke aerials was also assessed and the patent relating to these states '… by this means the stream of issuing gases may be made to form a very efficient aerial by means of which wireless telegraphic communications may be carried out over considerable distances'. It would have been ironic if Louis Mantell, the master of 'carburetion', had been the officer cajoled into mistuning engines to create the smoke. The 'Smoke Aerial' Patent states, 'Having now particularly described and ascertained the nature of my said invention and in what manner the same is to be performed, I declare that what I claim is:

1. A wireless electricity set in which the aerial is formed by the exhaust gasses of an internal combustion engine or other like stream of more or less minute carbon or other particles.
2. In a wireless electricity set as claimed in Claim 1, the provision of a number of spiked, pointed, or like elements past or over or between which the stream of particles flows prior to its escape to atmosphere.
3. In a wireless electricity set as claimed in Claim 1, the provision of an earth capacity to which the aerial is connected when the set is carried upon an aeroplane or other vehicle.

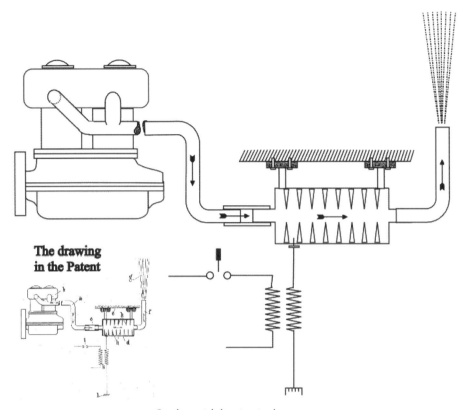

Smoke aerial drawing in the patent

4. An improved wireless electricity set, substantially as hereinbefore described and as illustrated by the accompanying drawing.'

In Bloom's *He Lit the Lamp*, Low provided a rather cryptic commentary on his inspiration for this development:

> Our modest works at this time was peopled by soldiers of a temporary nature, and I believe that the only amusement that I had during the few years, was when I stayed at an hotel with a charming lady whose characteristics were covered by a thin nightdress and a thick eiderdown quilt. It was the jerking of the latter covering, and the movement of the pencil which I had laid upon it to gratify a rather nasty love of making notes, which gave me the idea! I thought of handwriting from the sky by use of ether in place of a more solid wire. The eiderdown and my pencil. That was all there was to it.

In addition to the maintenance of the received signal strength at all altitudes of the AT as it manoeuvred, other aspects of radio reception were considered. For instance, text from the IWM exhibition labels relating to interference states that 'The wave length most suitable to operate the apparatus is put at a different value from the oscillations produced by any local sparks or by the spark of a magneto on any neighbouring engine'.

Counter-Measures and Security

Security of the transmission and enemy interference were considered to be a real threat. For the IWM exhibition the information displayed included 'the exact time of transmission of the signals … keyed by a letter-lock system' and Low referred to a letter-lock number system that defined the set-up of the system and could be varied every day. Kenneth George Munson said Low had told him in a letter in 1944 that the Sopwith AT contained a 'Key System' which prevented interference.

We know from the patents that the transmitter had a system that broke up the short transmitted control pulses into a specific number of even shorter pulses. The receiver then 'counted' these pulses and rejected the 'request' if it had the wrong form. The transmitted signal was sliced into a sequence of even shorter pulses by placing a fast spinning disc in the transmitter output that made contact for only a short period each rotation. A specific number of rotations of the disc fitted into the transmitted pulse length. In the receiver each short pulse moved a control a specific distance, driven by an 'inertia wheel'. If this control in the receiver did not move far enough or moved too far when all of the pulses had

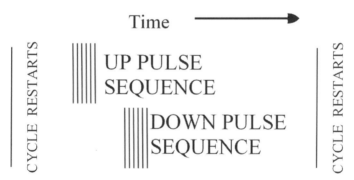

Diagram of pulses – secured cycle (simplified and only showing the up and down pulses)

been 'counted' no action resulted. It may be described as the chopper mechanism on the output of the transmitter and a form of electro-mechanical integrator on the receiver. Only if the correct number of pulses were received would action result. is one of the first examples of 'counter-measures' in radio (electronics).

In their book, *Unmanned Systems of World Wars I and II*, H. R. (Bart) Everett and Michael Toscano suggest how the 'letter-lock' may have been achieved:

> If each cam were assigned a letter and each time slot a number (or vice versa), the daily encryption key would be a simple alphanumeric lookup table that described the pairing of the two. The same changes made to the 'selector' would have to also be incorporated on the 'distributor' at the receiving end, perhaps by reassigning the electrical connections to the rotary switch.' They then say 'the most obvious approach would have been to simply mix up the various cam disks to change the time slot assignments for the individual commands.'

If we assume that they were referring to the cams on the operator's selective transmitter this would be similar to the later German Enigma machine where different rotors were selected. However, in the AT operator controller, the slipping clutch and braking mechanism that is associated with each of the rotors (cam disks) would make exchanging or interchanging them a time-consuming exercise. As touching the exhibits at the IWM is not allowed, they could not be articulated or handled to gain any further understanding of how the rotors moved but they certainly do not appear to be readily interchangeable.

A simpler explanation may be that the 'letter-lock' is a term used at this time for a 'combination lock' sealing the daily orders. There are contemporary patents that refer to such devices as 'letter-locks'. One of these patents, in 1908, utilised a letter-lock mechanism in a gaming machine to pay out winnings automatically if one of a number of 'correct' codes was selected by the player, its letter-lock having different outputs for different valid inputs. Alternatively, the use of the term 'letter-locking' refers to the old methods of folding and sealing written messages or orders to ensure that they could not be opened and resealed without the recipient's knowledge. Thus it merely refers to the 'envelope' used to deliver the days codes and not the hardware implementation of them. For Low's AT, the code to be used for the day by those in the control wagon transmitting station and by those readying the AT would be applied to their equipment by selecting the designated disc of a range of alternative chopper discs, all with different variations of coding, that were incorporated into the transmitter and at the receiver in the aircraft, the set-up that would activate the corresponding inertia wheel.

Low confirms this in his Patent 195,410, where he states:

> In order further to safeguard against outside interference I may have a number of inertia wheels of variable speed, only one being correctly adjusted to pick up the timed signals and actuate the mechanism. Again, the inertia wheel may have its teeth cut irregularly so that it will require a signal or combination of signals of particular form to operate; or I may have two inertia wheels side by side and arranged in conjunction with a contact member so that the same will be operated only when the wheels rotate with the same speed.

Items 3 and 4 in Figure 3 and 5 are the insulated and conducting sides of the angled contact plate in this electro-mechanical integrator. This coated plate may have been produced in a similar fashion to the 'roller' in the Televista system.

Two further extracts from Patent 195,410 are most relevant to this security measure:

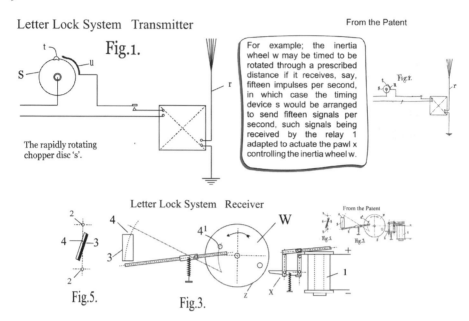

Transmitter chopper and receiver integrator with its inertia wheel 'W', taken from the drawings in the Patent 165,410

> The object of the present invention is to provide improved means for this purpose such that the control cannot be interfered with by outside influences or by an enemy or any unauthorised person.
>
> The invention consists in the provision of means whereby the switches or the like will not be operated unless a predetermined number of impulses or signals be sent in unit time.
>
> … the device cuts out the main current and thus the holding down of his key by an enemy operator will produce no ill effects.

A close inspection of the hardware in the IWM should identify the parts associated with these functions if they were fitted to these earlier equipments. It may be that they were only in later developments of the system such as the 1918 designs for the Royal Navy Distance Control Boats (DCBs). The base of the IWM receiver has slotted fixings to facilitate opening. It is unknown what is inside.

These designs and references to signal encoding are very early examples of electronic warfare measures and counter-measures and almost certainly another world first.

The following label text was used for the 1950s exhibition:

> By means of a combination of tuning, synchronism and key signals it is possible to obtain the wireless operation of a number of instruments without any reasonable possibility of interference, and by means of a simple, small and light apparatus.

Additional functions were considered. One of the 1950s exhibition labels stated:

Experiments were made with a view to finding a means by which messages could be transmitted from the missile back to the controller so that the missile could be controlled beyond the limits of vision.

This then is the basic operation of the AT and its ground equipment. All of these patents (and there are quite a few others not listed) describe in more detail the operation and to some extent the changes as the engineering evolved through the development. A great deal more could be learnt if the patents were to be studied in conjunction with the exhibits. Frustrating as it is for an engineer not to be allowed to touch or move, much less power up, the exhibits, it is understandable from a preservation viewpoint. If such a physical inspection is ever allowed it would have to be carried out under strict control and recording conditions.

It is clear that a great deal of work on the AT control systems continued after the March 1917 trial as many of the more advanced designs are contained in the patents raised later in 1917 and through 1918. For example, some of the patents imply the use of multiple channels operating simultaneously. This would allow the rudder and the elevator to be operated at the same time or two or more DCBs to be controlled from one aircraft and this may be why Captain Poole has a second set of operator controls in the illustration section image.

These then are the most salient elements of a weapons development programme that was ambitious, sophisticated, comprehensive, professionally managed and from what we can now see, was technically viable. All of this was advanced work carried out in the middle of World War I: a war for the very survival of the country.

To grossly understate the situation, control theory, signal processing and the host of related technologies have advanced somewhat in the past one hundred years but the creations of Low's Experimental Works were sophisticated systems; remarkable for equipment developed as early as 1917 and in the middle of that existential war. Their mechanical switch, rotary gyro and analogue technology from 1917 reached its peak in the routine auto-landings of commercial aircraft flying in the 1970s. At this time fragile and power hungry valves and discrete semi-conductor components were available but the acceptance of the digital solid-state transistorised world of integrated circuits into aircraft flight control only started in the 1970s. Sensors such as accelerometers and gyros are now available as micro-electro-mechanical systems (MEMS).

But along with the growing list of firsts, maybe Archibald Low was also at the forefront of this integrated circuit technology if we trace the following trail of evidence. Patent 195,410 on selective switches describes an inclined plate insulated on one side and conducting on the other. As alluded to earlier, Televista used a roller with conducting and insulating areas and in Patent 244,203, which precedes 195,410 by 11 months, there is a commutator with insulating and conducting zones. When the Low brothers had their laboratory in Paul Street, Archie raised Patent 27,599 on 30th November 1912, describing a method of reforming waste rubber. It could be that at this time he devised a method of reliably and durably embedding or coating part of a conducting substrate with an insulator and this was how he constructed the contacts on the roller for Televista. This surely is an early equivalent at larger scale of microcircuit deposition and etching? Low's 'Television' patent of 1938, number 149,011, shown previously, seems to confirm this.

Of the many challenges undertaken by the AT development team at the RFC Experimental Works at Feltham, those identified above give an indication of the maturity their designs had achieved by the time of the 1917 flight trials. It is astounding that such a volume of information and the physical artefacts have survived for 100 years.

CHAPTER 13

The Aerial Target Designers

A number of historians and authors have attempted to unravel the information and clues, matching these Aerial Target airframe designers and manufacturers to the photographs and descriptions of pilotless aircraft associated with the RFC. They have also assessed which aircraft were used for the trials at the various sites on the variety of dates that are in the records. There are some contradictions and gaps in this history but this is not always evident if the publications are read in isolation. Reviewing the few more recently written references to the AT Trials, it is evident that these are based principally on only two of the written sources for their information; Low's accounts, published in 1952 and another in 1955, and the Royal Aircraft Factory's records.

It is unlikely that we will ever be entirely certain of all of the facts. As far as can be ascertained these aircraft were all designed to utilise the radio control system devised by the RFC Experimental Works, Feltham commanded by Dr. A. M. Low. Indeed, their development was inspired by it. Low said in Patent 244,233 that the control system was 'one of a very large number that have been constructed'. He also stated in his 1952 article: 'The missiles that flew were made by de Havilland. We also attempted a biplane with Sopwith, and a few other experimental sets, prepared by what was then the Royal Aircraft Factory at Farnborough.'

The sources indicate that a number of copies of each of the post-1916 designs were produced. For example, the Royal Aircraft Factory produced six individual ATs of their design. The other designs were duplicated but it is not known exactly how many of each type were made.

The earliest attempted AT in 1916 was cobbled together by Low, Poole and their team from salvaged items and an available radial Gnome engine. This was probably the AT that Sir Norman reviewed in 1916 and maybe today we might call it a 'proof of principle' prototype. Archibald Low said that, initially, they had used a Gnome rotary engine for the AT but eventually gave up trying to overcome the electrical noise it emitted that disrupted their receiver and the communications from the ground transmitter. All of the later ATs were built by professional aircraft

The 1916 AT with some of its associated ground equipment. This was the first Aerial Target. It was assembled in Chiswick and completed at Brooklands. It had a tubular fuselage and was a monoplane utilising salvaged items (IWM Q 67987)

design firms and seem to have all used Bradshaw's 'Gnat' engine. The 'Gnat' was a horizontally opposed two-cylinder engine designed by Granville Bradshaw. Barry Jones, who had access to Bradshaw's papers, tells us that Thomas Sopwith asked Bradshaw to design an engine for his AT and the Gnat and its reduction gearbox were developed as a result of this request.

Often, what is missing from the records is as interesting as their content. There is, for instance, no mention of the aircraft designers being present at any of the trials of their AT designs but the fact that they devoted their expertise and time to the project at all is of significance and indicates that it had a considerable degree of high level support.

Low's account in Bloom's biography said the 1916 home-built AT had a pair of BE 2.c lower wings although in the 1950s they are described by Low as the lower wings of a Sopwith Pup. It was powered by a Gnome-type engine of about 60 h.p. and the 'air-screw' was from an SE5.

Sir Henry Norman said the trial he attended in 1916 at Netheravon was unsuccessful. This trial was most probably with this aircraft that Low's team made from spare and scavenged parts with no assistance from a recognised designer.

The Geoffrey de Havilland AT – the one that flew (IWM Q 67991)

However, Low and Kenneth Munson of 'Jane's Information Group' both stated that this aircraft went to Upavon but was never flown. Netheravon was a RNAS establishment so it is most unlikely that it was taken to Netheravon although it is just possible that Sir Norman saw either the Ruston Proctor or Sopwith AT there.

Post 1916, the Air Board reallocated serial numbers A8957 to A8962 for the production of ATs – the Experimental Radio Controlled Aircraft. These serial numbers had been originally allocated as part of a block A8950 to A8999 for orders of Armstrong Whitworth FX-10 Quad aircraft but the order for these was subsequently cancelled. There is considerable doubt over which number applied to which design. ATs from the various different designers' stables were trialled at different sites; Laffans Plain, Northolt, Netheravon and Upavon.

It is most clearly stated by Low in various sources that the aircraft that achieved the required level of reliability and that flew at Upavon in March 1917 was a Geoffrey de Havilland design.

This monoplane was launched from the compressed air ramp. There were several copies of the aircraft as Low states that 'the first machine had engine failure on the runway and flopped ungracefully into the mud' and 'eventually we got one into the air.'

Before aircraft design had become a serious career option for a young engineer, Geoffrey de Havilland had designed and built a motorcycle. In 1905 he sold the bike designs for £5. By 1917 he worked at the Aircraft Manufacturing Company

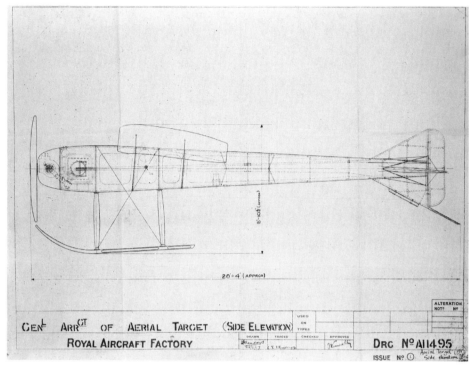

The Royal Aircraft Factory's AT drawing A11495, dated 1917 (IWM Q 68038)

'Airco' which he had joined in the autumn of 1914. However, prior to this Geoffrey worked with Henry Folland at the Royal Aircraft Factory just before the surviving 1914 AT drawing was produced (see Chapter 1). It is most probable that both de Havilland and Folland were involved in this design and used it as the basis for their versions of Aerial Targets. Airco were based at Hendon and as its chairman George Holt Thomas proudly stated when talking about his companies aircraft and their contribution to the war:

> The Airco and De Havilland designs were adopted by the government for a very large proportion [30 per cent] of the machines [trainers, fighters and bombers] used during the War. They were adopted almost entirely by the United States Flying Corps.

By the end of 1918 Airco claimed to be the largest aircraft company in the world. Sadly, after the war the British government did not support its indigenous industry, unlike the French.

Henry Folland joined the Royal Aircraft Factory in Farnborough in 1912, where he was assisted by Howard E. Preston. They built some of the classic aircraft of World War I and, it was noted, 'small monoplanes to test Mr. A. M. Low's design for wireless control' (*Flight*, 1920).

Six RAF aerial targets were built with the Air Boards, allocated serial numbers A8957 to A8962. In a 1958 lecture, Dr. George William Hoggan Gardner, director of the Royal Aircraft Establishment, confirmed that experiments with an aeroplane designed at the Royal Aircraft Factory were made at Northolt in July 1917. The design was tested in the wind tunnel at Farnborough in March 1917 which gave rise to a reduction in the fin and rudder area as detailed in the Royal Aircraft Factory BA Report 51 dated 2nd March 1917. This report also details the 150 ft-long launch track. The powered launch ramp devised by Poole, Bowen and Low was not used by the Royal Aircraft Factory and there is no evidence that it was used for any of the other trials. The RAF Superintendent O'Gorman and Low knew each other as they were both members of the five-man team of officials at the factory's race meeting at Brooklands on 23rd October 1915 but Low does not indicate that he or any members of his unit attended these RAF trials although it is likely that some of his mechanics were there to make adjustments to the control system if these were required. There was a cine film made of the RAF trials but only still frames from it have survived. These show the AT on its launch rails and some of the mechanics relaxing on the grass. The first launch on 5th July 1917 looped and crashed. With the trim corrected based upon the experience of the first launch, the second on 25th July did not lift off and ran off the track at speed finally crashing into a fence. On the 28th, with the trim on the third aircraft re-adjusted again, the aircraft was released but the engine started to cut out and the aircraft did not launch but slowly lost speed, ran off the track where the undercarriage broke and the aircraft broke its propeller. The last three aircraft were not trialled. Low's statement that the only design to fly was the de Havilland confirms that these RAF trials did not achieve controlled flight. Like the mnemonics for Henry VIII's wives we could say for the six RAF's ATs: launched, crashed, flopped, chopped, chopped, and chopped.

Folland also designed the pilotless aircraft built under contract by Ruston Procotor and Company Limited of Lincoln. It is possible that they may have made more than one copy of the aircraft and these could have been part of the six RAF Aerial Targets. A description in *Flight* (1955) says of Folland' Aerial Target (1917): 'Notwithstanding its name, this pilotless monoplane – the first of its kind – was intended as the prototype of an "aerial torpedo" and was powered by a 30 h.p. ABC Gnat. The airframe design was by H. P. Folland, and the radio gear by Professor A. M. Low.'

Meanwhile Thomas Octave Sopwith's AT never flew. Low tells us that this Sopwith AT was designed with the help of Harry Hawker, Sopwith's chief test pilot. It was the only biplane AT designed for Low's control system. The small biplane was mounted on a four-wheeled trolley undercarriage. It was abandoned but in 1917 it was modified for manned flight and became the Sopwith 'Sparrow'. However, as described by Barry M. Jones in *Granville Bradshaw: A Flawed Genius*, it was Sopwith who persuaded Bradshaw to design the small, short-life expendable 'Gnat' engine which was completed in 1916.

Sopwith's AT (IWM Q 67986)

Kenneth Munson revealed details of Sopwith's AT aircraft contained in a letter dated 4th August 1944 from Archibald Low, in part of which Archie describes his own control system:

> The Sopwith AT had a span of about 14 ft (4.27 m). The ABC engine drove an ordinary wooden propeller, about 3 ft 6 in (1.07 m) diameter, and the nose also housed an explosive charge weighing about 50 lb (22.5 kg)…The Sopwith AT was designed for full servo control in 1916. It was damaged before completion, and abandoned.

Thus, the Royal Aircraft Factory design drawing dated October 1914 for a monoplane with a 6 h.p. ABC engine is most likely the basis of both Geoffrey de Havilland's and Folland's later unmanned ATs. Low was then identified and transferred into the RFC to develop a system to control the AT from the ground.

Much more historical speculation on who made which aircraft seems to exists than is warranted by the hard facts but it is clear that with greater co-ordination between Low's control system team and the aircraft designers and with a better trials methodology, even more may have been achieved.

Building any aircraft was a complex undertaking, even for these 'simple' machines. Despite the complexity of the basic aircraft and the resources it consumed, material for construction and parts for repairs were readily available throughout the war.

Sourcing the parts from commercial directories and advertising had not stopped in the war. A buyer's guide in *The Aeroplane* 1917 issue is just one example. By 1917, aircraft production was big business and centred in places around sites like Brooklands and Kingston upon Thames. Farnborough and Hendon were two others.

The Aircraft Supplies Co. Ltd. advert (courtesy of Aviation Ancestry)

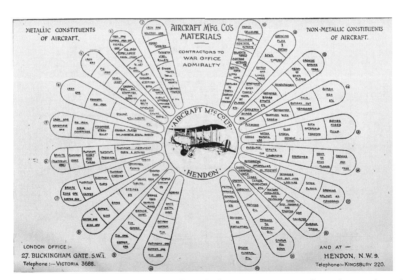

A Hendon Parts advert. Each blade on the left reads from outer to inner from the metal ore through the processes they undergo to make a component on the aircraft. The blades on the right describe the woods and other material. For example, 'birch, ash, etc.' become 'thin rotary cut veneers' that are 'cemented together with casein' and become 'plywood'. On another blade 'antimony, copper, tin' make 'white metal ingots' used for 'bearings' (courtesy of Aviation Ancestry)

An indication of the complexity of the basic aircraft and the resources it consumed are shown on an informative advertisement. For instance this tells us that airscrews, propellers (and presumably the pushers) were all made from walnut or mahogany.

One enterprising supplier of timber products was Messrs. Fentum Phillips and Co., of Guildford Electrical Works (Guildford's first electrical supply was started in 1891). Before Henry Fentum Phillips became mayor of the town and had a road named after himself, he 'added value' to his business by designing and making propellers. This illuminating *Flight* (1909) article also refers to the town's attitude to motor vehicles and, just like Brooklands, suggests flying near to sewage works is a good idea:

> Guildford Encouraging Aviation. Apparently Guildford's anti-motoring ideas do not extend to aviation, for we hear that the Town Council are actually helping a prospective flyer by lending him an aerodrome. Mr. Henry Fentum Phillips, who has been experimenting with propellers for twenty years, proposes building an aeroplane driven and partly lifted by specially designed propellers, and he has received permission to make his trial flights over the Corporation's sewage farm, which has an area of 250 acres. Although the land is rough, it has the advantage of being quite private and sheltered by trees.

Design was not just about building a prototype hoping 'on a wing and a prayer' that it would fly. In addition to wind tunnels, other design and development tools were being invented such as flight data recording. This 1913 system shows an example of the sophistication of the data that could be obtained.

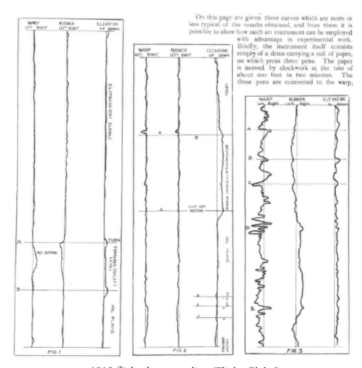

1913 flight data recording (Flight Global)

Nevertheless men were often injured or killed after making the simplest mistakes due to the quirks of these early aircraft, most of which were known to be flighty and unforgiving.

Initially, the aircraft were hand built by enthusiastic experimenters and then at the flight schools, who needed their repair and build facilities. The flying fields were in isolated areas where gas was not available so acetylene lighting was the norm unless sufficient funds were found for generators and electric lighting. Later these ad hoc workshops were superseded by dedicated production factories to meet the demands of the war.

Some powered tools were coming into use. For example, Russell Brothers of Littleworth, Redditch produced a powered screw driver with a hopper into which a handful of screws were placed so that the operator only had to position the work under the machine and apply the lever to drive the screw. A slipping clutch with a torque adjustment prevented over-tightening. Later in mid-1918, the company even devised a counter-balanced overhead support system so that the tool could be moved over the aircraft structure by the operator and claimed that this was an enormous boost to productivity.

The fabric covering of the wood-worked wings and fuselage frames served a number of functions, one of which was to stiffen the structure. The cloth had to be applied with just the right amount of slack to allow for the shrinkage when the protective stiffening lacquer known as dope was applied. Problems arose if the cloth was too tight, too slack or became brittle. Acetyl or nitrate dopes were not the only choices. Cody, like some others, started to use pegamoid waterproof varnish-coated fabrics, a product that was also used in bookbinding. The application of dope was a messy job and these liquids generally had a pungent odour, so while the Dope Shop was an essential and technically challenging place of work, it attracted more than its fair share of ribald attention.

All of these prototypes needed power and for many aircraft designs of the time, the only choice of aero-engine was literally the 'star', otherwise known as the 'radial' engine. This was a brilliant piece of 'lateral' thinking. The radial version of the internal combustion engine has the cylinders arranged in a 'star' fashion around its crankshaft. The rotating crankshaft in this design is still the drive output as it is in the more conventional 'in-line' and 'V' engines. The alternative implementation of the radial engine was to fix the crank shaft and spin the bulky hot cylinders around it, making them the drive output. This form of radial is known as a 'rotary' engine (quite different from and not to be confused with the Wankel engine). The spinning cylinders of the 'rotary' can be air cooled in their own fan-wise motion saving the complexity, and most importantly for aircraft, the weight of a liquid cooling system. The revolving mass of the cylinders act as a substantial flywheel to smooth the running of the engine but the gyroscopic effect of this gave some single-engined aircraft peculiar handling characteristic; lethal to some rookies but

Just one of the many Dope Shop cartoons (*The Aeroplane*, 14th March, 1917)

of benefit to those who survived to master their machines – machines such as the Sopwith Camel. Later, water-cooled engines showed greater potential than these air-cooled rotary radials which, as output power and therefore size increased, created unacceptable gyroscopic forces.

One of the first inventors to use a radial engine configuration used the rotary form. In 1895, Félix-Théodore Millet built and patented a motor-driven bicycle with a crank anchored to the frame and the radial cylinders forming the spokes of the rear wheel.

In 1889 the British-Australian inventor Lawrence Hargrave (of cellular kite fame) applied the rotary engine to the problem of powered flight without obtaining a powerful enough solution to be successful. In the late 1890s and on into the 1900s, Stephen Marius Balzer of New York and Fay Oscar Farwell of the Adams Co., Dubuque, Iowa patented various improvements in rotary engine design and there

After trials of over **TWO YEARS**

PEGAMOID

BRAND WATERPROOF

AEROCLOTHS

ARE PRONOUNCED PERFECT.

They are **ALL BRITISH** make, and have been adopted by Messrs. F. S. Cody, Howard Wright, and other prominent British aviators.

Samples, etc., from the sole manufacturers—

NEW PEGAMOID LTD.,

144, Queen Victoria Street, LONDON, E.C.

Pegamoid advert (Grace's Guide to British Industrial History)

were others working on such improvements. It had to be re-developed yet again in 1908 by the Seguin brothers, Laurent and Louis in France. They produced the 'Gnome' which was used extensively by many aircraft of the time and by the RFC Feltham group in their initial tests.

The complex valve actuation made accurate timing difficult so most early rotary engine aircraft had no throttle and ran at full speed continuously. To reduce that power, a 'blip' switch was used. This cut the ignition to some of the cylinders while the switch was held on. Sometimes if the 'blip' switch was released after being held on for an excessive time, the accumulation of too much unburned fuel igniting would cause explosive problems! Many landings were vol plané, meaning gliding flight with the engine switched off or faulty, now commonly known as 'dead stick' landings.

In the absence of an oil sump on rotary machines, lubrication was achieved by using a fuel/air/oil mixture. Castor oil was the best lubricant to use in this application, which was known as a total loss system. The oil rich exhaust got 'everywhere' and many said the famous flyers silk scarf was worn over the mouth and nose as filters to catch the oil as well as doubling as goggle cleaning implements and to prevent chaffing by the woollen collars on the jackets.

Victor Maslin Yeates in his book *Winged Victory* quoted one of his colleagues: 'These cursed rotaries, they do nothing but throw oil and foul plugs. I wish to God

CONFÉDÉRATION SUISSE

BUREAU FÉDÉRAL DE LA ✚ PROPRIÉTÉ INTELLECTUELLE

EXPOSÉ D'INVENTION

Brevet N° **9899**   21 janvier 1895, 7³/₄ h., p.   Classe **112**

Félix-Théodore MILLET, à PERSAN (Seine-et-Oise, France).

Une bicyclette à roue automobile.

Le système de bicyclette faisant l'objet de la présente demande de brevet d'invention se distingue par la disposition de la roue motrice qui porte en elle-même son moteur, et par les constructions de détail qui vont être expliquées ci-après.

Le moteur, qui est combiné avec une des sions intermédiaires de mouvements entre la roue et le moteur, les deux constituant un seul tout rigide. Enfin tout le mécanisme (manivelle, bielles, pistons) étant logé dans la capacité fermée constituée par le moyeu et des cylindres, ledit mécanisme est absolument à l'abri de la poussière, et les pièces qui le constituent

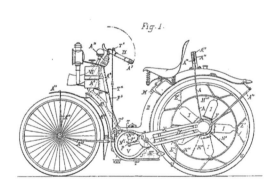

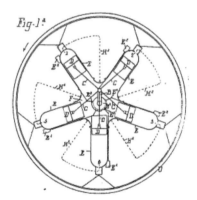

Extracts from Millet's rotary engine bicycle patent

I could get on SEs.' He was always neat and elegant, and hated castor oil. Any really adverse effects were dealt with by 'the castor oil merchant', that is, the doctor.

By 1918 and facing shortages of the organic-based oils due to the effective naval blockade, Germany used rapeseed, mineral-based voltol oils but these are thought to have been less than ideal and increased the failure rates of their aircraft engines.

Rotary engines developed a reputation for reliability – for example Charles Lindbergh put his faith and life in the single rotary engined 'Spirit of St. Louis' to fly solo across the Atlantic in 1927, having flown from San Diego to New York via St. Louis a few days earlier.

The marriage of the airframe, engine and other systems requires extensive consideration of the more subtle interactions that arise. The gyroscopic and resultant precessional affects of rotary engines on aircraft handling, and the radio interference that caused Low to change the power plant for the AT are two examples of this.

It is worth repeating that the ATs made to trial Low's control system were from extremely reputable and well-known aircraft design and construction companies. This AT work was undertaken despite the enormous pressure these same companies would have been under to deliver new designs and to meet production schedules to feed the demands of that insatiable war. The status of the AT project must have been significant to warrant this.

CHAPTER 14

The Trials

In March 1917, Geoffrey de Havilland's batch of AT aircraft, fitted with the engines designed by Granville Bradshaw and with Low's control systems, had been assembled and along with their associated ground equipment were ready for the trials. These trials, conducted at the RFC Central Flying School base at Upavon on Salisbury Plain on 21st March 1917, were the only ones to control the aircraft in flight. They were the only ones that we know for certain that Low attended and he (and others) declared them successful. It was also the only set of trials launched from the pneumatic-powered ramp (like the Queen Bees were a decade and more later). The other trials used rails laid on the ground so they didn't really stand a chance of reaching speeds that would produce aerodynamic control.

The success of these March trials ensured that the RAF AT development programme continued. Failure would have surely terminated the significant expenditure of talented manpower and scarce resources being invested in the six RAF ATs still in production. On the question of success, Archie Low said:

> The most surprising lesson learnt from our guided-missile achievement was that invention needs far more than success to make it successful. In other words, it takes time for 'desirability' to sink into people's minds – especially official minds.

Until recently, the only contemporary sources of information on the Royal Flying Corps, Aerial Target have been the evidence supplied by Low's Works, including their patents and the photographs in the archives of the IWM and RAF Museum together with the records and photographs of the Royal Aircraft Factory designs held in the archives of FAST along with the various reports in the National Archives such as BA Report No. 51. There are now two more, recently relocated, contemporary sources to add to this list. These are those evocative IWM-stored artefacts from the actual AT aircraft and Sir Henry Norman's report for General Smuts.

Supporting these contemporary papers, files and artefacts there are others; the Navy Post War Questions Committee, a 1920s' article by Denis Gwynn, a 1921 article in *The Aeroplane* by C. G. Grey which seems to refer to a mixture of the Royal Aircraft Factory's trials and the de Havilland trial at Upavon, and a 1930s' article by Miles Henslow on the Queen Bee referring back to the World War I project. There is also Kenneth Munson's notes on the Sopwith AT that were based upon the 1944 letter from Archie Low. There are the even later but more detailed items such as Low's 1952 article in *Flight* magazine and the IWM labels produced for their exhibition and of course, there is Ursula Bloom's biography of Low (a large part of which is, in reality, as she intimates, more like a ghost written autobiography). The other meagre collection of published articles and comments are extractions from these primary sources.

There is consensus that the RFC were carrying out trials of unmanned aircraft World War I. There has been less agreement on the degree to which these trials were considered to be successful. Before addressing the varying views on the trials in detail it is well to consider that the 1930s 'Queen Bee' RPVs came from the same stable as the AT that Low describes. These were both products of de Havilland, the RFC/RAF and their experimental units, the Feltham Experimental Works and the Royal Aircraft Establishment respectively. The other salient fact is that Low's system was subsequently employed on the Royal Navy's DCB programme, so successfully that the navy were at once delighted and concerned for the safety of their own capital ships until countermeasures could be devised. The preface of the 127-page Final Report of the Post War Questions Committee dated 18th May 1920 asked whether capital ships would survive submarines and aerial power. Its first conclusion concerned DCBs and Wireless Controlled Aircraft, their further development and the need for countermeasures. Of course one countermeasure was to produce the Queen Bee drone to perfect AA gunnery.

In the intervening 100 years, there are only a few who have written about the Aerial Target and very few of these that have given it anything more than a brief mention. Some of these historians have declared that the trials were a failure and they give a number of reasons for this, which fall into the following categories; it crashed, it didn't fly for very long, the war was coming to an end, the air services were too preoccupied with the reorganisation that created the RAF or they simply declare (erroneously) that development ceased.

In 1917, aircraft crashed all too frequently and so did the ATs. More significantly, the ATs were not designed to land and yet a few of the subsequent references to the AT declare that the project was terminated because they crashed. In fact, the project was not terminated after the trials. Before the de Havilland AT crashed it had been controlled briefly by the signals from the ground, the engine had been selected from half-power to full-power before take-off and it had responded, the pneumatic-powered launch ramp had launched the aircraft into the air and the elevators responded to the up command. The control system worked.

Sadly accidents were demoralisingly common. RFC fatal accidents in Britain around the time of the AT trials continued at a depressing rate. Two of these occurred at Upavon in a mid-air collision when Alfred Pocock Long's Sopwith 1½ Strutter was struck from behind in the air by the propeller and centre section of Philip Sellers' Sopwith Scout just a few days after the AT trials. Prangs were the norm and crashes shocked but no longer surprised serving officers. The aircraft coming into service at the time of the AT trials in 1917 were some of the first to offer a pilot the remote possibility of a career where the number of landings would equal the number of take-offs. Up until that era, aircraft were maturing from those that were robust but too heavy and under powered and others that were light but fragile; those that were stable but staid, with too little performance to fly out of trouble and others that were agile but fragile and unforgiving if mishandled. Faltering engines, particularly on take off, were the cause of many incidents and the desire to turn for home in such circumstances increased.

With this background, accustomed to the dangers and to some extent hardened by their experiences, it is most unlikely that the RFC and other officials witnessing the AT flight trials in March 1917 were, as some have suggested, 'surprised' that the aircraft crashed. It is more likely to have been the expected outcome for a prototype aircraft, of any description, to crash, especially one designed to explode rather than land! What mattered was that it had been 'under control' before it crashed.

We are told that a significant number of high-ranking officers attended the trial on 21st March 1917. Low recounts that 'the Plain was cleared by mounted police and I solemnly walked across to the lorry, accompanied by a glittering staff of brass-hats from Belgium, France and Italy, with a positive covey of our own generals.' Low says there were thirty to forty generals present. On this day, for the first time, they would see aircraft launched into the air without a pilot. These officers waiting for the trials to begin were watching a poor student pilot who was too scared to land his plane. You could almost forgive their impatient, half-joking comment, 'We'll have to shoot the _____ down!'

Archibald Low attributes this remark to Sefton Brancker and this speaks volumes when considering the attitudes and experience of those present at the trials. This black humour had developed over the years by those witnessing tragic prangs and dealing with the human consequences of shattered lives. On the other hand, considering the situation from the poor student's perspective, dazzled as he must have been by the illustrious audience gathered, as he must have thought, to watch his first solo landing, he was the cat up the tree with the dogs below barking.

The first AT machine flown that day had engine failure and flopped ungracefully into the mud. Major Gordon Bell, afterwards known as the 'Mad Major' due to his many crashes, remarked all too loudly, 'I could throw my bloody umbrella farther than that!'

So, to return to those who have questioned the AT's success 'because it crashed', we could answer that the designers and test pilots such as Frank Barnwell, Ted Busk and the many others had made great progress in the collective understanding of aircraft design but the complexities are such that even now a century later prototypes are built and tested and, while few fail catastrophically, it is doubtful that anyone would take a design straight into production.

Perhaps a more mundane reason can also be offered to explain 'the crash'. The army at the time of the AT trials did not allow an aircraft to be under the control of someone like Archie Low who did not hold a pilot's certificate. So Henry Segrave was selected to watch the AT and shout instructions to Archie at the controls. It will not have helped that the two men had not met before the trial. Henry would later joke with Low (and others) that he was the world's worst pilot, having crashed many machines while ferrying them from England to France. Many of those officers from flying establishments that were present at the AT trial will have been observant and will have been impressed that, despite the additional delays introduced by this chain of command process, the controls were responding to the commands shouted to Low by Segrave. Engines failed and prototypes crashed, it was the norm. What was clear was that a measure of control was achieved – it worked. Their endeavour was successful.

Some claimed the trial flight was too short to be counted as successful. Bart Everett acknowledges the RFC's achievement at the start of his book *Unmanned Systems of World Wars I and II* with this statement: 'As far as can yet be determined, Archibald Montgomery Low flew the first radio-controlled airplane on 21st March 1917, only 14 years after the Wright brothers made their inaugural flight at Kitty Hawk'.

However, he then brands this trial a failure while presumably accepting the Kitty Hawk hops as an historic success. If this is the case, the Wright brothers set the measure of success for 'firsts in flight' very low, claiming their four flights with a combined flying time of a little over one and half minutes in 1903 were the first heavier-than-air controlled flights. The first of these flights could have been flown down the economy cabin of a Boeing 747 Jumbo. This is especially significant as this was followed by a 5-year gap before they joined others, who were by then, flying in public.

The accounts of their 'first flights' were not widely reported or even considered credible, especially as the Wrights did not repeat their experimental flights in public. By 1906, even in their home country, the Wrights were being described as 'either fliers or liars.' But today you can visit the site at Kitty Hawk without being told that there was any doubt at all or that until 1942 the Smithsonian Institute did not recognise the Wright Brothers claims, celebrating Samual Pierpont Langley instead. Charles Edward Taylor, who built the wind tunnel and the engine for the Flyer, is rarely mentioned. He would have died in obscurity in the charity ward of Los Angeles General Hospital but was helped by eleemosynary assistance to spend his last months in San Fernando where he died at the age of 87 in a private sanitarium. Few know that 'Charlie' was key to the Wright Brothers endeavours.

Mr. Denis Rolleston Gwynn, the Irish writer and historian who had served in France and in the Ministry of Information, was not so reticent concerning the

Aerial Target's flight. He had a more sanguine analysis, declaring in 1921 that the manoeuvring of pilotless aeroplanes by wireless had been completely demonstrated and going on to describe fleets of wireless aeroplanes wreaking havoc on enemy cities.

Miles Henslow, the radio and aviation author of many books on radio developments, witnessed the Queen Bee in service and in 1939 referred to this being the result of twenty years' worth of development.

Some claimed the AT was terminated because the war was nearly over – but it was far from finished. The war was to intensify and hang in the balance for a further year or more, continuing to be in doubt even after the German offensive of early 1918 was repulsed. Indeed the outcome wasn't really 'beyond doubt' until much later in 1918 in the 'Hundred Days Offensive'. Brancker stated that he had noticed the public fear of a German victory on his return from the US in late August 1918 and Pemberton Billing exploited this public mood in his publications. The end came not just from decisive action on the Western Front but from the Southern fronts with the defeat of the Bulgarian army and the fall of the Ottoman capital Constantinople and, of course, from the consequences of the years of the blockade.

A more telling question arises if one assumes that the Aerial Target was indeed unsuccessful or was wound up because the war was ending. Why, if this was so, were Low and Bowen then given the task of developing the control system for the Royal Navy Distance Control Boats? The navy wouldn't have spent time and money converting their precious Coastal Motor Boats to remote control if the AT control system was a failure and the war was ending.

Some also say the AT project was curtailed because of the RAF re-organisation. The formation of the Royal Air Force could have curtailed the AT project but again the evidence is that it did not and the work on RPVs continued. The RFC radio work was consolidated at Biggin Hill. There were continuing experiments on the AT's control systems and modifications issued for changes to the design of the airframe of the Royal Aircraft Factory machines. Far from closing down, in September 1917 the Feltham Experimental Works moved all of its operations to the High Street works in preparation for the new naval work. Low wrote to Pritcher on 25th August 1917 confirming that the sets and gyroscopes were completed and the machines sent to Biggin Hill.

There is no evidence of any collaboration between the AT project and Prince's RFC wireless development team prior to this consolidation but Feltham were now to concentrate on the Navy DCB programme so the transfer was probably necessary. It was normal for Low to document his work in patents. If they were raised to pass the work to Biggin Hill it may explain why, as noted earlier, some of the AT patents contain additional details that would not usually be included.

Clues to the continuing work are obtained from the dates on these patents. The application for Patent 195,410 for the wireless control of weapons is dated 2nd

April 1918, the day after the creation of the Royal Air Force. The patent for the innovative 'Smoke Aerial' (number 191,406) was applied for on 9th January 1918. Most telling of all is Patent 244,498, again for improvements in the wireless control of weapons. This patent application is made by the 'RAF Experimental Works' (not the RFC) and is dated 3rd September 1918, fully 17 months after the flight trials.

The fact is work on RPVs was still very much alive in both the newly formed RAF and in the navy. Low said: 'The MID showed its mettle, for both Major Colley and Sir Henry Norman did all they could to cause the weapon to be developed and used.'

The Royal Aircraft Establishment drawings and photographs of the 1920s ATs are of similar design and show ramp launches off HMS *Stronghold* in 1924.

So, development did not cease, it continued and it led to the fleet of Queen Bee ATs of the 1930s and 40s on which the navy and army anti-aircraft batteries honed their skills.

There remains the question of whether these RFC trials of the de Havilland AT could have been an even greater success. The 8th June 1917 patent application 195,100 showed that a more robust construction of the system equipments had been designed. This redesign may have been for use in a mother aircraft controlling a DCB. Should they have waited for this modified system to be available? Was the AT ready for the trials or would it have been more successful given a bit more development time and trialled when the weather was better in the summer months? It is probable that the date of the trials had nothing to do with the progress being made on the equipment.

Top brass of this seniority and in these numbers reported would not have been assembled on a Wednesday in the wilds of Wiltshire in March just for these trials. It is likely that the timing of the trial was dictated by their presence rather than the reverse. It was and still is common practise to augment illustrious meetings with an initial selection of disassociated distractions as they allow interludes of informality in what are otherwise starchy proceedings. It is possibly no coincidence that the Imperial War Conference chaired by the Prime Minister David Lloyd George took place from Wednesday 21st March to 27th April. It included members from the Allied armies including those from most of the British Empire. For the first time at one of these conferences India had its own representatives but Australia was absent due to their federal election. It was at this conference that the epithet 'Commonwealth' was used for the first time in this context. Smuts, who had represented South Africa at the conference, was subsequently invited onto the War Cabinet and it was in this capacity that he compiled (with Henderson's great assistance) his report that led to the reorganisation of the air services and the formation of the RAF. While the principal attendees of the Imperial War Conference were greeting each other in London, a host of their senior advisors (generals) not required for the pre-ambles of the first days may have been, with representatives of the Allies, on a prearranged tour of British Army facilities that included a gathering in Wiltshire to witness the trial of the AT. So it is most likely that the trial date was not determined by the AT development team's progress but was out of their control and ordained by the higher authorities.

Although by March better weather could be anticipated, the windswept plains of Wiltshire must have seemed like a step back towards winter when Low's Unit moved there from the trees and relative shelter of Brooklands. The Meteorological Office report for the month was headed 'Cold and Unsettled. Frequent Snow.' Milder weather arrived during the middle of the second week, and on the 17th the maximum temperature rose above 13°C (55°F). However, the conditions had not become settled, and showers of rain or snow continued in nearly all places.

In addition to their exposed position, they were now also further removed from their supply source for their specialised, custom-made system. Pewsey Train Station was about 5 miles away and the Great Western Railway trains from London's Paddington station carrying any required personnel or spares would take a few hours to reach them if they were needed.

Was it sensible to have the operator at the controls of the AT inside the transmitter vehicle and unable to see the aircraft with 'the pilot' outside shouting orders? Of course not. We know Low had considerable flying experience as an observer and would have known that this was not an optimum method of control. The trial's methodology could have been much improved. In contrast to the enormous effort expended making the many ATs of each of the types from the various design groups and their control systems to be shot off the launching ramp, the planning of the trial itself appears to have been cobbled together on the day. Segrave 'was allocated' to Low to shout the control orders:

> I heard the command 'Let it go!' instructed by General Caddell, and at last the engine opened up. I pulled the launch-lever, and held one hand on the controls. With a roar the result of nearly two years' hard labour shot into the air. 'Up!' yelled Segrave. I jammed the 'Up' handle, and then hear the shout 'By God, it's working'. 'Up! Up!' instructed Segrave. 'Up! Up! Quick!'. So I upped, but the motor began to splutter. I knew that the wretched thing was far from reliable, and no wonder. It had been shot off an incline, pulled by compressed air gear, all contained within the lorry, so that the crew had only to stop the lorry to fire the weapon. The next thing I heard was a wild yell. They were shrieking 'Sort out!'. I peered out of the lorry again, and to my horror saw a positive covey of Generals running for their lives! I had no idea what could have happened, but in a matter of seconds my beloved AT came into view, and with a beautiful loop under control, the engine packed up, tore into the ground and crashed the works! Many thousands of pounds and all our work gone west in a split second, but it was worth it, for we now had a guided missile.

And so the unit returned to Feltham and at the end of these momentous trials the AT project changed. Feltham had to prepare control sets for the Royal Aircraft Factory units that were just about ready for their debut. This could be carried out with renewed confidence knowing that controlled flight could be achieved once the machine was airborne with its engine running reliably.

Two of the most contemporary accounts of AT trials were written against the background of hidden agendas.

The first of these started on 6th September 1917 when Sir Henry Norman received a request on behalf of Lord Alfred Milner. This asked for a report based upon Sir Henry's extensive connection with the flying services to aid General Smuts in his review of the organisation of these forces. Sir Henry's report, marked SECRET, was delivered to Smuts on 11th December 1917. The section on inappropriate management notes the curious histories of some officers. 'The Officer Commanding the Organisation of Gunnery, Air Board was a short time ago an actor at the Gaiety Theatre.' 'An officer in the Central Indian Horse commands the (RFC) Eastern Training Brigade.' 'The Deputy Director of Air Organisation was a civil engineer in Hong Kong and has no air experience whatsoever.' On page 11 of this 26-page report, Sir Henry concludes this section:

> I will give a further example. In March 1916 I was requested by the Comptroller MID to go to the RFC Experimental Station at Feltham to report upon the invention of Capt. A. M. Low D. Sc. RFC for the wireless control of a small aeroplane to carry a large charge of high explosive, and to be steered and controlled from the ground entirely by wireless telegraphy.
>
> I reported that the invention was remarkable and novel, and that there appeared to be every reason to suppose that it would do all that was claimed for it.
>
> The invention was duly installed upon a model aeroplane and tested in my presence at Netheravon. As soon as the local flying officers saw the machine, they remarked, 'that thing will never fly' and this proved to be the case.
>
> But from that time till September 1917 the RFC never provided Capt. Low with a machine that would fly, and then the whole experiment was abandoned and Capt. Low was transferred to the Navy, which proposes to use his invention for steering torpedoes by wireless – one year and five months wasted!

This report was written to influence the general into supporting Sir Henry's particular point of view on the re-organisation of the air service. It suited Sir Henry's argument to imply that nothing was achieved on the Aerial Target due to 'inappropriate management' but he would certainly have known some of what Low's group were doing after his 1916 direct involvement in their work. Sir Henry had access to information of a sensitive nature at the highest level. It was his job to monitor innovations and he was an accomplished radio designer and engineer so he understood Low's control system. He knew that Low had transferred in late 1917 to the Royal Naval Volunteer Reserve, so it is almost certain that he also knew about the 1917 AT trials although it didn't serve his purpose to mention these in this report. In addition, at the time of this report, Henry Segrave, the 'pilot' who had observed the Aerial Target and directed Archie Low from outside the control lorry during the first trials in March 1917, was working for Sir Norman. Sir Norman formally requested the loan of Captain Segrave on 31st January 1918 to confirm an existing position. This request was granted.

THE COMEDY OF THE AERIAL TORPEDO.

The heading from Charles Grey's article (*Aeronautical Engineering*)

In March 1918 Norman wrote to Low, saying: 'I know of no man who has more extensive and more profound scientific knowledge, combined with a greater gift on imaginative invention than yourself'

The second account was by C. G. Grey who wrote about the trials nearly four years after they were conducted.

C. G.'s article appears to relate to the work conducted by the Royal Aircraft Factory and it incorrectly concludes that the project was stopped. The author was obviously unaware or chose to ignore the work of other establishments who continued with trials or that the Royal Aircraft Establishment also continued to work on RPVs.

His article was titled 'The Comedy of the Aerial Torpedo' and it was published in the 21st December 1921 edition of *Aeronautical Engineering*. C. G. was the founding editor of the British weekly *The Aeroplane* and was known for his vituperative comments and his critical references, especially those concerning the government establishments and institutions. This article seems to be related to the ATs trialled at Luffan's Plain and Northolt but as it mentions the 'generals' fleeing which occurred at Upavon months earlier, it suggests it was based upon combined hearsay from all of the various secret AT trials.

The article is really about a claim for a financial award for work on the Gnat engine. In it, C. G. notes 'a wireless expert, identity unknown, designed a suitable controlling gear.'

After the war Norman, Segrave and Low went into business together, in the Norlow Engineer Company which all suggests a degree of friendship, of mutual respect and confidence in each other's ability.

The documentation and recording phase of the AT project was initiated, preparing the draft patents for submission. New refinements to the design were considered as the development work continued.

The 'spark' of Low's system was still burning bright as another urgent 'need' was identified and the triangle's 'means' would come from both the army and the navy from now onwards. The AT project was successful and the British development work on RPVs would continue through the 1920s and 1930s and onwards.

CHAPTER 15

A Drone by Any Other Name

The ultimate successor to the RFC's 1917 AT was the 'Queen Bee.' These were flown in large numbers by British forces from 1935 through to the end of the 1940s. Ironically, they were true Aerial Targets; used to train, improve and guage the effectiveness of ground-based and ship-based air defences.

The Queen Bees were wooden fuselage versions of the De Havilland Moth biplane. Without close inspection they were difficult to distinguish from the Tiger Moth and they were the first Remote Piloted Vehicles in the world to enter service and be deployed in large numbers. Queen Bees were full-sized aircraft that could be flown in three modes, either conventionally by a pilot, allowing them to be ferried to their operating bases or by a pilot using the onboard remote control panel for testing and training or at their operational base, they could be launched and operated remotely as targets … but they were not called 'drones'.

In the 1919 post-World War I rush to peace, the AT programme did not get completely trodden into obscurity and lost to our history. As a concept it belonged firmly in the future and indeed, that is exactly where the RAF and the research establishment at Farnborough placed it.

Regarding this long development towards the Queen Bee, Low's 1952 article on the AT prompted E. G. Riddle (ex-RAF) to write of his experience on the aircraft carrier *Argus* in 1922. He reported that a number of small pilotless monoplanes were hoisted on board and when they were launched off a rail, several actually flew for about two or three minutes. These were probably the RAE's 1921 ATs that are described as 'Royal Aircraft Factory 1917 type AT with a 45 h.p Armstrong Siddeley engine'. This was the 'Ounce' engine. Three years later when Riddle was stationed at Gosport, a unit known as the Glider Flight launched small aircraft. These were probably part of the Farnborough, Armstrong Siddeley 'Lynx' engine-powered, 'Larynx' programme. After this, three Fairey IIIF aircraft were fitted with radio control and this variant was known as the Fairey Queen. At about the same time in America three of the Standard Aircraft Corporation E-1s were converted for unmanned flight trials.

In 1924, while he was still under security restrictions, in his book *Wireless Possibilities*, Archie predicted: 'The time will come when low-flying wireless planes will explore, and render visible at many miles distant, places where no human pilot could remain for any length of time in safety.' The realisation matured in the inter-war years that Capital ships and other significant high value and prestigious military assets were becoming ever more vulnerable to air attack in the new age of air warfare. Inertia prevents nations from adopting new strategies. The larger the historic investment in a substantial arsenal of weapons of one type, the more painful is the realisation that they are obsolete. Despite the threat, the production of Capital ships did not stop but emphasis was placed on improving their defence against aircraft. This created a market for Aerial Targets to test these defences.

These projects coalesced in Britain into an aircraft that met this new and urgent operational requirement. The De Havilland Aircraft Company Limited produced the DH82B, the 'Queen Bee' Aerial Target for anti-aircraft firing practise. The first attempt at pilotless flight was made from HMS *Orion* and it was a qualified success. This aircraft, the Queen Bee, was the world's first realistic target aircraft to be used extensively.

Geoffrey de Havilland was a keen entomologist so many of his aircraft designs had insect names such as Moth, Mosquito or Dragonfly. The Queen Bee probably came from the Fairey Queen and the 'B' variant of the DH-82.

The Queen Bee was the world's first target aircraft to be produced in significant numbers. 420 were built but many were salvaged, repaired and reused so any count of the total numbers is bound to be somewhat confused. A Queen Bee base and five permanent Queen Bee units were established round the coasts of Britain at sites such as RAF Waybourne in Norfolk. They were used for army and navy exercises and the navy also used Queen Bees in exercises abroad.

Many Queen Bees ended up being used commercially, as camera platforms for filming by Pathe News and later after the war during the making of movies such as the 1957 *Spirit of St. Louis*. There are clips of Queen Bee launchings and of them undergoing bombardment in naval target practice. Other projects followed with the Airspeed prototype Queen Wasp and then the joint Anglo-Australian development of the Jindivik drone.

From 1935 onwards this secret Queen Bee aircraft had been revealed to the press. Statements in these articles citing events of 'twenty years ago' can only be references to the RFC's development of the AT in World War I. The servicing of the control system was separate from that of the aircraft for security reasons, as it was in World War I. The compressed air launcher for the Queen Bee is not too dissimilar to Low's 1917 AT launch ramp. We also see in these articles mention of flight data recording; capturing the actual command inputs to the aircraft controls as they are transmitted – albeit on the ground at the point of transmission. The World War I AT patents also stated: 'A record of the signals may be made, if desired, by any

Churchill at a Queen Bee launch (IWM H 10307)

well-known means.' Bloom's book quotes Archibald Low talking of a video link '…
for there is a radio-controlled Queen Bee plane, which sees the view, and transmits
it to base without any pilot on board.' In addition to all of these early examples of
innovations, we know that the Queen Bee had a form of automatic landing and
that its control system was powered from a ram air turbine enabling it to land if
the engine failed. Concorde also had a RAT.

Back in 1902, the play *The President* ran at the Prince of Wales theatre in London
from 30th April to 16th May. Robert Loraine had played 'Enrico Carbojal' and a
very young 11-year-old British actor named Reginald Leigh Denny had the part of
'the Midshipman'. Reginald was born Reginald Leigh Dugmore and by the time of
World War I he had, like Loraine established a career as an actor in the US.

In 1917 Reginald, now a famous 25-year-old movie star, became another atypical
recruit when he joined the Royal Flying Corps where Robert had been serving since
the start of hostilities. They had both left successful acting careers to enlist so it is
probable that they were reacquainted at his time.

After the war, Reginald's acting and movie career prospered and, in addition, in
the late 1930s he started a company called 'Radioplane' making target drones for
the US military. These were large 'model' aircraft. The US Army ordered them and
so did the US Navy whose version of the design was known as TDD, for 'Target

Norma Jeane Dougherty (taken by David Conover)

Drone Denny', nicknamed Tiddledy-dee. These were the first mass produced drones after the Queen Bee and many thousands of them were produced after the first orders were placed in 1940.

The army version of the TDD was produced at a plant near Los Angeles where Norma Jeane Dougherty worked. A publicity opportunity at the plant was organised through Denny's acting contacts with Ronald Wilson Reagan who commanded a World War II army film unit. The photographs of Norma Jeane, taken by the 25-year-old 'Shutterbug' David Conover in late 1944 at the factory in Van Nuys, were the first professional 'exposures' of the phenomenon that became Marilyn Monroe.

It is possible that there is direct link between the 1914 Royal Aircraft Factory Aerial Target drawing and the Global Hawk, one of the most advanced drones in operation today. After the war in those roaring twenties, even before Lindbergh fanned the public fascination with flying, Robert Loraine and Reginald Denny were both in the USA. Reginald combined his successful acting career with the adrenaline fuelled thrill of stunt flying, joining 'The Black Cats' union as one of the film pilots in the "Thirteen Black Cats". The movies bought together aviators in the industry making films such as *Young Eagles* which was inspired by Elliott White Springs' books about the Lafayette Escadrille. The talkies invigorated the movie industry and a few years later Loraine returned to Hollywood, joining the great move west from the Broadway stage, a migration made by many after the Great Depression. Here he was naturally attracted to those actors who had aviation in their blood and he became friends with Paul Lukas and others in this group. Sparked again with the joy of flying, on 31st October 1933 Robert got his American flying licence. Duncan le Geyt Pitcher was one of the officers who recruited Archie on to the AT project. He was the officer involved in 1918 in Low's moves to the Royal Navy and back to the RAF and Duncan was a close friend of Robert Loraine, close enough to have been his best man at Robert's wedding in 1921. From 1916 onwards General Pitcher was the Controller of the Technical Department of the Air Board and served on the Advisory Committee for Aeronautics. Pitcher was an Air Commodore when he retired in 1929, senior enough to be aware of the work leading to the Queen Bee. Robert, the first in Britain to transmit radio messages from the air, would have been interested in radio-related developments. Denny and Loraine had known each other in 1902, both were veterans of the RFC and both were British actors in Hollywood in the early 1930s. They were both still flying and both had connections with relatives living around Richmond Park in London. So it is an extraordinary coincidence that in the whole of the US it was Denny who opened a model aircraft shop in 1934, starting a company that went on to design and produce the first American mass produced drones in the 1940s. It is possible to imagine, despite the other stories explaining his new commercial interest in model aircraft, that through Pitcher and Loraine, Reginald Denny heard the story of those generals at Upavon in 1917 gathered to see the Aerial Target trials and was alerted to the introduction around 1935 of the Queen Bee into service in Britain. Eventually Denny's Radioplane drone company was absorbed into Northrop who now produce the RQ-4 Global Hawk.

To date, the largest historical impact of the drone on world politics was probably not due to their use but was the result of a tragic accident in WWII, the details of which were not made public at the time. John Fitzgerald 'Jack' Kennedy may not have become President JFK if a 'drone' had not exploded prematurely. A specialised US Eighth Air Force program code named 'Aphrodite' used 'Doolittle's Doodlebugs', a nickname derived from their commander, the famed US flyer James Harold Doolittle and the German V1. These US Doodlebugs were bomber aircraft converted into remote control 'drone' bombs that required a two-man crew for take-off. Joseph (Joe) Patrick Kennedy Jr and his flight engineer Wilford John Willy were killed when their Doodlebug exploded. They were on a secret mission on 12th August 1944 when, having reached the required altitude, they activated their aircraft's radio controls and armed its massive explosive charges. They were killed before they could make their scheduled parachute exit and leave the Liberator 'drone' aircraft under the control of its chase mother aircraft. Joe Kennedy Jr was the oldest brother of

JFK and would almost certainly have entered politics and eclipsed his brother's career had he survived.

The etymology of the term 'drone' is uncertain. For instance, the name may have originated from the aircraft's sound. A 1939 *Flight* magazine article described the Queen Bee launch: 'Suddenly the engine roars at full throttle, there is a hiss of compressed air, and the Bee drones away over the sea, climbing steadily as flying speed is maintained.' In 1932, the British Aircraft Company produced the 'drone' which was a manned ultra-light aircraft and this is another possible, although unlikely, derivation of the generic naming of RPVs. This 'drone' had a small engine mounted right above the pilot – that no doubt 'droned' in his ears. Robert Kronfeld was an Austrian who, due to post-World War I restrictions, was trained as a glider pilot. Of Jewish descent, he emigrated to Britain in the early 1930s and took over the design of an earlier version of this BAC aircraft, and the company that made it. BAC became Kronfeld Ltd. One Kronfeld drone, registration G-AEKV, which last flew in 1984, is in the care of Brooklands Museum in Surrey. Robert died in yet another flying accident testing a flying wing glider in 1948.

But the most generally accepted origin of the generic name 'drone' is that it derived from the Queen Bee but was coined in the US. US Admiral William Harrison Standley, while he was attending the London Naval Conference between 7th December 1935 and 25th March 1936, witnessed a live-firing exercise of anti-aircraft gunnery involving Queen Bee targets. Back in the US, Lieutenant Commander Delmer Stater Fahrney working on Standley's reports is thought to have named their projects 'drones' as a deliberate nod to the de Havilland Queen Bee. It may be a lucky happenstance but in the US 'Q' was used to signify a target drone. Of course, the prime missions of drones, both RPV and Anthophila, are potentially fatal.

CHAPTER 16

Controlled Distractions

The AT project was the primary product of the Feltham Experimental Works, the concept that it was created to realise. But Low did not give up on his 'private' work. By the time the war started, Archibald had an extensive list of patents to his name. Some were potentially very relevant to the impending situation, such as that machine for de-aerating and re-forming waste rubber referred to earlier. A number of these patents had been raised jointly with other engineers and he continued to collaborate on patent ideas during the war and to submit his own. An interesting example was the patent he raised in June 1917 for improvements in signalling apparatus. It can be found in the European Patent Register and it reads:

> This invention relates to signalling apparatus of the kind in which signals may be transmitted from a sending station to a number of receiving stations in such a manner that only one of the receiving stations is able to receive signals at any one time.

Another in August 1918 was a patent for improvements in radiographic transmission which describes a form of facsimile transmission. It reads:

> This invention relates to the radiographic transmission of signals and the like, and has for its object to devise a simple and efficient apparatus by means of which signals, messages, markings or the like made at one place may be transmitted to a distant station at which they will be automatically reproduced upon paper or other receiving medium. The invention is of particular utility in the case of signalling from aeroplanes.

Sidelines aside, after its formation, the Feltham unit soon became involved in a great many other official projects and its expertise was called upon to assess the viability of new developments and suggestions. For instance Low was requested to investigate a report that surfaced in Paris, a request that may well have originated from Henry Norman's intelligence network. Archie was supplied with introductory documentation along with about £100 in gold sovereigns for emergency use and sent to contact an Italian naval attaché, Commandatore Ernesto Binetti. The reported 'secret device' that was to be investigated was quickly dismissed by Archie but by then it had appeared in print in *Le Matin*, a respected French national newspaper of the day. On 15th November 1915 this carried a report under the banner 'Jules Verne In Action' which stated that Professor Louis Rota, an Italian engineer residing in Marseille, had invented an apparatus which simply by using Hertzian waves triumphs over the law of gravity and is able to hold a considerable weight immobile in the air at a height of up to 1000 metres or to move it at a prodigious velocity in any direction and stop it at any point.

Today it seems strange that such claims could be given any credence at all and that they could be peddled as news in national newspapers. However, such instances occasionally occur. A more recent example of a sensational report was the 1989 'Cold Fusion' experimental results that promised unlimited clean energy for the planet but were ultimately proved to be an erroneous anomaly.

Between 1917 and 1921, Luigi Gino Valerio Rota worked in the research laboratories of the British Admiralty. He did not give up his 'Jules Verne' invention and on the 14th August 1917 Rota and Binetti filed a patent application titled 'Apparatus for the Concentration of Electric Waves in a Single Direction or upon a Fixed Point'.

After this wild goose chase to southern France, Low was called upon for further diversionary adventures which he seems to have considered to be unwarranted distractions from his main task – the AT. One of these involved a considerable amount of travelling. He was sent to Bayonne in the Basque Country region of southwestern France to investigate a report concerning a 'death ray' which Low was sure would be another 'red herring'. To pursue this assignment, Low was required to make a visit across the border to San Sebastian. Crossing into the Kingdom of Spain required non-military dress, so he had to borrow civilian clothing which he managed to arrange. However, Archie found the pointed patent leather shoes obtained as part of the loan were very painful. His compensation was what he described as an 'unbelievably luxurious dinner' in the Maria Cristina. This splendid hotel building conceived in the spirit of the Belle Époque had only been open for three years and was now a centre of intrigue and information on an international scale, with guests that had included Margaretha Geertruida 'Margreet' MacLeod, better known as Mata Hari. As a neutral Netherlander, she was able to travel across the lines and was destined to be accused of spying for Germany and executed by the French on 15th October 1917. So, this was an appropriate venue for Low's clandestine mission but amid the sumptuous food and his aching feet, Archie noted that the hotel's clientele were not a nest of spies and international agents but consisted primarily of German submarine officers. The 'death ray' of course did not exist.

Assignments such as these that were allocated to Archie emanated from a variety of controlling organisations. After it was announced on 28th July 1915 that the Ministry of Munitions was to set up an inventions branch, its first Advisory Panel meeting was held on the 20th August 1915. This new Munition Inventions

Department (MID) attempted, with mixed levels of success, to co-ordinate the work that was being undertaken by the significant number of less centralised technical departments despite ongoing distractions over questions of authority and organisation. The conflicting responsibilities of the MID and the War Office were only concluded in February 1916 after a ruling by the Prime Minister Herbert Asquith to make the MID responsible for all of the management and control of inventions for the Army.

Under the separate naval re-organisation, the 74-year-old Lord 'Jacky' Fisher was appointed as chair of the new 'Board of Invention and Research'. Other departments were formed such as the Australian Imperial Force (AIF) Research Section established in November 1916 and later located in Esher, Surrey under the command of William Henry Gregory Geake.

While the Navy research priority was clearly the curtailment of German U-boat activity, the Army had no such single innovative focus. Controlling the creative process without extinguishing the flame that fed it became an ongoing balancing act for those who understood that the scarce resource of technical innovation had to be managed but not stifled.

By 1918, the BIR had dealt with over 41,000 submissions of ideas and inventions. The MID's work was summarised in a series of comprehensive reports. As the date of the Armistice was approaching (although no one knew that the end was so near), the 37th monthly report of the MID dated 1st November 1918 was issued. Its introduction stated that from its formation in August 1915, the MID had received 47,112 inventions, ideas and suggestions of which 46,104 had been examined, 45,985 considered and just 4,026 reported as worthy of further consideration. The work of the MID ended in April 1919.

Reading this classified tome that was specifically intended for and addressed to the minister of munitions of war on a monthly basis would have had a lasting affect upon an imaginative recipient. At this time this recipient was Winston Churchill. Churchill held his series of late night meetings around the start of World War II with all manner of attendees and as soon as he could, he set up in his role as the minister of defence an establishment called MD1. As described in Robert Stuart Macrae's book *Winston Churchill's Toyshop*, MD1 was used to prevent protocol delaying the development of any device that was critical to Churchill's more radical plans. Indirectly, it was Archie Low who caused Macrae's involvement in MD1, as we will see.

However, in World War I submissions to these various inventions departments were not just large in quantity. They were extensive in their range of topics and categories that were not just munitions and weapons. They included suggestions as diverse as alternatives for scarce or critical materials through to improvements in artificial limbs. Items judged worthy of further investigation were passed for assessment to the relevant specialist groups, sub-committee or organisation associated with that area of speciality.

This attempt to centralise the inventive process was a significant contribution to the efficient use of development resources but some officials continued to be frustrated that the systems were not comprehensive, leading to a lack of co-ordination and a waste of precious time. However, while it might be said that 'invention' always tends to be initially subdued when it is put in a bureaucratic bottle, luckily, it almost always contrives to pop the cork and flourish anew.

In addition to appointing committees to consider suggestions or inventions, the Royal, Chemical and Physical Societies created 'War Registers' of their fellows to perform these assessments. Despite Britain's heritage being forged in the Industrial Revolution, such was the status of these engineering and scientific boffins, it was then assumed by the administrative mandarins that the services of these 'trades people' would be voluntary and they announced 'it is to be understood that all service would be unpaid, being given for the good of the country during this period of emergency.'

Comparisons were then drawn concerning the scale of the wages paid by the government for the performance of less responsible, learned and essential labour such as government consultants and medical doctors.

Although many of these academics joined the forces, a great many did not and were not paid. The use of laboratories and other facilities for military development in most cases was provided free of charge.

However, this new national web of expert authorities, paid or unpaid, was utilised.

Archie Low commented that 'chemists were looked upon as merely "pill fellows", and engineers only "carriers of germs".' A 1916 item stated: 'Our whole system of education is anti-technical. Our newspapers put politics, sport, society gossip, fashion puffs and theatrical rubbish in front of science and technical affairs, and it is really a marvel that we have held our own so well against Germany, where so much has been done to foster invention and industry'.

It must be said the political establishment in this respect led by example with upwards of four out of every ten MPs in some sort of military service. The benefits of closer cross party co-operation and a deeper understanding of the military position provided by these 'officer MPs' were arguably offset by an erosion of their objectivity and independence – although there is no evidence that this was the case.

One of these officer MPs, Sir Henry Norman of the MID who assessed the AT project in 1916, had a moderately privileged and very productive life. He was a long-time advocate for the organisation of Britain's technological innovation and was an influential member of the MID. Sir Henry was in his late 50s during the war, an imposing figure in the smoking room at 'his club' or at a high society event in

Paris. He was the author of the 37th MID report. His background and the varied work in which he was engaged are enlightening. The following gives us a glimpse of this fascinating period before and throughout the 'war to end all wars' that started in a period when about 60 per cent of the wealth in Britain was in the hands of, at most, 1 per cent of the population.

Henry's parents were from modest backgrounds. He lost his father when he was in his early teens. He had attended the Quaker establishment, Grove House School in Tottenham, London. Then he was educated privately in France, in Leipzig and at Harvard University. He was a journalist for the *Pall Mall Gazette*, the *New York Times* and the *Daily Chronicle*. In 1891, when he was 33, he married the 24-year-old writer Ménie Muriel Dowie who, having just returned from her adventures in eastern Europe, was publishing her book *A Girl in the Karpathians*. Henry also travelled a great deal after their marriage, visiting North America, Russia and the Far East and some of his photographs have been published on-line by the Royal Commonwealth Society.

As a journalist and with his connections in France, Henry was instrumental in exposing the truth behind the Dreyfus affair and this bought him a degree of celebrity in both the French and English world press.[1] Henry wrote, edited and published a great deal on subjects that ranged across a very wide field of interests. Much of his earlier work concerned his travels, particularly in the Far East but it did include books like *The Witching Time: Tales for the year's end* that was published in 1887. He had coal mining and iron industry interests and was elected to parliament as the Liberal Party MP for Wolverhampton South in 1900. By 1903 he had given up journalism and was divorced following his wife's adultery with the mountaineer and adventurer Edward Arthur Fitzgerald who had been a family friend.

Following the divorce he had custody of their son Henry Nigel St Valery Norman and they would spend time together in his workshop on one of their various projects. By 1904 he lived at 33 St. Thomas's Mansions, Westminster Bridge, London and drove a 24 h.p. Darracq. This and his other cars will have been a delight to work on and he became the vice-president of his constituency's Wolverhampton Automobile Club. According to Grace's Guide, a note records that:

> He was formerly devoted to horses, but the pleasures he derived from the possession of an 8-horse Panhard were so fascinating that he has now transferred his affections to the motor but has now discarded his old car for de Dion, Clement and Darracq cars. He has his own workshop in the country and does his own car repairs. He has many times strongly championed motorists' rights in the House of Commons.

Among his many other ventures, he founded and edited *The World's Work*, a British illustrated magazine of 'National Efficiency and Social Progress'. The first issue appeared in December 1902 and it continued in publication until 1932.

The
World's Work

AN ILLUSTRATED MAGAZINE OF
NATIONAL EFFICIENCY AND SOCIAL PROGRESS

Edited by Henry Norman, M.P.

VOLUME II	JUNE 1903	NUMBER 7

The World's Work banner

Henry Norman was knighted in 1906. In 1907 he married the 23-year-old Florence Priscilla ('Fay') McLaren.[2] The wedding of the newly knighted Sir Henry and Fay was a high society widely reported event.

By 1908 Sir Henry was busy with his work and raised a patent for the selenium photocell lighting controller.

N° 17,540   A.D. 1908

Date of Application, 21st Aug., 1908—Accepted, 10th June, 1909

COMPLETE SPECIFICATION.

Method of & Apparatus for Automatically Igniting & Extinguishing Electric & other Lamps by the Action of the Sun's Rays.

We, Sir HENRY NORMAN of Honeyhanger, Haslemere, Surrey, Member of Parliament, and THOMAS BERTRAM READER, of Hindhead, Surrey, Electrical Engineer, do hereby declare the nature of this invention and in what manner the same is to be performed, to be particularly described and ascertained in and
5 by the following statement:—

This invention relates to a method of lighting & extinguishing automatically

Extract from Norman's automatic lighting sensor patent

1909 bought with it a major political innovation. The Chancellor of the Exchequer Lloyd George began his attempts to implement a progressive programme that quickly became known as the 'People's Budget'. This Liberal initiative taxed the rich to fund social welfare reforms. The lobbying group, the Budget Protest League, became pitted against the Budget League in the tussle over its introduction. Sir Henry, at the behest of Churchill, became heavily involved in the campaign supporting the budget. The ensuing constitutional crisis led to an election at which Sir Henry lost his seat in the Commons on 10th February 1910. This created a record for the shortest term appointment of an Assistant Post Master General, as Sir Henry Norman had only just been appointed to the role in the January in recognition of his technical and organisation expertise. However, the new government was short lived and Sir Henry stood again and was elected for Blackburn in the December 1910 election, a seat he then held until 1923. The People's Budget was finally approved.

Sir Henry was now a man of some authority and worth, and with the responsibility of a son by his first wife. Sir Henry setup a wireless receiving station at their home, 'Honeyhanger' near Hindhead. At the start of the war there were only a few such British amateur wireless enthusiasts with sensitive facilities that could detect continental transmissions. Sir Henry ran his as a monitoring station and his was one of the establishments at the start of the war that fed radio intercepts to the intelligence community in London. The British Admiralty worked with the Marconi company to obtain German radio messages through a network that grew to over 200 locations designated as 'Y' stations, work in which George Wright made a major contribution.[3]

The Admiralty, traditionally associated with external diplomacy and intelligence work due to its 'reach' overseas, had its own, now famous but then secret, codes and ciphers organisation and this was known by its location, 40 O.B. (Old Building) in the Admiralty or more simply 'Room 40'. With their submarine communication cables out of action, Germany relied more on radio messages transmitted by their agencies such as 'Transocean'. Intercepted messages were prioritised, the most important being recognised by their use of the most secure codes. The Director of Naval Intelligence in Room 40 was William Reginald Hall (called Blinker because of his facial twitch). He was able to read these codes and had to ensure that knowledge of this ability did not become apparent to the Germans. He was responsible for the tradition of recruiting a wide mix of varied expertise including civilians into the decoding organisation and for insisting every effort be made to acquire enemy code books when the opportunity presented itself. Many were involved in such work, even on occasions, very senior officers. Between 1908 and 1913 Admiral Sir Percy Scott patented machines for simultaneously printing ordinary language and cypher texts. But cryptography in World War I was still a paper and pen affair with the 'Playfair Square' that had been invented by Charles Wheatstone in 1854 still widely used by the British military in the field. As the war intensified at the start of

1918 and with the growing concern in Germany to keep business communications secret, the prolific inventor Dr. Arthur Scherbius patented his 'Chiffrier- oder Dechiffriermaschine' (Ciphering or Deciphering Machine) and the technology of the famous 'Enigma' sparked into life. The world had entered the new machine age of cryptography.

Having had their three children, Willoughby Rollo, Laura Rosalind and Anthony Charles Wynyard by 1912, in the first months of the conflict Fay Norman worked in a requisitioned hotel by the coast in France that they had converted into the No 4 British Red Cross 'Sir Henry Norman' Hospital. A substantial illustrated publication about the establishment was produced after the opening of this hospital at Wimereux in November 1914. In addition to pictures of the building and some of the patients, it listed the facilities which boasted an x-ray machine and a radiographer among the more than 70 staff. Florence wrote glowingly of its merits and the eminent visitors who inspected the establishment in its first weeks, hoping that these might even include the king if he crossed to the continent at some future date. Some say that the king and queen did visit the hospital, but if so, it seems that it must have been late in 1915 during the royal visit to France on 21st October to 1st November. The hospital took Allied and enemy wounded men and at one point the Normans received a modest donation from the family of a German patient, given it seems in anticipation of his repatriation. As the needs of the war developed, this hospital, funded as it was by private donations and having fulfilled a desperate need during its tenure, was closed in December 1915. In the IWM records, in a letter of 10th January 1916, Sir Henry noted that he was still 'busy with affairs, winding up the Hospital'.

Before the war, x-ray facilities had become more common but were still a new technology emerging quickly after Wilhelm Conrad Roentgen had discovered in 1895 the x-rays emanating from a Crookes tube. The war required the supply of more x-ray machines and introduced the portable x-ray machine championed by Marie Skłodowska Curie. Fearing that the German Army would conquer Paris, the double Nobel Prize winner put her work on radium in a shielded box and deposited it in a bank in Bordeaux. With donations made by the Union des Femmes de France she produced the first of her 20 'petites Curies', field x-ray radiological vehicles. For the duration of the war she organised the Red Cross volunteers who staffed these units. There were many other medical improvements that saw their first widespread application in the war. Blood transfusions had a poor press until 1907 when Jan Janský introduced his blood classifications enabling the procedure to become moderately routine during the war. However, in retrospect the liberal supply of cigarettes was not such a great innovation. For a time the hospital at Wimereux received its supplies of these from an appeal organised by the *Westminster Gazette*, an appeal that maintained a flow of 100,000 a week to the troops at the front.

Lady Florence Norman, a suffragette, on her motor scooter in 1916

On 22nd June 1915, Henry was created Baronet of Honeyhanger in the Parish of Shottermill in the County of Surrey. Fay became Lady Norman. She had followed her grandmother and her mother's passionate support of the women's suffragist movement and she made sure she was photographed on her new motor scooter in 1916 on her way to work through London. This vehicle was a birthday present from Henry and these scooters became very popular at this time.

Fay's brother, the MP Francis McLaren, arrived in Turkey in 1915 with the RNAS Armoured Car Section. He wrote frequently to Fay and his fellow MP and brother-in-law Henry Norman. Churchill and Charles Samson thought that they might find in Turkey a suitable theatre of war in which to use the armoured car in what they envisaged would be a more mobile campaign. The section was to support the Royal Naval Division when it was deployed in Gallipoli. Francis's letters described the efforts made to use the vehicles which they finally succeeded in doing and a transcript of these letters was kept by the Normans.

The RNAS had arrived with eight vehicles on the island of Tenedos on 5th April 1915 and by the 8th they were on Lemnos. In his letters Francis included as a heading 'Note to Censor – all things described in past – no reason for not letting through'. The section was finally employed on 4th June in the third battle of Krithia. The attack with cars was planned with the vehicles running in to the front line and crossing the various obstacles at defined locations. It all started at noon and Francis said the car he commanded arrived in the spearhead of the attack at the assigned point and exactly on time. The detail in his narrative was comprehensive and graphic. During the advance they had to drive over four dead Turks on what he described as the 'Bandits McLaren Road'. Bullets burst their cases and jammed his gun and they had to waste a crucial minute or two using the unjamming tool. They had to abandon the car when they hit a bridge but they managed to jump into a 'sap' taking their wounded. Despite the fact that they did not negotiate this bridge successfully and lost the vehicle, Francis was encouraged by the use of the new technology.

Another account of the battle is contained in the book *With the Twentyninth Division in Gallipoli – A Chaplain's Experience* by the Reverend Oswin Creighton. He describes a ruse that was supposed to make this attack more likely to succeed than the previous two battles. It was that 'at 11 a.m. the artillery started to fire for a quarter of an hour, then paused for another quarter, when the troops in the trenches were supposed to shout and wave bayonets so as to get the Turks into the firing line, then another half-hour's bombardment.' It was not a success. Oswin had emigrated to Canada in 1910 but he, like so very many who had fought in Gallipoli, died elsewhere later in the war, in France on 15th April 1918. He left a widow in Alix, Alberta, Canada.

The precise action that Francis describes is one of those rare instances where we have yet another eyewitness account seemingly of exactly the same few yards of a sap in the battle. This report however was from a very different perspective. Captain Albert Mure, 1/5th Royal Scots, 88th Brigade, 29th Division was in his trench and recalled in his book, *With the Incomparable 29th* (1919):

> An armoured car came with them, spitting and puffing and lumbering along. Nothing so ugly or so awkward ever was seen outside a zoo! The very amateur bridge the Engineers had tossed up for them was just by my phone. The car made for it. She got on the planks all right; then her off hind-wheel slipped over the side, and down she came on her axle, and pretty well on my head. Nothing could be done, so the naval officer in charge and the gunner climbed out. In getting out the naval petty officer was seriously wounded.

Captain Mure described the horrific aftermath from the Turkish shells that the stranded car attracted. His unit was badly mauled and his mission to report back over the phone lines was completely scuppered by the arrival of the armoured vehicle once it came to grief at his trench.

These two accounts offer very different opinions on the effective use of the first available motorised armour on the battle field in 1915. The development of effective armoured vehicles for the battlefield was just beginning, with the Landships Committee into its 4th month.

In 1922, Sir Henry and Fay purchased Ramster Hall in Chiddingfold near Guildford in Surrey. Britain's pre-eminence in glass that Brabazon noted, grew from places like Chiddingfold which had been a centre of glass-making in England since the 1600s. Ramster Hall had been built in the 1600s by a wealthy glass manufacturer.

Sir Henry Norman, the Liberal MP, cabinet minister, writer, explorer and amateur scientist who was involved in the introduction of wireless telegraphy, was a great support to Archie Low. In the 1940s many of the IWM pictures of the war to end all wars were taken to Ramster Hall for safe keeping from the bombs of World War II and artefacts from Sir Henry's explorations are still kept in Ramster today.

Major Clarence Colley claimed to have been appointed by Admiral 'Jackie' Fisher as chief experimental officer and artillery adviser to the Munitions Invention Department. He worked with a variety of inventors. With Hiram Maxim he raised a patent in 1916 to improve multi-charged guns so that they could fire a mix of different bullets in quick succession. Low mentioned that in addition to the work with Colley and Pomeroy on the PSA bullet they tested gear for firing through the airscrew. The major was working with another inventor, George 'Gogu' Constantinesco, a Romanian who, with the support of Colley, Sefton Brancker and Walter Caddell from the Department of Military Aeronautics, produced the Constantinesco-Colley Fire Control Gear – the 'C.C. Gear'. This was the synchronisation (interrupter) gear fitted to British fighters that allowed them to fire forward through the rotating propeller. Proving to be a great improvement over previous devices in both the rate of firing achieved and the ease of installation on different aircraft types, in November 1917 this C.C. gear became standard, being fitted to all new British aircraft with synchronized guns for the next twenty years up to 1937. The mechanical systems that had preceded it could not compete with the 'C.C. interrupter gear' once it was introduced in the latter half of 1916.

During development the mechanism was thought to suffer occasional problems with some rounds but these were found to be caused by defective bullets. So accurate and repeatable was the Constantinesco mechanism that a form of it was then introduced as a quality control tester for ammunition production, thus improving the performance of all guns using these rounds.

The C.C. gear had its origins in a collaboration that started just before the war. Gogu and Mr. Walter Haddon had established an experimental laboratory for the study of the wave transmission of power in fluids. This laboratory was in the Haddon Engineering Works near Ealing. Walter had business interests connected with Fleet

Street in the world of printing and its machinery. He was well connected and had considerable influence and funding. Investigations were conducted at Honeypot Lane into the application of Gogu's wave transmission to printing machinery. This was most probably the site where the C.C. gear was developed and where the RFC tests of the bullets were conducted by Low. In 1925 the Royal Commission on Awards to Inventors awarded Messrs. G. Constantinesco and W. Haddon £70,000 for their work on the synchronising C.C. interrupter gear and a further £15,000 from the US fund.

Walter and George worked together on George's theories of the wave transmission of power. This used induced waves (vibrations) in the fluid to transmit power rather than the mass movement of the fluid as used in classical hydraulic systems. The C.C. gear used this principle, as described in Patent 129,299. Constantinesco had designed buildings and bridges before the war, a car with automatic transmission in the 1920s, was responsible for over a hundred inventions and published his book on the theory of wave transmission. He died in Britain, beside Coniston Water in the Lake District in December 1965.

Other improvements were also associated with fire power, although Low's unit were not involved in all of them. Major George Hazelton was an inventor from Woodhouse Street, Portadown in Northern Ireland and when he was based at the RAF Experiments Shops in Kirtling Street, Battersea in London he designed improvements and raised his patent on a muzzle booster that increased the rate of fire of machine guns. This was introduced into service in May 1917. Later he transferred and became a lieutenant commander in the Royal Navy. At the end of February 1920, George's case for an award was considered, as reported in *Flight* magazine (1920):

> Before the Royal Commission on Awards to Inventors last week, Maj. George Hazelton, late of the RAF, entered a claim in respect of an invention for quickening the rate of fire of a Vickers machine-gun. … The invention was mainly used on aeroplanes machine-guns, and increased the rate of fire from 500 rounds per minute to 1,000 rounds per minute. The Government had ordered 50,000 sets, of which 27,000 had been supplied. … On one occasion a rate of fire of 1,385 rounds per minute was obtained. Maj. Harold Balfour, RAF, who had brought down 15 German machines, said that the use of the gear in aerial fighting increased the chances of a pilot by 100 per cent. … The Treasury admitted the invention, and they did not suggest that it was part of the claimant's duty to invent.

Harold Harington Balfour would go on to a career in politics, becoming the under-secretary of state for air and was involved in the development of London Heathrow Airport. He was the brother-in-law of John Dennis Profumo, the disgraced minister at the centre of the 1960s famous 'Profumo Affair'.

As the C.C. gear worked with all the different rates of fire, it and Hazelton's adapter (muzzle booster) were compatible. Prideaux's links, Constantinesco's synchronisation gear and Hazelton's improvements in the firing rate were complimentary improvements to the Vickers guns and were deployed in service from late 1917 onwards for use on most of the British aircraft.

After the trials at Upavon, Archie Low's Feltham Works was briefly given over to a task of a totally different and more social nature. They arranged and hosted a charity concert. With their wealth of home grown talent and with other supporters, they had no difficulty staging a complete evening of entertainment. The ornate concert programme (cost 2d.) was printed in colour, announcing 'The R. F. C. Chorus Concert'. The performance on Tuesday, 17th April 1917 was held 'by permission of Capt. Low RFC D.Sc. O.C. R.F.C. Feltham' and it was 'In aid of Lady Henderson's Fund for Wounded RFC Men'.

The many acts included some eminent musicians and performers, a smattering of acts by 2nd Lt. Bertie Charles Adamson, acts involving some of the airmen and NCOs and the unit's Radio Officer 2nd Lt. George William Whitton in the role of 'The Old Soldier'. There was a cello solo by Mr. Jack Squire who was then the musical director of the Apollo and Royalty Theatres.[4] In the interval, another of the units officers, 2nd Lt. Louis Mantell, played the piano.

The musician, Henry Poole, was not on the programme but maybe it was his connections behind the scenes that engaged the professional acts for the Feltham Work's concert. Of the other performers George Whitton and Louis Mantell were 'old boys' in Low's unit but the 35-year-old Bertie Adamson had only joined the works on 3rd January. By the time of the concert he was 'well in' and confirmed in his post as a special reserve experimental officer. After the war Bertie was posted to the Inland Area Aircraft Depot (IAAD) at RAF Henlow until he was demobbed. On 21st September 1939 he rejoined with the rank of Sq. Ldr. but he was killed on active service on 20th April 1940.

The day after the RFC concert the newspapers reported that the hospital ships *Donegal* and *Lanfranc* were both attacked by U-boats and torpedoed when carrying wounded across the English Channel with significant loss of life, many of them Germans. The second battle of Gaza had begun and Japanese flotillas had joined the Allied forces in the Mediterranean and on the Western Front the battle of Arras was about to enter its tenth day. The RFC would call it 'Bloody April'. The concert was a charity event but it also provided just a little respite from the grind of the war.[5]

Low utilised land behind No. 86 and they moved the large building from the Ivory Works into this yard to use as the new laboratory. By 1st September 1917, Low's unit had vacated the commandeered facility near Bedfont Lane and was based at Low's premises in the High Street.

The laboratory was a corrugated iron and timber frame building, 4.5 m high with a concrete floor area of 200 square metres. The yard had York Stone Paving and there were store rooms and a urinal. The property already had a substantial garage. There is also a record of what each room in the house was used for. The plan of these High Street Works still exists because it was required by Lt. Leslie George Bullock who inspected the property after the war when Archie Low claimed £3000 retrospectively for the use of his personal facilities. It is Bullock's report that confirms that the commandeered factory was also in Feltham and there is other evidence to support this. However, Sir Henry's visit to see the 1916 prototype suggests that Low had set up in Feltham well before the RFC requisitioned the factory.

CHAPTER 17

The Clifton West Affair

Archie made much of General Pitcher's remark, recorded in *He Lit the Lamp*: 'My idea of Low is to put him in a room with his feet on the mantelpiece, and make him think out his ideas.' In the circumstances, this was not the wisest advice to give Archie, not that he could in anyway be described as otiose. Far from it, he could never have been accused of being lazy or unfocused.

However, he was accused of a few other significant infractions and one bordering on larceny but the most serious of these alleged offences involved a form of 'misconduct in public office'.

The first formal stain on his record occurred in June 1916 when Archie allowed Mr. E. M. P. Boileau to photograph his unit's vehicles for Boileau magazine *The Motor Cycle*. Sefton Brancker, the Director of Air Organisation (DAO) 'wanted something done' about Archie Low. It was obviously a complaint made by an authority of some weight to merit the DAO's attention. On the 14th, Blotto wrote, 'This appears to call for some disciplinary action' and he suggests Low's 'M.T. establishment might be reduced, substituting a Studebaker for the Crossleys'. On the 19th, the DAE Duncan MacInnes replied, 'This matter has been dealt with. Lieutenant Low has been instructed that he is not in future to write any articles for publication without W.O. permission. The Factory at Feltham has only 2 3-ton lorries, 1 light tender and 1 motor bicycle, and as the experiments are to commence next week it is not necessary to reduce them at the moment.' Sefton had visited the works at Feltham so he knew what was being attempted there and Henry Norman had also been shown the works prior to witnessing the subsequent AT trials. It is possible that these experienced officers, Brancker and MacInnes, suspected that this was a calumnious accusation and considered it prudent to record that punitive action was considered but not taken.

These terse file notes held in the National Archives, for all of their brevity, provide the details of the Motor Transport (MT) resources of Captain Low's establishment. We also know from the IWM exhibition labels that by March 1917 their MT pool had acquired a 5-ton lorry that they fitted out to hold all of the trial's ground transmitting system and launching ramp.

Ursula Bloom's biography does not include any mention of Low being the subject of disciplinary action so it would appear that Low either did not advise his author of any such detail or she decided to expurgate such content. This carpeting of Low was in itself a relatively trivial incident. However, in light of what was to follow it is revealing and it was perhaps just the start.

Archie seems to have always ploughed his own very distinct furrow through life. His qualifications were 'unusual' and his oft-used title 'Professor' was questionable. At times his attitude to his colleagues was fatherly to the point of being patronising. However he was always willing to share his knowledge and does not seem to have been at all aloof. His later 'careers' in literature, motor sports organisations, as a magician and as a Master of Ceremonies at many social events suggest, if anything, a positively gregarious nature.

Possibly because he had fond memories of Australia, he formed an affection for John and Mary Pomeroy, saying, 'Pomeroy was a marvel; he made all his own materials with the help of his wife, working in the kitchen at home.' But as an example of his self promotion he does refer to John as 'his assistant' when they were testing the explosive bullets and, being the designer and manufacturer of the ordnance under test, John was hardly just Archie's assistant.

Low often referred to the work of his unit as his own work, as in Patent 244,233 where he states: 'The apparatus which I will now proceed to describe is one of a very large number that have been constructed by me, and has been successful in prolonged experimental trials.' The sheer complexity of these equipments and the number of sophisticated custom-made parts are clearly not the work of one man but the output of his entire establishment and probably a number of sub-contractors. This apparent arrogance possibly stems from the insecurity of the period and perhaps we shouldn't overemphasise this trait as one confined to Archie. It may be that he had a proclivity for self promotion. There was no government welfare so you had to work to eat and being self employed, promoting your personal expertise and intellectual property demanded a culture of personal advertising; an element of selling one's self.

In defence of his character, after his promotion Capt. A. M. Low RFC was mentioned in despatches on 24th February 1917. The announcement stated that Low 'had been bought to the notice of the Secretary of State for War for valuable services rendered in connection with the war.' On 29th August 1919, Low was mentioned again in the Air Ministry's long lists of those who gave valuable services in connection with the war.

By the end of 1917, two other senior officers, the 42-year-old John Hardman Morgan, a distinguished lawyer, and the 49-year-old Ernest Dunlop Swinton had had many interesting and unusual experiences in the war and they were about to become involved, for all of the wrong reasons, in the dealings of Archibald Low.

John Morgan was born in South Wales in 1876. Having been educated at Caterham School in Surrey, the University College of South Wales and at Balliol College in Oxford, he was rarely in any one place for very long. In the first years of the new century he was in London undergoing his legal training at the Inner Temple, before spending time as a research scholar at the University of Berlin, so that he was a much-travelled and experienced gentleman. 1908 saw Morgan succeed Sir William Searle Holdsworth as Professor of Constitutional Law at University College, London. With his journalistic and liberal background, Morgan commented on many of the social issues of the Edwardian period and upon the Irish situation. In 1912 for 'The Eighty Club', Morgan edited the 'New Irish Constitution – An Exposition and Some Arguments' and he coined the phrase: 'Irish history is a thing for every Irishmen to forget and for every Englishmen to remember.' This phrase was later popularised by Horace Plunkett.

In the second half of 1914, as the path to war broadened, Morgan was busy as the principal author of *War: Its Conduct and Legal Results*, published in January 1915 as a 'guide' for Sir John Allsebrook Simon, 1st Viscount Simon, the Attorney General (AG) at that time. This 555-page work is unusual as it internalises international law, reviewing the consequences that the state of 'being at war' would have or should have on the laws of Britain. This extensive and carefully researched legal appraisal probably influenced some of the legislation that was then introduced under the Defence of the Realm Act (DORA) of August 1914. The law, and particularly international law, is always playing catchup as national relationships, technological innovation and other social factors create new issues. For instance, the Dutch decision in 1914 to release Francis 'Cecco' Hewlett from Holland was one such small precedent. The issue arose again in 1943 when seven American airmen ditched off the coast of Turkey after a bombing raid in Operation *Tidal Wave* on the oil fields in Romania.

At the outbreak of the war, Morgan joined the army and for five months he was attached to the General Headquarters Staff as Home Office Commissioner with the British Expeditionary Force. It was here that he investigated allegations of misconduct and offences committed by the opposing forces. This record, of evidence formally gathered at the front, contributed to the British national publication known as the 'Blue Book' or the Bryce Report or more formally the 'Report of the Committee on Alleged German Outrages'. Viscount James Bryce chaired 'The Committee on Alleged German Outrages'. The Central Powers produced their own 'books' and would point to activities such as Sefton Brancker's fact-finding pre-war cycle-riding mission into Belgium as evidence of warmongering. Much of this outpouring by each of the warring nations was aimed at the neutral countries and principally America to obtain advantage and alliance.

Morgan also published a number of his own books in the early years of the war including *Germany's Dishonoured Army* and *German Atrocities; An Official Investigation*.

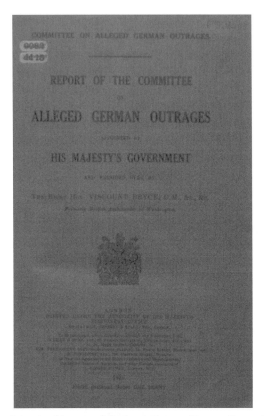

The 'Blue Book' cover of the Bryce Report (Crown Copyright)

Frederick Edwin Smith, previously of the Press Bureau, succeeded Simon as AG in the Herbert Asquith's government and on taking office he crossed the Channel to Boulogne. On 30th January 1916 he was promptly arrested by 'his own' military police as he did not have appropriate paperwork to be there. Once this bizarre episode was resolved, he visited General Haig and then Churchill. Apparently, it was here that Smith, Churchill, Lloyd George and Andrew Bonar Law met and agreed that Asquith was ineffective and should be removed from office. F. E. Smith was destined to become Lord Birkenhead, the Lord Chancellor. He was somewhat 'larger than life' and a powerful influence; he must have been as he so impressed his friend Churchill.

So it was Smith, as the new AG, who inherited Morgan's *War: Its Conduct and Legal Results*, which picked apart the complexity of the new situation, identifying legal ambiguities. Before the war, the lawmakers and the general population were still absorbing the implications of man's new-found dominion over the alien aerial dimension. On aerial navigation, it illustrated how retroactive the legal systems were (and still are) in addressing issues arising from innovation. A year after its publication, when German bombs began falling on Britain, Morgan's guide for the AG referenced the international legal authority for Britain to implement defensive action.[1]

When war came it was fought on all fronts by the whole population. Just as invention itself would be bent to the benefit of the war, so to, by officials such as Morgan, was the law. Some of the first changes were in banking and the introduction of paper money. Other changes introduced by direct legislation were complimented by social changes enabled under DORA. From conscription and rationing to the introduction of Daylight Saving Time, the new laws were applied. In addition, as we have seen with explosive bullets, changes wrought by the sudden advances in technology required legal consideration.

While Morgan was based at General Headquarters at Montreuil-Sur-Mer at the start of World War I, his work as a home office commissioner bought him into contact with an officer he later described as 'that brilliant soldier, Colonel E. D. Swinton, DSO'. Their mutual love of storytelling may have led to the bond of friendship between Morgan and Swinton.

Ernest Swinton was a professional soldier whose father Robert was in the Indian Civil Service. Ernest had been born on 21st October 1868 in Bengaluru, Karnataka, India. He was educated in England and became an officer in the Corps of Royal Engineers in 1888, serving in India.

By February 1896, Ernest was stationed at Brompton Barracks in Chatham where he patented a neat little attachment for cotton reels that cut the tread and secured the end ready for the next length to be unwound and cut to length. Ernest received the DSO in 1900 during the Second Boer War. After this African war, in 1904, he wrote *The Defence of Duffer's Drift*, a classic short book on tactics that has been used in the Canadian, British, US and other military training establishments.

During the 1800s George Cayley, Bramah Joseph Diplock, James Boydell and others reinvented the wheel, which led to the 'dreadnaught' and early forms of caterpillar track.

In 1900 Jan Gotlib Bloch's book *Modern Weapons and Modern War* was published. This concluded that a future conflict would be a static war of attrition as the available weapons would create impenetrable lines of defence. Three years later H. G. Wells provided the theoretical antidote to this in his story *The Land Ironclads*, even incorporating a reference to Bloch in the first few lines of the text. Wells' Ironclads were metal forts that crawled over the battlefield on pedrail wheels. Ernest would have been aware of these suggested developments and also, the reports of the trench warfare in Manchuria. These probably influenced him in his ongoing work. He continued to write and adopted the pseudonym 'Ole Luk-Oie' for his many articles.

Ernest was in contact with other authors such as Captain C. E. Vickers whom he was able to assist. Despite the disparity in social class and rank, Swinton referred to Vickers as his 'pal' and they were among the authors of this period who, in retrospect, portrayed future conflicts in the most prophetic way. In his 1908 work *The Trenches*,

Vickers foresaw the grinding inertia in the military bureaucracy with dialogue such as 'sending it to the Inventions Committee. To the Grave of Invention eh?' He also envisaged the use of trenching machines from the US.

Ernest published the story *The Point of View* in 1908 and included it in his compilation *The Green Curve*. *The Point of View* graphically described the trench warfare to be experienced five year later and to an extent explains the perceived detachment shown by the staff officers from their wards in the fire trenches or out in the deadly disputed territory. It suggests a more sober assessment of the role of these staff officers than the stereotype sycophant offered to us in the popular media. In World War I, which relied so heavily upon telephone lines, communications invariably deteriorated rapidly from the start of the inevitable artillery bombardment before 'H' hour. Radio was unreliable and runners, the mobile pigeon lofts and message rockets did not fill the communications gap created by broken telephone lines or engagements forward of these fixed lines of communication. In *The Point of View* Swinton re-introduced to the language of war the ancient term 'no-mans-land' in his graphic depiction of the area between the trenches, 'the dreadful No-Man's-Land between the opposing lines'. *The Point of View* is a work of 'future fiction', graphic in its portrayal of trench warfare and insightful in its reference to the use of radio on the battlefield.

Through the years leading up to World War I, Swinton was serving as a staff officer and as an official historian of the Russo-Japanese war. This work involved the weapons, tactics and trench warfare observed by Sefton Brancker and to be seen again in World War I.

The War Minister, Lord Kitchener, was an impressive man, 6-feet 2-inches tall with his large white moustache, blond hair and a squint in his left eye. This striking appearance (without the squint) was used to great effect in those famous posters of the prolonged recruiting campaign. It was perhaps through their Royal Engineer connection, or more likely due to Ernest's many publications, that Kitchener, at the start of the war, appointed Swinton as an official journalist on the Western Front whose reports were to be published under the anonym 'Eye Witness'. Most 46-year-old officers given such a posting would sink into obscurity. However, Swinton was destined for knighthood and would retire as a major-general. He would also become involved fleetingly but crucially with events surrounding our Aerial Target. A little time after Swinton's assignment in 1914, Henry Major Tomlinson, a journalist working for the *Daily News*, was recruited and joined Swinton as an official war correspondent. To remain on the front, these journalists had to accept government control over what they wrote.[2]

As predicted in Vickers' story, tractors from the US made by the Holt company did sterling work on the battlefields of the first war but not for trenching. Ernest started campaigning for the development of a mechanised, armoured vehicle; 'petrol tractors on the caterpillar principle and armoured with hardened steel plates' that would be able to counteract the machine-gunner. Side stepping opposition from General Sir John French, he got support from Churchill who, in February 1915, set up the secret Landships Committee – secret that is from all those who would have closed it down which was most of military and the government. One of the committee's three members was Flight Commander Thomas Gerard Hetherington of the RNAS Car Squadron.

In 1915 Ernst Swinton was to become very busy with the development of the tank. By the autumn of 1915 Vickers' 1908 story of a 'turtleback of steel' was a reality – in the form of Little Willy, the prototype of the British Mark I tank.

The Mark I became the first tank to be used in combat during the battle of the Somme on 15th September 1916. This was in the battle of Flers-Courcelette which also witnessed the first use by the Germans of their new Albertros D aircraft and Richthofen's first victory on the 17th flying an Albertros D II at the start of what was to become a prolonged period of air superiority for the German forces on the Western Front. Ernest made several visits to the US in 1917 and 1918. Disembarking down the first-class gangway from the American Line SS Saint Paul when it docked at Liverpool on 12th November 1917, along with Lord Northcliffe and the Lord Chief Justice Viscount Rufus of Reading, Ernest would have been made aware of another imminent battle, another one that would use 'his' tanks in significant numbers. Three days later the battle of Cambrai began.

The issue of who should be credited for the invention of the 'tank' was determined by the Royal Commission on Awards to Inventors convened on 6th October 1919 under the chairmanship of Sir Charles Henry Sargant. There were 11 claims but 12 claimants as 2 were named on one of the claims. The commission bestowed the ultimate honour for the invention on Ernest with an award of £1,000. Awards were made to some other claimants and some of the claims were dismissed. The largest award went to Sir William Ashbee Tritton and Major Walter Gordon Wilson. They were jointly awarded £15,000 and were recognised for 'designing and producing a concrete practical shape, the novel and efficient engine of warfare known as the 'Tank'.

One claim by Lancelot Eldin 'Lance' de Mole, a prolific inventor born in Adelaide, South Australia but living in the state of Victoria, was treated somewhat differently.

In 1919 this Commission on Awards recorded the fact that Mr. L. E. de Mole, an Australian engineer, had made and reduced to practical shape, as far back as the year 1912, a brilliant invention which anticipated, and in some respects surpassed, that actually put into use in the year 1916, and that this invention was in fact communicated at the time to the proper government department, but was not then appreciated, and was put aside and forgotten. They did not recommend the payment of any award to Mr. de Mole but on 20th November 1919 – a few days after the date of their report on the matter – the commission expressed the opinion that the case of Mr. de Mole was quite exceptional, and that, if he should make an application for the payment of his expenses, the matter should be dealt with with a generous spirit; and it was in accordance with this opinion that the payment of £987 to Mr. de Mole was subsequently authorised. Lance stood accused of the same failing that many applied to 'Professor' Low; that of being too far ahead of his time for his inventions to be taken seriously.

Though usually referred to as the 'father of the tank,' Swinton remarked that 'it was the 'Caterpillar' track-type tractor' which inspired his idea and helped change the course of the war. He would never have achieved his goal had it not been for the vision and drive of Winston Churchill. Defending the tank as a weapon that saved rather than squandered lives, Churchill deplored the disarmament conventions that declared tanks offensive weapons.

The case that would involve Morgan with Archie Low brought Archie to the attention of the right people for the wrong reason. All of Feltham's hard work could have been vitiated by this much more serious and murky incident than Brancker's rebuke of June 1916. This potential fly was dropped into the ointment of the Feltham Experimental Works in late 1917.

On a surprisingly mild Wednesday 5th December 1917, a private citizen named Mr. Clifton 'Antivaccinator' West, confirmed the details of his earlier verbal complaint against Low in a letter to Mr J. W. Weigall of the legal department of the Ministry of National Service (London Region). West was born in Rochester on 24th August 1879 when his parents were among the original 'conscientious objectors' of the Anti-Compulsory Vaccination League. He didn't use his extraordinary middle name as an adult!

Weigall submitted West's case to Auckland Campbell Geddes, the director of recruiting at the War Office who passed it on to the Adjutant-General Cecil Frederick Nevil 'Make-Ready' Macready and in early 1918 Captain John Morgan was handed the brief.

Morgan, this eminent senior legal officer, now had the statement made by West in which he described how on 10th May 1916 he was introduced to Low by a Mr. Renison to discuss his aerial torpedo invention that he claimed Low subsequently submitted in his own name. But more seriously, West explained that he was given a certificate by Low for exemption from military service on the grounds that he was carrying out experiments for Low's unit. West presented this certificate to the City Tribunal on 22nd June and, after celebrating the birth of his third child in early August, submitted it again on 15th September which exempted him till 6th January 1917. On 27th December, West applied for further exemption on the same grounds, and on 26th April exemption was granted till 26th July 1917. West's request for a further exemption had then been turned down owing to a letter which, he said, Captain Low addressed to the tribunal deriding his inventions and requesting that he be placed in the army.

Clifton must have been angry, hurt and a little desperate to approach Weigall to make his complaint. However, Clifton could not delay in his attempt to avoid conscription and the months since his exemption had expired must have been very trying and emotional for him, as he wrestled with the sense of injustice at his present predicament. Clifton had been a corporal in the Army Service Corps when he married Annie in 1902 and was a lieutenant in 'The Legion of Frontiersmen'[3] when he made his complaint. What was at stake for him was a secure home position in London with their three children and a collection of Annie's relatives from Poole in Dorset.

West had patented a number of inventions. One of his first was in 1907. On 12th September 1913 in Britain as an engineer living at 36 Torriden Road, Hither Green, London and again on 13th July 1914 in the US as an inventor at 132 Churchfield Road, Acton he patented projectiles that extended cutters to tear the envelope of a balloon or airship and then sparked to ignite its gas. These 'shells' with clockwork mechanisms were specifically for use against balloons and dirigibles but they could not be the aerial torpedoes he refers to in his complaint because he already had the patents for these.

The term 'aerial torpedo' is now almost exclusively reserved for self-propelled ordnance dropped from aircraft into water and aimed at shipping. In World War I it was a term that referred to certain types of bombs dropped from airships and aircraft onto urban targets over land. The Germans developed a 300kg aerial torpedo and one was dropped in Moorgate but it did not detonate. Attracting no official attention it lay in the gutter for an hour and half and with no cordon the more curious members of the public could come along and see it. There was no established bomb disposal organisation and the removal of UXBs (unexploded bombs) was an improvised affair unique to each incident that, prior to World War I, only had to deal with small devices related to suffragette, Irish and other militant action. The authorities in London had facilities at Duck Island in St. James Park that had been established in 1894 and they could also call on experts from Woolwich. An aerial torpedo dropped on 19th October 1917 on Albany Road in Walworth, London killed two children and 10 adults. The aerial torpedo that landed in Moorgate was dealt with and dragged off to Hackney Marshes to be detonated safely.

West also mentions a land torpedo invention that Low later confirmed was a rolling device like a large cable drum, such as many others that had been submitted. A different successful example of a land torpedo is the Bangalore which was devised by Robert Lyle McClintock before World War I and it still has uses today.[4]

In considering West's case against Low, Morgan noted that Low was 'a professional inventor and a mechanical engineer engaged in a good many commercial enterprises which he continued to pursue after being commissioned and to have used his position in the army as a kind of "jumping off board" for them and for self advertisement in a way which has already incurred the displeasure of the Air Force authorities and been the subject of disciplinary action' (which we can assume referred to the 1916 incident). West claimed that Low had used the threat of conscription to coerce him into helping a business run by Archie and his father John (who also served

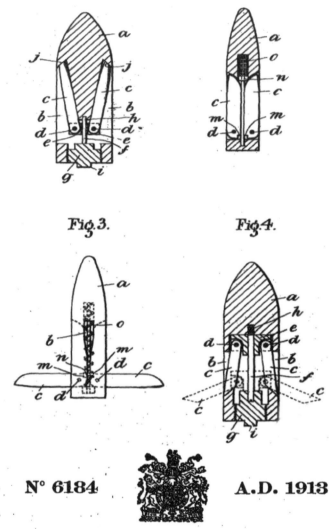

Nº 6184   A.D. 1913

Date of Application, 12th Sept., 1913—Accepted, 20th Aug., 1914

COMPLETE SPECIFICATION.

Improvements in Projectiles.

I, CLIFTON WEST, of 36, Torridon Road, Hither Green, London, S.E., Engineer, do hereby declare the nature of this invention, and in what manner the same is to be performed, to be particularly described and ascertained in and by the following statement:—

5   This invention relates to improvements in that class of projectiles for rifled firearms which are intended for the destruction of dirigible air-ships, or the like, and which projectiles comprise folding radiating arms which are normally retained within the circumferential limits of the projectile, but are released so as to assume an open or extended position when the projectile leaves the firearm
10   after it has been fired, whereby the effective destructive or tearing action of

West's patent

in the RFC and is referred to as a consulting mining engineer). As evidence, West submitted a note sent to him by Low from Pellow Lodge asking Clifton to give £5. 0. 0d to Low's father as a commission.

It was then Morgan turned to his friend Ernest Swinton. Ernest had already provided his formal opinion of West's capabilities and had got the Munitions Inventions Department to do the same, so John Morgan asked his friend for a more personal opinion of West. Morgan received Swinton's prompt reply on 26th January 1918 saying, 'West is a clever man and very ingenious, but tends towards the type of inventions "crank". He is also the most perfect mug in the world, as I have told him and is like a bit of toasted cheese to all the rats and crooks within a hundred miles: they smell him coming and get out their Bowie knives.' This note is interesting both for its subject matter, its use of language and as an example of the 'old boy network' in action.

Prior to another of Swinton's trips to Holt in California, Morgan had suggested he visit the 'Old Man' of Crater Lake. Ernest said that he would not forget the suggestion and wished Morgan well on his new appointment to a posting in India. So, a year after the US had entered the war, Ernest went out to the States again in April 1918, to Stockton, California, to formally and publicly honour Benjamin Leroy Holt and to relay Britain's gratitude to him and the Holt Manufacturing Company for their contribution to the war effort. Benjamin was the inventor of the track mechanism used on tractors being used on the Western Front that had inspired the use of such tracks on the British tanks. A model of Little Willy had been constructed to grace the occasion.

Before leaving for India, Morgan suggested that Low might be prosecuted for offences under 'The Military Services Act 5 & 6, Sec. V. Geo. V Ch. 104 Sec. 3, subsection 4' and 'Section 16 of the Army Act' but he then went on to suggest why Low may prove to be the innocent party.

Rationing, conscription and other new laws created opportunities for abuse and called for measures to curb such activities and the trials of life under fire challenged tradition disciplinary remedies. Two years before these allegations against Low, Morgan had addressed the questions being posed in law by the new situations of this vast prolonged conflict. In his book *War: Its Conduct and Legal Results*, Morgan had anticipated the challenges that innovation and the war presented for the legal system and the story 'Stokes's Act' in his book *Leaves from a Field Notebook* illustrates a part of the Military Service Act that was reinterpreted on the Western Front. Sergeant John Stokes' previous exemplary record would normally have overridden his serious misconduct but his offence in the face of the enemy could not be ignored. The pragmatic resolution of this conundrum results in an 'Act to suspend the operation of sentences of Courts-martial.' In this way the court would reach a militarily acceptable verdict to maintain discipline but the sentence would be suspended in the knowledge that the, by then more enlightened, rank and file would not take

Holt and Swinton at Stockton

advantage of such leniency. Morgan says, 'In the Temple they call it 5 & 6 Geo. V. cap. 23. But out there they call it "Stokes's Act".' Of course, Stokes was not the real name of the defendant.

Low's initial apparently insouciant attitude to the accusations changed and on 30th May 1918 he submitted an 18-page dossier with supporting memos that dealt seriatim with the allegations. In this dossier Low declared that far from using his position to further his career he had personally funded much of his unit's work. He described West 'whom I did not consider to be of strictly British descent' as a coloured gentleman with an aggressively friendly manner, citing as an example West's animated explanation of his newly invented game of 'putting Charlie Chaplin's trousers on the Kaiser.' Ironically, West's patent for this game was published in November 1918 just as the war ended and the Kaiser went into exile.

By 1st July 1918 the authorities were looking for Clifton and Low's reply to an official request for a description of West was: 'A large built man, loose limbed, not stout. Height about 5' 10½. Age about 40. Very dark hair not quite straight in front. Dark swarthy complexion of slightly negroid characteristics to observers of the subject. Manner – usually excitable.'

After the war, Morgan was at the Paris Peace Conference in 1919 following which Marshal Ferdinand Foch said, 'This is not a peace. It is an armistice for twenty years'.

On 4th March 1920, Bobbie Loraine left St. Moritz flying as a passenger in a Condor machine and reported that as they were flying over Germany he was 'very much impressed by the extreme activity that was everywhere noticeable. At all the

In the 1950s drones began to move into popular culture. In 1953, a year after Prof. Low's articles on the WWI Aerial Target, this cartoon of General Jumbo Johnson and Professor Carter started in this British children's comic, *The Beano*. The cartoon was still being published into the 1980s (By kind permission of DC Thomson & Co Ltd)

manufacturing towns chimneys were belching forth smoke and quarries were being worked very actively.'

Morgan was in Berlin until 1923 and in 1924, he monitored Germany re-arming, contrary to the agreements. He published *The Disarmament of Germany and After* and he was concerned even then with the blatant way that the Germans were allowed to flout their agreements regarding re-arming. Subsequently, the rush for peace and the diplomacy of appeasement started with the Locarno Treaties of 1925. The Weimar Republic agreed to respect the borders of other countries. After the withdrawal of the Control Commission, international enforcement of the conditions of the Armistice were replaced by conciliation. On 9th September 1926, Germany joined the League of Nations. William Collin Brooks, known as simply CB, recorded in his 'Journals' publication that the speakers on the international situation at a dinner in the House of Commons on Thursday 5th December 1935 riled him and he responded first. He admitted that he had been on the verge of rudeness in his rebuttal but Morgan, who followed him, was even hotter, addressing one of the principal earlier speakers, Morgan said, 'It was preposterous that any man, even Rennell Rodd, should discuss the foreign situation on the assumption that Hitler was a pacifist and that Mermel, Prague and the Eastern Mediterranean do not exist.'

In 1946, Morgan reworked some of his earlier work and published it as *Assize of Arms: The Disarmament of Germany and Her Rearmament (1919–1939)*. He said, 'It still annoys me that we didn't stop them well before 1939'. Morgan served as a legal adviser to the United Nations War Crimes Commission at Nuremberg from 1947 to 1949.

But on a brighter prospect than this march towards World War II, back in 1919 Swinton retired as a major general to serve in the Civil Aviation department at the Air Ministry before he joined Citroën in 1922 as a director. He was Chichele Professor of Military History at Oxford University and a fellow of All Souls College, Oxford from 1925 to 1939; he was also colonel commandant of the Royal Tank Corps from 1934 to 1938. Ernest and his wife Grace remained married until his death in 1951. They would have been proud parents in September 1918 when 2nd Lieutenant Robert Clayton Swinton, their eldest son was awarded the Military Cross for conspicuous gallantry, evacuating his wounded under heavy shell fire and manning the Lewis gun to cover the retreat of his section. Grace died within 18 months of Ernest's passing.

Clifton did not disappear and he was living in Bournemouth and still raising patents in the 1930s and the secret Feltham Experimental Works business was not interrupted by West's case against Archie Low. Far from it, for as we have noticed, Archie was promoted to captain.

CHAPTER 18

Distance Control Boats

One of the two intended sacrificial old submarines used in the Zeebrugge attack on 23rd April 1918 was able to destroy its target, the viaduct linking the Mole to the mainland. This vessel was steered into place and exploded by its captain, Lieutenant Richard Douglas Sandford, who was awarded the VC, one of the eight awarded to participants in the raid. The citation read:

> This officer was in command of Submarine C.3, and most skilfully placed that vessel in between the piles of the viaduct before lighting his fuse and abandoning her. He eagerly undertook this hazardous enterprise, although, well aware (as were all his crew) that if the means of rescue failed and he or any of his crew were in the water at the moment of the explosion, they would be killed outright by the force of such explosion. Yet Lieutenant Sandford disdained to use the gyro steering, which would have enabled him and his crew to abandon the submarine at a safe distance, and preferred to make sure, as far as was humanly possible, of the accomplishment of his duty.

Sandford, who was 27 years old, survived the raid and the war, but only by 12 days. He contracted typhoid fever and died on 23rd November 1918.

Before this raid to block the Zeebrugge U-Boat port, the Royal Navy were developing their anti-submarine technology. Capt. Cyril Percy Ryan of the HMS *Tarlair* research establishment on the Forth of Firth in Scotland was involved in hydrophone research but on 11th November 1917 he submitted a patent on 'Controlling the Movements of Ships…by Wireless Telegraphy'.

Even before Ryan's patent was submitted, at the request of the Admiralty, on 2nd October 1917 Low and Bowen had been released from service with the RFC and they were seconded to the Royal Navy Volunteer Reserve. We do not know whether Archie was recruited primarily to assist Commander Brock in his work to organise effective remote-controlled smoke screens or to develop their remote-controlled boat or for one of the other projects he undertook. We do know that the Royal Navy had reason to develop an unmanned boat as the Germans had used their Fernlenkboot against them off the Belgium coast. This FL boat was wire-guided from a shore-based controller and it was a great aid to their shore defences out to a range of about 12 miles (20 km).

All of this planning and re-planning of operations against German shipping and their North Sea ports must have identified the 'need' for an unmanned navy vessel able to steer to its target and explode. From Sandford's citation we can see that the Navy clearly did not trust the automatic steering devices in service at the time, even for the final straight run in to the target. There were no electronic navigation aids so any complicated attack by an unmanned ship in coastal waters where complex tides and currents abound would need remote guidance by an operator. If, as was suggested, Clarence Colley was liaising between MID and 'Jackie' Fisher's Naval Board of Invention and Research (BIR), he may have prompted the Admiralty to take an interest in the AT control system following its successful trials in March 1917.

The conversion of Coastal Motor Boats (CMBs) to be radio controlled by an airborne operator was a triumphal endorsement of the Feltham Works' control systems by a new sponsor, the Royal Navy. The Royal Navy's development was an RPV that was not tied to a land base and was less restricted because it was controlled from an aircraft and could be operated with other similarly controlled vessels as a flotilla. So the inspiration for this development may have arisen from the planning for the raid on Bruges.

Following the development and trails on 13th March 1918, an order had been generated for Low's clock-driven impulse senders for DCBs, the Distance Control Boats. Five of these top secret DCBs were made, three of them by converting CMBs. The CMBs were 40-foot-long fast torpedo boats that had stepped hydroplane hulls making them capable of 40 knots and were propelled by a single screw and armed with one 18-inch torpedo. They were built for the Royal Navy by companies such as Thorneycroft. DCBs were controlled from a mother aircraft. The bow and about a third of the hull of a CMB travelling at speed were out of the water and too high to launch a torpedo at the target off the bow. So they were designed to release the torpedo off the stern, but with the torpedo deployed tail first and hence aimed at the target. The CMB then had to turn quickly out of the path of the torpedo as soon as it was launched. The CMB had a distinguished career and a 55-foot version with two torpedoes was added to the fleet.[1]

However, as Low explains in Bloom's book:

> We built a tuned system which was applied to the control of wireless-operated motor patrol boats; all these inventions were long before the days of the Queen Bee target aircraft and the radio-controlled battleship experiments by the Admiralty. ... I was transferred to the RNVR as a lieutenant-commander, only two days later to be again transferred, this time to the newly formed RAF.

Sir David Henderson's letter of 23rd August 1917 to The Honourable Sir Edward Stafford Fitzherbert, K.C.B., Lord Stafford, the Director of Torpedoes and Mining (DTM) had described Low as 'an exceptional officer' and continued 'I don't half like his going. I hope it will be possible to give him suitable position as regards pay and rank.' The records show that Low's transfer lasted far longer than a couple of days, totalling about six months but so much was achieved in that time it must have flown by. It is also interesting that Archie Low was with the RNVR when the army were investigating Clifford West's accusations. Low asked for a return to the RAF to prevent a reduction in pay but he retained the command of the Feltham Works throughout, as they were by now located in his own premises and it was where most of his work for the navy would have been conducted as confirmed in a letter of 21st March 1918 from Fitzherbert:

> Captain Low has been a 1st class Experimental Officer for over two years and he has assigned about 14 complete Patent to the Services. He was gazetted as Lieut. Commander as from 2nd October 1917 recommended by Sir David Henderson, Brig. General Caddell, Brig. General Pitcher and Major, Sir Henry Norman, M.P., P.C .... Low has voluntarily lent his entire laboratory and staff to the Admiralty where manufacturing is now carried out .... Three distinct inventions have now been accepted into service after being tested, namely:
>
> Complete sending control gear for DCB.
>
> Electrical Gun Timing Apparatus
>
> Gun Silencer Audiometer Measuring Device
>
> ... Captain Low's request to General Pitcher he went back to RFC to prevent reduction in pay and go for duty to Admiralty there being (apparently) at the time no Officers RNVR attached to RNAS .... It is also requested that Lieut. E. Windsor Bowen be attached for duty to Captain Low.

Two months after he sent this letter, Admiral Fitzherbert became commander-in-chief on the Cape of Good Hope Station on 20th May 1918.

One of the DCBs was transferred to the RAF. Another was the converted CMB9 that became the Distance Control Boat DCB1. This naval drone developed in World War I still exists today thanks to its owners and dedicated enthusiasts Bob and Terri Morley who saved it and spent years restoring it and researching its history. Now, more than 100 years later, we can reinstate the link between CMB9/DCB1 and Low's control system once again, which is most fitting as CMB9 was built by Thornycroft at Platts Eyot in the Thames at Hampton in 1916, less than five miles from Low's secret Feltham Experimental Works. DCB1 was part of 'The Avenue of Sail' at the Queen's Diamond Jubilee Pageant on 3rd June 2012.

Low's control system will have required considerable redesign for this DCB application. The receiver may not have needed the added complexity of incorporating gyroscopic stabilisation that was necessary for its aerial implementation but it could have incorporated one. Patent 244,258 for the AT states 'The control mechanism is preferably mounted in position by means of springs or in diarubber or other resilient suspension bands or strips and may be contained in a box or casing having a celluloid or other suitable cover ....' In a 40-knot motor boat the receiver system protection and durability will have been more important than its weight and power requirements than for the AT. However, shock and vibration protection, as well as

DCB1, yet another world first (Robert Morley and Liner Lookout Cafe)

weight and power would have all been design issues for the transmitter and control system to use it in an aircraft. But as the letter states this was achieved and it was tested and accepted for further development but it was never used, as far as we know, as World War I finally ended some months later.

Tuning systems enabled multiple channels so that two or more weapons deployed in the same vicinity could be separately controlled.

The 1917 patents contain a description of 'a modified form of the apparatus' when referring to these drawings. While the original ground based sender unit shown in illustration 4 was suitable for use by the operator on the bench in a control vehicle, this modified unit is evidently a more robust and compact construction of the sender equipment – probably designed for use in harsher environments – such as the mother aircraft controlling ATs or the DCBs.

The DCB image in the illustration section shows port, starboard, ½ speed and explode as selections on the controller and a gimbal mounted gyroscope. Further investigation may reveal the role of this gyroscope in the guidance of the DCB.

The Final Report of the Post-War Questions Committee, 27 March 1920, recorded that 'it is very difficult for an enemy to interfere with their control by means of wireless jamming, since to discover the tune on which one of them is working is a delicate operation' and 'these weapons are already capable of being handled in numbers: two of them can be controlled by one aircraft, three of them have been manoeuvred close to one another simultaneously without mutual interference, and probably as many as eight can be handled in a group if the groups are not within about four miles of one another'. This Questions Committee concluded the DCB

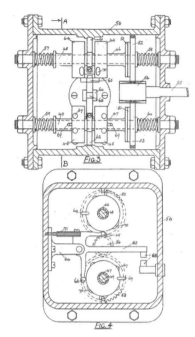

A drawing from Patent 195,100

'is in a different category from all others in that it is capable of control up to the moment of hitting, and this fact alone justifies close attention to development.' Work on the DCBs was continued in the inter-war years.

On 19th March 1918 Low had received a 'thank you' letter from the Royal Navy concerning another job on audiometers, a letter that contained praise indeed with phrases like 'very pretty' and 'come to the rescue for the second time'. Archie's work on audiometers stemmed from one of his many phobias. He had a fear of the dark and confined spaces, a disgust with the act of eating, literally a loathing of the process of putting food into one's mouth and … he hated noise. This phonophobia gave him a great interest in sound and he did a great deal of research continuing this work into the 1950s. He gained contracts to record and analyse noise for many organisations such as the London Underground and was even involved in the law courts. A Mr Stanley Vine was summonsed for having an ineffective silencer on his motorcycle. Low's audiometer evidence was presented by the Auto-Cycle Union in Vine's defence, showing that his was no noisier than other motorcycles. The court wasn't interested enough to forgo its fine of ten shillings!

The Feltham Works, with its projects, experiments, inventions and, of course, a considerable volume of production to fulfil a growing order book must have been a hive of activity that intensified as the work expanded and the war dragged on. Their radio control system, far from being abandoned as a failure as a few authors have assumed in the past, was by the end of the war the 'spark' completing the triangles of both the new RAF's and the RN's needs and means in their ongoing development programmes. Just three years into the post-war period, with all of its financial constraints, in 1921 the Royal Navy were so confident in the technology that they converted the semi-dreadnought HMS *Agamemnon* to radio control and used as a target ship until she was replaced by the King George V-class dreadnought battleship HMS *Centurion* when she was converted to radio control in 1926. The work continued through the inter-war years leading to the Queen Bee and continuing naval programmes.

However, the drone, like every other product, is only of use when the need persists. For many decades brave young men could be found to fly into danger although work on drones continued for specific uses. Today many factors make drones the device of choice for a range of operations and the global reach of GPS and satellite communications, the level of automation that can be achieved and the desire to observe and act at arms length have provided military drones with potent operational capabilities.

Archie Low could look back with mixed emotions on the war. He was employed by the army to develop the AT and the other systems they worked on, so after the war he couldn't claim a penny from the Awards Commission. He was obliged to seek recompense by claiming for the use of his premises. However, this most unmilitary chain smoker with poor eyesight had now served in the British Army, the British Army's Royal Flying Corps, the Royal Air Force, the Royal Navy Volunteer Reserve and had been an agent on a secret 'undercover' mission in neutral Spain.

CHAPTER 19

Determination and Resolution

Dulce et Decorum est Pro patria mori

Many of World War I's social and technological innovations were pre-war ideas nurtured and given a market by the conflict. However, in Britain, World War I was, in the truest sense, 'the Mother of Invention'. It created 'the War Machine', the single-minded synergy of production and delivery involving every sinew of society's muscle and every member of its population, a total war in which 'invention' itself was identified as a resource to be managed. The Aerial Target development was just one of a great many projects run by a disparate collection of back-room engineers, academics and inventors. But as a consequence of this it was the British Army that flew the first drone successfully in March 1917, launching it from a powered ramp. This drone was created by De Havilland's, Bradshaw's and Archie Low's teams.

Back then everything was natural; made of wood, metal or bone and powered by wood, coal or increasingly by oil. Newpapers were the only 'media'. The city's odours came with a strong whiff of 'horse'. Controls on alcohol, chemicals and drugs had been initiated. Children and animals had a measure of rights and protection that women also craved. Following the end of hostilities in 1918 the war-weary world turned its back on military matters and believed in the other 'old lie', that this was the conflict that would end warfare. Most of what had been created to service the war, at great cost in wealth and effort, was discarded. This included ousting many personalities who, up to that point, had been much in demand.

At this time Archie noted that some of the bombers were converted for civilian use. They carried airmail and some passengers such as the peace negotiators to and fro between London and Paris. These may have been some of the first international air passengers. In 1919, on Monday 25th August, 'Aircraft Transport and Travel, Ltd.' started their regular service using an Airco DH4 machine. It left Hounslow at 9:10 a.m. carrying an *Evening Standard* newspaper reporter, a number of daily newspapers, a consignment of leather from a London firm to a firm in Paris, several brace of grouse, and a considerable number of jars of Devonshire cream. It arrived at Le Bourget, the Paris terminus, at 11:40. At 12:30 p.m. a DH16 left Hounslow with four passengers and landed in Paris at 2:45 p.m.

Archie Low did not linger with the radio control projects after the war and was, as always, drawn to the next interesting project. Throughout his life he would lose interest in most of his work well before it became profitable and usually at the point where he had extracted all of the 'fun' from it. As we have seen, Archie started off earning money by applying for retrospective payment from the government for the use that was made of his premises in Feltham during the war.

Through Sir Henry Norman, Low met Henry Segrave again. In collaboration the three of them formed the Norlow Engineering Company with headquarters in Conduit Street in Mayfair, London and with the Hon. Victor Austin Bruce they produced the Norlow motor scooter. Norman and Low even raised a joint patent on scooters.

Henry Segrave went on to his life of legend; breaking the world land speed record three times, gaining his knighthood and meeting his tragic end attempting the world water speed record in 'Miss England II' on Lake Windermere in the Lake District on Friday 13th June 1930.

The 1919 Norlow motor scooter (Bloom, *He Lit the Lamp*)

144,384

PATENT **SPECIFICATION**

Application Date, Mar. 10, 1919, No. 5947/19.

Complete Left, Sept. 10, 1919.

Complete Accepted, June 10, 1920.

PROVISIONAL SPECIFICATION.

Improvements in and relating to Auto-scooters.

We, The Rt. Hon. Sir HENRY NORMAN, Bt., M.P., P.C., of The Corner House, Cowley Street, Westminster, and ARCHIBALD MONTGOMERY Low, D.Sc., Major in His Majesty's Royal Air Force, of High Street, Feltham, in the County of Middlesex, do hereby declare the nature of this invention to be as 5 follows:—

This invention relates to auto-scooters and similar devices, and the object is to provide an improved structure thereof and novel arrangements and combinations of parts with a view to facilitating and cheapening the cost of pro-

Extract from Sit Henry Norman and Archie Low's patent

With Victor's older brother, Clarence Napier Bruce[1] (the Real Tennis and rackets champion and who was later titled Lord Aberdare), Archie started the Low Engineering Co. with offices at 92a High Street, Kensington and, most notably, their works at Feltham. Another director was Low's old 'boss' in the RFC, Walter Caddell.

In 1922, the company produced an in-line, air-cooled, four-cylinder, two-stroke engine and with Victor Bruce they designed and trialled a prototype all-enclosed motorcycle using this engine, but it proved too expensive to produce.

Advert for Low Engineering (Grace's Guide to British Industrial History)

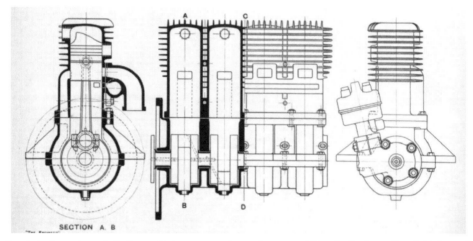

Low's in-line, air-cooled, four-cylinder, two-stroke cycle engine (Grace's Guide to British Industrial History)

In 1923, Henry Stafford Fred Robert O'Brien's Fortis and Partners was acquired by Low Engineering and O'Brien was appointed chief designer to the firm. He stayed with them until 1926. In the war he had been the chief draughtsman in the aviation department of Vickers where he had worked on the Vickers Vimy development.

Low had a broad range of interests including his acoustic work with his 'audiometer'. Following the success of his two-stroke engine book, in 1924 he published *Wireless Possibilities* followed by many other publications on 'popular science' and 'science fiction'.

By now Low was doing well financially and he moved from the Goldhawk Road to a large property called 'The Yews' at 1 Woodstock Road around the corner from the Bowens.

In 1929, the periodical *Armchair Scientist* was launched and this would occupy a good deal of Archie's time right up to the start of the next war in 1939. His involvement with 'popular science' tarnished his reputation as a serious academic. Some of his other activities are listed in those 'updated' records held by Imperial College (Appendix 1).

For his less public life and relationships we rely upon the anecdotes of his friends, most notably his biographer Ursula Bloom. Life was good to Archie though most of the 1920s and 1930s and Ursula refers quite often to the women he was involved with, sometimes in detail and other times just alluding to his various relationships. Although undoubtedly lonely at times he was rarely 'alone'.

He was on holiday in Margate when his father died in 1934. A car had been despatched to fetch him but he arrived too late to be at his father's side. After this his mother moved into a house almost opposite 'The Yews'. Low was 48 when, after all the years of separation, he and Amy filed for divorce. Low was in a deep and meaningful relationship when these proceedings were instigated but the affair did not last. These very personal relationships were very publicly and unpleasantly reported to the great distress of all of those affected.

1938 started an even harder period for Archie. In April he was taken ill and diagnosed with pneumonia and it took him a very long time to recover. He needed a nurse and Dorothea Lucie Bitton was one of those who attended. Ursula Bloom notes that Archie called her 'Aggie' who would prove to be a very capable, much respected and loved companion for Archie.

'Aggie' was born in Shanghai, China in October 1904 and had two older brothers. Her father William Nelson Bitton was a missionary with the London Missionary Society (LMS), Dr. David Livingstone being probably their most famous missionary back in the 1840s. Nelson Bitton's mission went to Shanghai in 1897 and Aggie's oldest brother was born on 16th October 1898. His parents then married on 23rd December. Aggie was only two years old when her mother died back in England. Her father remarried in 1913 and she was then to gain two much younger half brothers. Nelson Bitton became the 'Home Secretary' of the London Missionary Society in 1914 and remained in that post until 1936 having gone on a deputation visit to Australia, New Zealand and Samoa in 1933.

Dorothia Bitton is listed in the 1943 Register of Nurses as number 76140 and this records her training at the Royal Northern Hospital, London from 1931 to 1934 and her qualification on 15th March 1935 'by examination'. It also shows her address as 1 Woodstock Road, Archie's house.

As Archie was recovering, later in 1938 his ageing mother took a liking to his new nurse. Gertrude had 'Aggie' move in to her house at 15 Marlborough Crescent 'to be close for Archie', her home being just a few minutes' walk away from Woodstock Road. Subsequently, Aggie stayed in Archie's employment right until the end in 1956. Aggie was soon taking on more duties by looking after Gertrude as her sight was failing. In January 1939, Gertrude 'had a fall' and broke her thigh. For the next six months Aggie attended to her as her health declined further and she died in September.

Amy Woods (by now using her maiden name) was living in the same road as Gertrude. In 1940 the divorce was rescinded, airing the situation again to the distress of those concerned. Subsequently Amy and Archie's relationship, although never close, was at least businesslike. So much so that Archie let Amy use one of his cottages when recovering from surgery.

Archie said that he 'shrank from those at home knowing about it, even his secretary.' This was 'Aggie' who had extended her roles from nurse to those of lab assistant, secretary and in his later life, chauffeur. He dedicated a number of his other books to her, simply as D. L. Bitton, presumably because she must have spent many hours assisting him in their production.

One of Archie's special long-term acquaintances was John Beverley Nichols. Best known for his gardening books, he had spent time with Low down the years. On the face of it, the two were such complete opposites so it is amazing that they became such firm friends. Neat and tidy versus carefree. When they first met, Nichols was writing for the *Sunday Despatch* newspaper and interviewed Low in 'the shambles of a study in Chiswick'. At that time Low was a very young man with a shock of black hair, a pale impish face, a stoop and a nervous blink. These two will have shared some mutual associates such as the Normans as Beverley knew the Bodnant estate, Fay Norman's family home. Beverley said that it was amazing that a man who knew so much about his beloved cars could drive so badly. A drive through Shepherd's Bush terrified Nichols as Archie seemed to ignore the needs of other traffic while reminiscing and chattering about the times when flowers grew in the woods there and the nightingales sang on April evenings. All long gone by the time of their excursion in the rapid urbanisation of London's hinterland.

Low investigated spiritualism but he did so from a scientific standpoint. There were and still are many eminent and famous believers. For example, Nichols would go on to publish *Powers That Be* in 1966 and Hugh Dowding, who had survived the training and active service in the RFC and directed RAF fighter command through the World War II Battle of Britain, was very involved in the subject in later life. Oliver Lodge, the radio pioneer, was another with a fascination for this subject. Low conducted his own experiments at the 'scientific' laboratory of George Walter de la Warr in Oxford who had expanded on the work of Albert Abrams. The de la Warr laboratory remained in operation until 1987. Low was at once open minded and sceptical, bemused by the apparent contradictions such as that exhibited by a medium who had just boasted that he could contact Mars but then, on taking his leave, asked for directions to his home in North London!

After his studies of the paranormal, Low mused that 'he had learnt that the greatest discovery of the last decade is not nuclear fission but that we know almost nothing about anything!' This is close to but not quite a restatement of the Socratic paradox.

Some of Archie Low's thoughts, predictions and views are cited by Peter J. Bowler in his *A History of the Future*, including Low's belief that women should and would be a growing force in society.

In the summer of 1937, Low invited Stuart Macrae, who was just quitting as the editor of a different publication, to join *Armchair Scientist* and take over as its editor. As a young man Macrae had worked on munitions design in World War I and, due to an article on the new powerful magnets he had published in the *Armchair Scientist* magazine, he became involved in the design of river mines that were urgently required in 1939 for Churchill's Operation *Royal Marine*. Low was 'bursting to get into the army' and help with the war effort although he was well over the age limit. Macrae managed to use Archie as a kind of unofficial helper and Low then involved Albert Henry Midgley and Midgley's two sons. It is likely that Midgley, an electrical engineer, a prolific inventor and patriarch of Midgley Harmer Ltd, located at Warple Way, Acton Vale close to Low's new abode, had been involved in the design and production of items for Low's projects. It is even possible that he was known to Low during the development of the Experimental Works' AT systems in World War I.

Macrae, to avoid a claim after the war, phoned Low in the afternoon of Friday 22nd December 1939 to get him to withdraw his patent application for the marine flavial mine. However, Low's patent was approved. Macrae and Midgley were subsequently awarded the patent they applied for on 11th January 1940. Macrae went on to join Churchill's Toyshop – Ministry of Defence 1 (MD1) when it was created by Churchill later in 1940.

Aggie had proved to be most capable and became interested in Low's work when acting as a lab assistant, secretary and housekeeper. By the time he was assisting MD1, Low said that Aggie thought nothing of carrying prototype bombs on the train up to a test ground near Bedford.

Archie Low's World War II application letters that he submitted in his quest to find a role in which he could contribute show a growing frustration and even a sense of desperation as he was rebuffed and passed over. He mentions time and time again his old champions such as Lord Brabazon as references. Low finally gained the rank of major in the Royal Pioneer Corps stationed in Wilton in Wiltshire where he lectured.

Archie was a fascinating man. He was 'into' so many things and he could have been a bellwether of his generation. He was a brilliant inventor and looked the part. In appearance in later life after World War II he gave the impression of a somewhat shambolic man although, in a photograph taken at the Isle of Man Tourist Trophy race with HRH the Duke of Edinburgh, he looked quite dapper. He was the chairman of the Auto-Cycle Union for 24 years and the Duke was the Patron. He signed the foreword in the program as 'Professor A. M. Low'. He had his failings and one was this; he cocked a snook at the establishment by calling himself 'Professor'. Another problem was that he didn't see things through, didn't stick with his inventions to get any payback. He wrote dozens of books and he edited the *Armchair Scientist* publication for 11 years. He gained his membership of the Magic Circle on 5th September 1950 and he had what amounted to a career touring the country as an after dinner speaker, in great demand because he was witty, accomplished, well known and probably almost always available! However, he did show his more philosophical side. In the final chapter of his book *Modern Armaments* he argues that war is wasteful in every sense but this is repaid with interest and is of overall benefit to mankind by its legacy to peacetime use of its developments in a myriad of fields, from medicine to agriculture and transport to mining.

Low's output of new titles continued into the bookshops throughout World War II and on into the Cold War period. He and Amy even collaborated on one of

Amy Low's illustration of Oliver Lodge (*They Made Your World*, Low 1949)

these as she produced the illustrations for *They Made Your World: Short Histories of Famous Scientists* that was published in 1949. He dedicated the book to his mother Gertrude Anne Duncan Low.

Archie's literary output, though impressive, was eclipsed by that of his friend Ursula Robinson (nee Bloom) who was not only known for her books but also for the quantity of them: there are over 500. She had known Archie Low for at least 35 years and in the 1950s she lived in Crammer Court, Chelsea and was ideally placed to record a history of Low's life which she did in her book, *He Lit the Lamp*. However, Ursula was the first to admit that she was not technical and so like the mountain of papers he gave her access to, it is a bit 'jumbled'. One book review in *Motor Sport* magazine in May 1958 describes it as 'a sad book' and in many ways it is somewhat melancholy for she was obviously very fond of Archie and felt that he spread himself over too many activities and that he could have been 'a great scientist' if he had been just a little more focused.

Ursula notes that Archie asked that no biography should be written but then he provided her with a great deal of its content, a copious archive and a dedication for the book which reads: 'Dedication to my Mother and Father whose book this is'. Ursula declares in the Author's Note of *He Lit the Lamp* that it is 'his book'.

In their separate homes in Chiswick, Amy and Archie were not far from their grandchildren. On 14th December 1953, Amy was on her way to see the schoolmistress at the school their granddaughter Ann attended when she was knocked down by a motorcycle on a zebra crossing. She never regained consciousness and died on the 16th.

At this time, Alick, the grandchildren's father, was the resident architect at the new buildings of the University College of the West Indies in Jamaica. These replaced the old Gibraltar Camp site huts that had been used by the UCWI. for its first few years after its instigation and before that, during World War II, they had housed German and Italian internees. More than 3,500 drawings were required to specify the new campus buildings and the site employed 1,200 workers. After surviving Hurricane Charlie in 1951, the campus was largely completed by the time Queen Elizabeth II visited in November 1953, just 5 months into her reign.

After purchasing The Yews in the 1930s, Archie acquired further properties, at Liphook in Hampshire and then in West Sussex at Trotton and a bungalow right on the coast in Tamarisk Walk, East Wittering. He fell in love with Devon, 230 miles and many hours from The Yews, at a beautiful secluded location called Hartland Point. Ursula Bloom visited him there at the house he had built on a site that had no access except on foot across the fields. She was not certain whether it was his infatuation with 'the local lady' or the view across to the island of Lundy that was the real attraction. However, she found that the only one of these that endured was the view of Lundy. A couple of Archie's books were dedicated to Cynthia and one ends 'Hartland 1939'. This house on the cliff edge didn't even have a water supply and later, Ursula described it as a melancholy memorial – a ruin.

The two cottages he bought near Liphook he converted into a house known as 'Old Barn Farm' in Hammer Lane, Hewshott. Aggie often drove him down to the farm in the 1940s and 50s when he was getting more frail. Archie patented one last improvement – to bedpans. In his book *They Made Your World* he signed off the final chapter – 'Hewshott 1947.'

The Aerial Target exhibition at the IWM in the mid-1950s displayed the exhibits that the museum now have in their stores, including 'the actual controls invented during the early part of the 1914/18 war and flown in 1917'.

Initially Archie had met with officialdom in his quest to publicise the RFC's Aerial Target achievements in World War I. He wrote about the work and he was persistent. He tried to put these items into an exhibition and was passed on to the IWM by the London Science Museum. Finally, he persuaded Leslie Ripley Bradley, the Director General of the IWM to visit his laboratory at The Yews. This visit overcame the museums reluctance to display the AT. In 1954 models of the missile (Low's invention of July 1918, Patent 191,409) and the AT were made. The AT remote controlled aircraft model was produced by J. T. Robson who lived in Sunderland. He was an amateur model maker who had worked for the de Havilland company and from his correspondence it would appear that he gained his information for the model

Professor Low and Lord Brabazon on 29th June 1955 presenting models of the Aerial Target and Guided Missile to the Director General of the Imperial War Museum (Bloom, *He Lit The Lamp*)

directly from Archie. The museum opened its prestigious new gallery dedicated to the flying services that same year.

Leslie was clearly fascinated by Low's cluttered and intriguing laboratory and he was keen to revisit and get the exhibits into the IWM gallery. However, he needed Low for all the detailed labelling and explanations to make sense of the planned display but Archie Low was suffering prolonged periods of ill health. On 27th February 1956, Leslie wrote to Low saying how pleased he was to 'read in the Times yesterday that you are home after two months in hospital' and Low replied 'good to be home'. After Leslie's next visit to that intriguing laboratory in Chiswick, the planning of the AT displays at the IWM finally went ahead. Archie submitted the text for the labelling and the museum had the models to go with the hardware exhibits from the AT for public exhibition.

Low gave his last lecture in the club room of the Magic Circle on 23rd April 1956. Throughout that summer Aggie took him down to Hewshott to rest as often as possible. Ursula Bloom described the farmhouse in the autumn of 1956 as secluded, 'there would never be intruders, for the approach to the place made that practically impossible'.

In the closing chapter of his book *Men Who Shaped the World*, Egon Larsen described Low as the last of the lone inventors, a silver haired, friendly, be-spectacled character who, if you were a film director looking for someone to cast as a scientist, you would have found the man who looks the part. The Yews was by this time much neglected and entering the property required visitors to duck under the overhanging branches, adding to the seclusion that Low valued. Egon found the house a treasury of contrasts with antimacassars but central heating radiators, an old-fashioned gramophone but with a state of the art public address amplifier and books everywhere. Entering the laboratory, a large shed across the garden from the house he exclaimed 'What a sight!'. It was crammed with apparatus on long work benches, some marked DANGER or DO NOT TOUCH among less threatening items; such things as an illuminated dog collar he had made for Ursula Bloom's dogs. Obviously, much impressed by his visit he said Low 'makes no mystery and will show you anything'.

During their conversation Archie remembered the pitfalls of measuring success, when he took his newly invented marble game to school and in short order won off every boy their collections of the precious glass balls. His very successful game did not survive the ensuing retribution extracted by his irate classmates. Success depended on the objective; an addictive method of 'rooking the punters' or a game to add to one's popularity at school? Among other wonders he was shown one of Archie's early inventions which used marsh gas to light the cars acetylene lamps without getting out of the driver's seat. He saw a miners' lamp sent to Low by the grateful coal workers who were using his firedamp detector and the press cuttings about the demonstration of Low's Televista. Inventions in later years included those in Wolrd War II, not many years before he and Egon met. A notable humanitarian example involved the incorporation of a flap on the carrier pigeons cage secured by sugar so that if the bird was trapped after a crash or was not soak into the sugar and release the creature. Of his World War II service, Larsen says that Field Marshal Lord Harold Rupert Leofric George Alexander complained that Low's lectures were too entertaining, which he considered to be out of place but Low espoused the value of imparting entertaining information.

Aggie was with Archie at the farmhouse in Liphook where he died. Ursula had phoned Aggie in the evening of 12th September 1956 to be told that all she could do for him was 'keep him asleep' adding, 'It will be much easier for him that way'. The next day Ursula read the announcement of his death in the 'stop press' of the newspaper.

However inventive, Archie Low never shook off an undercurrent of resentment from the establishment. So what was Prof. A. M. Low; a charlatan or a genius? In his personal life he was to most of his acquaintances, a confirmed bachelor and they were surprised, on the death of his wife, to find that he was still a married man. He liked the limelight as an inventor, an author, an after-dinner speaker, a magician and a long serving official of a number of organisations. Undoubtedly gifted but as his many friends admitted, flawed. Maybe he was happy enough to have been almost famous. True fame may have unravelled his claimed but dubious academic honours. He disliked the low status of engineering and science in British society, especially as these pursuits bestowed such wealth and prestige on the

The view from Old Barn Farm

country. Maybe he was upset by the attitude of some towards him but there is little evidence that he was.

With the possible exceptions of a few like Louis Walter, Raymond Phillips, Jack Hammond and Anton Flettner, Archie Low was the only spark who initially saw the real possibility, beyond science fiction, of what we now call a drone. Most of these others submitted patent applications but they did not address by experiments to any great extent the problems of launching, radio reception and the host of other challenges facing the production of a vehicle ready for trials.

In his 1949 book *All I Could Never Be,* Beverley Nichols reveals the origin of the characters in *Down the Garden Path,* his best-selling classic of 1932. Only two were taken from life and these were based upon his childhood governess and Professor Low. Low was 'a sort of scientific Shelley' in Beverley's assessment, although he seems aware of the slur on Low's professional reputation as he pointedly admits that 'of Low's scientific achievements I am not competent to speak.' Finally, he writes in the most affectionate manner, 'some of the happiest hours of my life were spent walking, in imagination, with the Professor down the garden path, and recapturing the echo of his conversation through the whisper of the wind in the trees.'

So, Archie almost slipped through the fingers of history. Amy and Archie's children died; John died in 1979 but Alick lived until 1997. It is not known what happened to Alick's children Ann and David A.

But having now particularly described and ascertained the nature of his said invention and in what manner the same was performed, we declare that what we claim is:

1. As an achievement, the first flight of the AT was on a par with that of the Wright brothers, although it was a far more difficult and challenging task to achieve.

2. The first heavier-than-air flights (powered or on gliders) were made by a significant number of inventors and investigators, many of whom were sharing their knowledge and findings. In contrast to this, the RFC AT was produced in secret, in isolation and was not assisted by any substantial depository of existing experience or knowledge.

3. Deriving from the AT work, continuing development by de Havilland, the Royal Aircraft Establishment and the RAF ultimately produced the Queen Bee and this was used in numbers, in service and extensively for many years before any other 'drones' were created.

4. The most likely derivation of the term 'drone' derives from the Queen Bee.

5. It is truly astounding that the Feltham AT control system still exists in the IWM stores and that the Distance Control Boat DCB1 has been identified, saved and lovingly restored.

6. There is agreement that the RFC AT of World War I was the world's first 'drone'. This is acknowledged in all the serious literature on the subject and is universally accepted … but not celebrated – yet.

However, there is international acknowledgement of Prof. Low's achievements. The British inventor was one of the original inductees in 1976 into the New Mexico Museum of Space History's 'International Space Hall of Fame', listed as 'ARCHIBALD M. LOW "The Father of Radio Guidance Systems"'. This is a very exclusive listing. The entries are selected by the 11 member New Mexico Governor's Space Centre Commission in the US. It is a Hall of Fame that now, over 40 years later, still has only 173 entries, including of course, the 12 men who have walked on the moon and many others of the notable firsts in space. It even has a couple of others who feature in this book.

After 100 years the drone's dawn is still awaiting its place in the sun. Highly capable robotic probes in the vacuum of space and in liquid depths of our seas have extended our reach and autonomous cars are being trialled. But the early visions of vast fleets of drones in our skies have not materialised. Drone technologies are used in construction, agriculture, film and other industries for imaging, surveillance, inspection and search tasks. Forests are being efficiently seeded, monitored and sprayed on inaccessible hillsides using drones. The exploration of Mars by drones is continuing. Drone taxi services are starting. Drones are edging into our commercial and civilian world.

Their engineering is challenging but these technologies raise issues ranging from moral questions of drone misuse to the insurance implications of operating drones. Dawn is still just breaking for the drone but, to be fair, the vast majority of air traffic worldwide contain levels of autonomy and automation boarding upon full UAV capability. Since the late 1960s, commercial aircraft carrying fare-paying passengers have been performing automatic landings and the reluctance to implement pilotless operation is to a great extent due to understandable human sensitivities. By the application of technology, the dangerous business of flying has paradoxically been converted into one of the human race's safest modes of commercial mass transport.

Appendix 1: Archibald Low's Imperial College Record

Extracted from 'Students of The City and Guilds College 1884–1934'

LOW, A. M., A. C.G I. (C. & M. 1905–08). F.C. S. M.I.A.E. F.R.G.S. F.I.P.I.

With Messrs. E. Chester Co., Ltd. With the Low Accessories Co., Ltd. With the Low Coal Engine Co., Ltd Major, RAF. Hon. Assistant Professor of Physics, Royal Artillery College. Founded the Low Generator Co., Ltd. Technical Director, The Low Engine Co., Ltd. Consulting and Research Engineer.

Special work: Acoustic work in connexion with Gaumont Studios; Mayfair Hotel; Plaza Theatre, London; Alhambra. London; Empire. London; London Underground Railways. Investigation of noise for Imperial Airways. Founder and Editor, Armchair Science.

Inventions: Low Coal Engine; Low Forced Induction Petrol Engine; Flexible Adjustable Curve; Automatic Acetylene Generator; Radio Aeroplane Control; Catapult Aeroplane Launcher; Oscillographic Monograph; Audiometer; Echo Mirror; Synchronous Cinematograph. Vibrometer.

Books and Papers: Joint author of 'Radio Log'; also 'Wonder Book of Machinery' etc (Ward Lock Co.). Author of 'Tendencies of Modern Science' (Elkin Mathews.); 'Peter Down the Well' (Grayson & Grayson); 'Wireless Possibilities' (Kegan Paul); 'The. Two Stroke Engine' (Temple Press); 'The Wonder Book of Inventions'; 'Scientific Recreations' (Ward Lock & Co.); 'Our Wonderful World of To-morrow' (T. Nelson & Sons); 'The Future' (Routledge); 'On my Travels' (Armchair Science). 'The Cinematograph and Engineering Design' I.A.E., 'Some Experiments and their bearing upon the Design of Automobile Parts' I.A.E. 1914. 'Science in Wonderland' (Lovat, Dickson & Thompson). Demonstrated method of television before the Inst. of Auto. Engineers in 1914.

Special distinctions: Formerly Hon. Assistant Professor Physics Royal Artillery College as result of research on radio control and radio base position finders.

Commanded R.F.C. Experimental Works. Was responsible for twenty secret patents. Twice mentioned for valuable services (European War), Chairman, Auto Cycle Union. Fellow and Vice-President, Inst. Patentees. Vice-President, Brooklands Motor Cycle Racing Club, Chairman, Royal Auto Club Motor Cycle Committee. President, S.E. and S, Midland Centres Auto Cycle Union. Former President, Harrow, Scientific Society. Patron and Fellow., Institute of Wireless Technology. Doctor of Science (Chicago Law School) for research on Internal Combustion Engines with methods of infra red photography. Noise recording and method of engine indication electrically.

Appendix 2

List of A. M. Low's Relevant Patents

Note: most of the Aerial Target patents were secret and publication was consequently delayed.

Patents related to the Aerial Target

Of course, none of these patents say that they relate to the 1917 RFC AT. However, the descriptions and the drawings that they contain match in so much detail the exhibits in storage in the IWM boxes that there is no room for doubt that they form a contiguous set.

It is difficult to draw any inference from the sequence numbers of these patents. The 191 sequence has for example 191,756 with an application date of the 9th January 1918 and the supposedly much earlier 191,406 has the same application date.

Patent 128,119 Improvements in Electrical Relays
Application date: 21st November 1918
Publication date: 19th June 1919
The subject of an article published in *The Engineer* on 25th June 1919

Patent 191,402 Improvements in Signalling Apparatus
Application date: 22nd June1917
Publication date: 8th February 1923

Patent 191,404 Improvements in Coherers for Detecting Electrical Radiation
Application date: 10th August 1917
Publication date: 8th February 1923

Patent 191,406 Improvements in Wireless Telegraphic Apparatus
Referred to as the Smoke Aerial
Application date: 9th January 1918
Publication date: 8th February 1923

Patent 191,407 Improvements in Electrically Driven Gyroscopes
Application date: 22nd January 1917
Publication date: 8th February 1923

Patent 191,410 Improvements in Electrically Driven Gyroscopes
Application date: 25th July 1918
Publication date: 8th February 1923

Patent 191,753 Improvements in Electro-magnetic Relays
Application date: 22nd June 1917
Publication date: 15th February 1923

Patent 191,756 Improvements in Electro-magnetic Relays
Application date: 9th January 1918
Publication date: 15th February 1923

Patent 195,100 Improved Apparatus for Selectively Sending Pre-arranged Electrical Signals
Application date: 8th June 1917
Publication date: 19th April 1923

Patent 195,101 Improvements in Electrical Controlling Apparatus
The Actuator used on the AT to move the aircraft control surfaces
Application Date: 22nd June 1917
Publication Date: 19th April 1923

Patent 195,102 Improvements in High Frequency Transformers
Application Date: 19th January 1918
Publication Date: 19th April 1923

Patent 195,410 Improvements in the Wireless Control of Selective Switches or the like
Application Date: 2nd April 1918
Publication Date: 26th April 1923

Patent 195,991 Improved Apparatus for Launching Aerial projectiles or the like
Application Date: 10th April 1918
Publication Date: 10th May 1923

Patent 244,203 Apparatus for Operation of Switches by Means of Signals
Application Date: 22nd May 1918
Publication Date: 14th January 1926

Patent 244,258 Improved Aerial Projectile
The primary Aerial Target Patent – defining the aircraft and the placement of control equipment within it.
Application Date: 9th January 1918
Publication Date: 14th January 1926

Patent 244,302 Improvements in the Control of Torpedoes and the like
A Gyro Control mechanism
Application Date: 2nd April 1918
Publication Date: 14th January 1926

Patent 244,498 Improvements in the Control of Switches and the like
Application Date: 3rd September 1918
Publication Date: 14th January 1926

Other related or specifically mentioned patents by Low

Patent 191,409 Improvements in Rockets
Application Date: 12th July 1918
Publication Date: 8th February 1923

Patent 244,497 Improvements in the Radiographic Transmission of Signals and the like
A facsimile machine
Application date: 26th August 1918
Publication date: 14th January 1926

Patent 742,826 Bedpan
Was this A. M. Low last laugh? He says in it '...the invention for which I pray that the patent may be granted to me...'
Application Date: 22nd September 1953
Publication Date: 4th January 1956

Note: For other patents by A. M. Low and other inventors, many of whom have been included in the text see the European Patent Office website at http://worldwide. espacenet.com/

Abbreviations

AA	Anti-Aircraft
ABRS	Air Bandit Reporting System
ACGI	Associate of the City and Guilds Institute
Ack Ack	Anti-aircraft Fire
AG	Attorney General
AID	Aeronautical Inspectorate Division
AIF	Australian Imperial Force
Airco	Aircraft Manufacturing Company Hendon
ASDIC	Anti-Submarine Detection Investigation Committee
AT	Aerial Target
BARC	British Automobile Racing Club
BBC	British Broadcasting Corporation
BEF	British Army Expeditionary Force (the Old Contemptibles)
BIR	Board of Invention and Research
BSc	Bachelor of Science
CID	Committee of Imperial Defence
CMB	Coastal Motor Boat (fast torpedo boat)
CRT	Cathode Ray Tube
DAE	Director of Aircraft Equipment
DAO	Director of Air Organisation
DCB	Distance Control Boat
DF	Direction Finding
DH	De Havilland or De Havilland Aircraft Company Limited
DORA	Defence of the Realm Act
Dsc	Doctor of Science
DSMA	Government Defence and Security Media Advisory Notices ('DA' Notices)
DST	Daylight Saving Time (summer time)
DTM	Director of Torpedoes and Mining

ERDC	Empire Resources Development Commission
FAST	Farnborough Air Sciences Trust
Fax	facsimile
FRS	Fellow of the Royal Society
GHQ	General HQ
HF-DF	High Frequency Direction Finding (Huff-Duff)
HQ	Head Quarters
IAAD	Inland Area Aircraft Depot – RAF Henlow
IAF	(Inter-Allied) Independent Air Force
IEE	Institution of Electrical Engineers
IEEE	Institute of Electrical and Electronics Engineers
Isle of Man TT	Isle of Man Tourist Trophy
IWC	Imperial Wireless Chain
IWM	Imperial War Museum
JLWS	Jewish League for Woman Suffrage
LADA	London Air Defence Area
LMS	London Missionary Society
MD1	Minister of Defence 1
MEMS	Micro-electro-mechanical systems
MI-5	Military Intelligence, Section 5 (UK Internal Counter Intelligence Service)
MID	Munitions Inventions Department
MIIMS	Member of the International Institute of Marine Surveying
MOS	Metropolitan Observation Service
MP	Member of Parliament
MT	Motor Transport
NPL	National Physical Laboratory
PPM	Pulse Position Modulation
PSA	Pomeroy Small Arm
RAE Farnborough	Royal Aircraft Establishment 1918–
RAF	Royal Aircraft Factory 1911–18
RAF	Royal Air Force 1918–
RASC	Royal Army Service Corps (Ally Sloper's Cavalry)
REC	Railway Executive Committee
RFC	Royal Flying Corps (1912–18)
RMA	Revolution in Military Affairs
RN	British Royal Navy
RNAS	Royal Naval Air Service
RNVR	Royal Navy Volunteer Reserve ('Wavy Navy')
ROC	Royal Observer Corps
RPC	Royal Pioneer Corps

RPV	Remote Piloted Vehicle
RS	Royal Society
RTC	Royal Tank Corps
SIGINT	Signals Intelligence
SONAR	Sound Navigation Ranging
TDD	Target Drone Denny
TNT	Trinitrotoluene
VC	Victoria Cross
UAV	Unmanned Aerial Vehicle
UXB	Unexploded bomb
WSPU	Women's Social and Political Union

Bibliography

Books and publications

Abbot, C. 1942. 'The 1914 Tests of the Langley "Aerodrome"'. *The Journal of the Royal Aeronautical Society,* 46(384), 291–296. doi:10.1017/S0001924000100168

Admiralty Committee – President Sir Richard Fortescue Phillimore. 1920. 'Final Report of The Post War Questions Committee'

Allen, D. W. Unmanned Aircraft – FAST Monograph No 003

Archibald, N. 1935. *Heaven High, Hell Deep 1917–1918.* New York: Arno Press

Ayrton, H. M. 1902. *The Electric Arc.* New York: D. Van Nostrand Co.

Balfour, H. H. 1973. *Wings Over Westminster.* London: Hutchinson

Balfour, H. H. 1985. *An Airman Marches.* London: Greenhill Books

Bangay, R. D. 1914. *The Elementary Principles of Wireless Telegraphy.* London: Marconi

Baring, M. 1930. *Flying Corps Headquarters 1914–1918.* London: Heinemann

Barnwell, F. S. 1917. *Aeroplane Design.* London: McBride

Bickers, R. 2017. *Out of China: How the Chinese Ended the Era of Western Domination.* Cambridge: Harvard University Press

Bloch, J. G. 1900. *Modern Weapons and Modern War.* London: Grant Richards

Bloom, U. 1958. *He Lit the Lamp: A Biography of Professor A. M. Low.* Burke

Bloom, U. 1959. *Youth at the Gate.* London: Hutchinson

Bowler, P. J. 2017. *A History of the Future: Prophets of Progress from H. G. Wells to Isaac Asimov.* Cambridge: Cambridge University Press

Brabazon, Lord. 1956. *The Brabazon Story.* London: Heinemann

Brooks, C. 1998. *Fleet Street, Press Barons and Politics: The Journals of Collin Brooks, 1932–1940.* London: The Royal Historical Society

Bryan, G. H. 1911. *Stability in Aviation.* London: Macmillan

Burns, R. W. 1998. *Television: An International History of the Formative Years.* London: Institution of Electrical Engineers

Cayley, G. 1809. *Nicholson's Journal of Natural Philosophy,* Chemistry and the Arts, September 1809

Churchill, A. 2014. *Blood and Thunder: The Boys of Eton College and the First World War.* Stroud: History Press

Collier, B. 1959. *Heavenly Adventurer: Sefton Brancker and the Dawn of British Aviation.* London: Secker & Warburg

Constantinesco, G. 1922. *Theory of Wave Transmission.* London: Haddon

Corbet-Smith, A. 1917. *The Marne—and After.* London: Cassell

Creighton. Rev. O. 1916. *With the Twenty-ninth Division in Gallipoli*. Sydney: Wentworth Press

Currie, J. 2004. *Lancaster Target*. Manchester: Crecy Publishing Ltd (first published: 1981)

Dolgin, E. E. 2015. *Shaw and the Actresses Franchise League: Staging Equality*. Jefferson: McFarland & Co

Draper, Michael I. 2011. *Sitting Ducks and Peeping Toms: Targets, Drones and UAVs in British Military Service Since 1917*. Tonbridge: Air Britain Historians Ltd

Driver, H. 1997. *The Birth of Military Aviation*. Suffolk: Boydell & Brewer Ltd

Emmerson, C. 2013. *1913: The World before the Great War*. London: Random House

Everett, H. R. 2015. *Unmanned Systems of World Wars I and II*. Cambridge: MIT Press

Francis-Williams, Lord. 1974. 'Propaganda 1914–15' in *Purnell's History of the 20th Century*. ed. A. J. P. Taylor. 792–801. New York: Purnell

French. D. 2006. *British Economic and Strategic Planning 1905–1915*. Abingdon: Routledge (first published: 1982)

French, P. R. B. 1995. *The Life of Henry Norman*. London: Unicorn Publishing Group

Gardner, G. 1958. The Forty-Sixth Wilbur Wright Memorial Lecture: Automatic Flight—The British Story. *The Journal of the Royal Aeronautical Society*, 62(571), 476–496. doi:10.1017/S0368393100069145

Gibbs-Smith, C. H. 1966. *The Invention of the Aeroplane*. New York: Taplinger

Harper, E. H. and A. Ferguson. 1911. *Aerial Locomotion*. Cambridge: Cambridge University Press

Hawker MC, T. 1965. *Hawker VC: The First RFC Ace: The Life of Major Lanoe Hawker VC DSO 1890–1916*. London: Mitre Press

Heiferman, R. 1972. *Flying Tigers: Chennault in China*. London: Macmillan

Henshaw, T. 1995. *The Sky Their Battlefield*. London: Grub Street

Hewlett, G. 2010. *Old Bird: The Irrepressible Mrs Hewlett*. Leicester: Matador

Howard-Flanders, R. L. 1924. 'Reminiscences of the Early Days of Aviation at Brooklands'. Abstract of paper read by Mr. R. L. Howard-Flanders, before the Institution of Aeronautical Engineers on 11 January 1924 in *Flight*, 4(16), 52–54

Johnson, H. 1981. *Wings over Brooklands*. London: Whittet

Jones, B. M. 2008. *Granville Bradshaw: A Flawed Genius?* Bangalore: Panther

Jones, H. A. 1931. *The War in the Air*. Vol. 3. London: Oxford University Press

Joubert de la Ferte, P. 1961. *The Forgotten Ones*. London: Hutchinson

Lambert, N. A. 2012. *Planning Armageddon*. Cambridge: Harvard University Press

Lanchester, F. A. 2008. *Aircraft in Warfare: The Dawn of the Fourth Arm*. New York: Budge Press

Larsen, E. 1954. *Men Who Shaped the Future: Stories of Invention and Discovery*. London: Phoenix House

Leeming, J. F. 1936. *Airdays*. London: George G. Harrap & Co

Lewis, P. 1962. *British Aircraft 1809–1914*. London: Putnam

Liggera, L. D. 2013. *The Life of Robert Loraine: The Stage, the Sky, and George Bernard Shaw*. Newark: University of Delaware Press

Loraine, W. 1938. *Robert Loraine: Soldier Actor Airman*. Glasgow: Collins

Low, A. M. 1939. *Modern Armaments*. London: Hutchinson

Low, A. M. 1945. *Benefits of War*. London: The Scientific Book Club

Low, A. M. 1949. *They Made Your World: Short Histories of Famous Scientists*. London: John Gifford

MacCarron, D. 2006. *Letters from an Early Bird*. Barnsley: Pen & Sword

MacKersey, I. 2012. *No Empty Chairs*. London: Weidenfeld & Nicolson

Macmillan. N. 1935. *Sir Sefton Brancker*. London: Heinemann

Macrae, Colonel S. 2012. *Winston Churchill's Toyshop: The Inside Story of Military Intelligence*. Stroud: Amberley

Mallinson, A. 2016. *Too Important for the Generals: How Britain Nearly Lost the First World War*. London: Bantam

Maloney, A. 2014. *The World of Mr Selfridge: The official companion to the hit ITV series*. London: Simon & Schuster UK

Miessner, B. 1954. *On the Early History of Radio Guidance*. San Francisco: SFP

Morgan, J. H. 1916. *Leaves from a Field Notebook*. London: Macmillan

Morgan, J. H. and T. Baty. 1915. *War: Its Conduct and Legal Results*. London: John Murray

Munson, K. J. 1996. *Jane's Unmanned Aerial Vehicles and Targets*. London: Jane's

Mure, Major A. H. 1919. *With the Incomparable 29th*. Edinburgh: W. & R. Chambers

Negev, E. and Y. Koren. 2011. *The First Lady of Fleet Street: The Life of Rachel Beer: Crusading Heiress and Newspaper Pioneer*. New York: Bantam Books

Nichols, B. 1951. *All I Could Never Be*. London: Jonathan Cape

Norris, W. 2001. *A Grave Too Many*. Colombia: SynergEbooks

Norton, R. 1908. *The Vanishing Fleets*. New York: D. Appleton

Pain, B. E. O. 1917. 'The Kaiser and God' in G. H. Clarke. ed. *A Treasury of War Poetry*. Boston: Houghton Mifflin

Peel, C. S. 1929. *How We Lived Then, 1914–1918: A Sketch of Social and Domestic Life in England during the War*. London: John Lane

Pixton, S. 2014. *Howard Pixton: Test Pilot and Pioneer Aviator*. Barnsley: Pen & Sword

Pritchard, L. J. 1953. 'The Wright Brothers and the Royal Aeronautical Society' in *Journal of the Royal Aeronautical Society*, 57(516)

Raleigh, W. 1922. *The War in the Air: Being the Story of the Part Played in the Great War by the Royal Air Force*. Oxford: Clarendon Press

Raleigh, W. 1928. *The War in the Air*. London: Oxford University Press

Reese, P. 2014. *The Men Who Gave Us Wings: Britain and the Aeroplane 1796–1914*. Barnsley: Pen & Sword

Reynard, C. 1994. *Yesterday's Shopping: Selection from Gamages General Catalogue for 1914*. Ware: Wordsworth Editions

Sanders, I. L. and L. Clark. 2011. *A Radiophone in Every Home: William Stephenson and the General Radio Company Limited, 1922–1928*. Scarborough: Valley Press

Sayers, W. H. *A Simple Explanation of Inherent Stability*

Scott, J. D. 1994. 'The British Press and the Holocaust, 1942–1943', PhD dissertation. University of Leicester. http://hdl.handle.net/2381/35594

Squire, John (Jack) Henry. '….And Master of None'

Swinton, E. D. 1904. *The Defence of Duffer's Drift*. London: W. Clowes & Sons

Swinton, E. D. 1914. *The Green Curve*. New York: Doubleday, Page & Company

Taylor, A. J. P. 1963. *The First World War: An Illustrated History*. London: H. Hamilton

Taylor, J. W. R. 1977. ed. *Jane's Pocket Book of Remote Piloted Vehicles*. Collier

Tiltman, R. F. 1927. *Television for the Home*. With an introduction by Professor A. M. Low. London: Hutchinson

Tokaty, G. A. 1971. *A History and Philosophy of Fluid Mechanics*. Edinburgh: Foulis

Van der Kloot, W. 2011. 'Mirrors and Smoke: A. V. Hill, His Brigands, and the Science of Anti-Aircraft Gunnery in World War 1' in *Notes Rec. The Royal Society*, 65(4). https://doi.org/10.1098/rsnr.2010.0090

Van Emdem, R. 2000. *Prisoners of the Kaiser*. Barnsley: Pen & Sword

Wells, H. G. 1903. 'The Land Ironclads' in *Strand Magazine*, December, 1903

Wells, H. G. 2005. *The War in the Air*. London: Penguin (first published: 1908)

Woodhead, L. 2008. *Shopping, Seduction & Mr Selfridge*. London: Profile Books

Yeates, V. M. 1934. *Winged Victory*. London: Jonathan Cape

Zaloga, S. 2008. *Unmanned Aerial Vehicles*. London: Bloomsbury

Websites

Chris Baker: http://www.longlongtrail.co.uk/
Espacenet: European Patent Register: https://worldwide.espacenet.com/
Flight: Flight Global Archive: https://www.flightglobal.com/pdfarchive/
Grace's Guide to British Industrial History: https://www.gracesguide.co.uk/
Hansard: UK Government
and well-known genealogy websites

Endnotes

Chapter 2

1. The famous inventor Rudolf Christian Karl Diesel's turbulent young life was affected by this 1870 invasion when his family fled from Paris to London. His tragic, mysterious and possibly sinister death occurred a year before the start of WWI. Like Charles Rolls, another great name in motoring who died before WWI.
2. Claude did however win the Gordon Bennett air race that year in Belmont Park, New York flying his Blériot XI and Alexander 'Alec' Ogilvie, a great champion of the Wright's machines, came third. Alec developed improvements to air speed measurement on aircraft from 1912 onwards. He continued to fly his Wright machine and in 1913 he took Herbert George 'H. G.' Wells up as a passenger.

Chapter 3

1. A graphic depiction of such a London laundry business appeared in the 2016 movie *Suffragette*.
2. *The Building* News, 18th November 1881.
3. The turbulent history of the invention of the telephone started in 1886 and Alexander Graham Bell was not the only participant in the race for recognition. After the court cases, the commercial scramble to cash in on this new form of communication began. This was barely twenty years before the young Archibald noted the phenomenal proliferation of telephones in Sydney.

Chapter 4

1. As a result of Robert's career, 'Stonehage Fleming' the London-based wealth management company and James Bond live on.
2. 6d or 6 pence was commonly called a tanner and 40 of these made £1.
3. At the start of 1910 Alliott's younger brother Humphrey Verdon's business acumen had gained the family's trust and through him the Roe family funded A. V.'s developments. The Lancashire firm of A. V. Roe & Co. was launched. Their pre-war AVRO 504 design was in production throughout the war right into the 1930s.
4. Friern Hospital (formerly Colney Hatch Lunatic Asylum) was a psychiatric hospital in Colney Hatch, Barnet, London. The hospital was the second Middlesex County Asylum and was in operation from 1851 to 1993.

Chapter 5

1. The Hunterian Museum in Glasgow has a collection of 18 Kerr cells. Archie spent time in Renfrew and it is almost certain that he will have been aware of the work of the Rev. John Kerr. In another connection, Brabazon lamented the loss of British skills in glass making in the latter part of the 1800s and as an example of this, Kerr had to employ a German glass worker who had settled in Glasgow to make his cells.

Chapter 6

1. Duncan's uncle Henry William Pitcher as a 22-year-old lieutenant won the Victoria Cross during the Umbeyla Campaign on the infamous North-West Frontier for his action on 16th November 1863.
2. Much later, when Sefton was a major-general, he made a poor landing at the training airfield he was visiting for an inspection. Flying suits were a great leveller, making it less obvious the rank of the soldier residing inside their plump covering. On his way from the aircraft an instructor ordered Sefton to go up and do it again. Brancker promptly did as he was told. History does not record the subsequent career of the hapless instructor once 'the students' senior rank was exposed. However, after the recounting of the incident had produced its maximum capital and boosted morale in the wider RFC community, it would have been Sefton's way to pen a letter of encouragement to the instructor in question.

Chapter 7

1. The Red Baron died when an air battle strayed over the Allied lines in an unusual easterly wind and Richthofen was shot at by both ground fire from the Australian trenches and by the an ace Captain Arthur Roy Brown. It is thought by some that the ground fire killed the German. Brown had the distinction of being the only commander on the Western Front not to lose a single man from his flight while he was in post.
2. Today, these processes are being used again to produce biofuels. After World War II, Chaim Weizmann became the first president of Israel.
3. The first *Monitor* (shallow draft heavy gun naval ship) was the USS *Monitor* designed in 1861 and used in the American Civil War.
4. Franklin continued to make significant contributions to radio and television in the inter-war period and in 1949 he was presented with that year's Faraday Medal. The *Lusitania* was sunk on Friday 7th May 1915 when it was torpedoed by German U-boat *U-20* sailing from New York on its 202nd crossing.
5. Maurice Wright's son, Peter Maurice Wright, was born in the middle of WWI on the 9th August 1916. He became a scientific officer in the British Counter Intelligence Service (MI-5) and wrote the 1980s book *Spycatcher* which the government attempted to ban. The historian A. J. P. Taylor said: 'The only lasting mark which the First World War made on mens' lives: Daylight Saving it was called then, Summer Time as we call it now'. Others have stated that censorship was the most enduring WWI mark on British Society, citing the introduction of Government Defence and Security Media Advisory Notices (DSMA's) now known as 'DA' notices. However, the 'DSMA' notice system was introduced before the war as a voluntary system in 1912.
6. After the war HJ continued his innovative work, eventually working on acoustic submarine detection systems known as ASDIC (Anti-Submarine Detection Investigation Committee) in WWII and now called Sonar (Sound Navigation Ranging).

7. Bangay's book has 176 pages and it was for the target audience of 'students and amateurs, members of the Boys' Brigade, Church Lads' Brigade and the Boy Scouts Association'.

8. After the war Eckersley had a long and illustrious career in broadcasting with the newly formed BBC until personal problems complicated his position.

Chapter 9

1. Later requisitioned by the navy, HMS *Alcantara* was sunk in a battle in the North Sea on 29th February 1916. She was one of four British ships despatched to catch the German SMS *Greif*, which was also sunk.

2. Lanayre D. Liggera attributes this quote to Elliott Springs in her biography, *The Life of Robert Loraine: The Stage, the Sky, and George Bernard Shaw.*

Chapter 10

1. John Bernard Léon Foucault is credited with naming the gyroscope. The first known apparatus similar to a gyroscope, called the 'Whirling Speculum' or 'Serson's Speculum,' was invented by Captain John Serson in 1743. The 'whirling speculum' provided an artificial horizon for marine navigation, consisting of a mirror, attached to a spinning top, that attempted to remain in a horizontal plane despite the movement of the ship. This device was not a gyroscope but it was used as a level, to locate the horizon in foggy or misty conditions. Serson was lost at sea from HMS *Victory* in 1744.

2. The Creed Telegraph Works had its roots back in 1901 when Frederick George Creed developed a receiving re-perforator which recorded telegraph signals as perforations in a paper tape, at speeds of up to 200 words a minute. This automated the re-transmission of messages and in 1902 the company had delivered the first Morse-keyboard perforators to the General Post Office. Incidentally, Sir Henry had been Assistant Postmaster-General for a very brief period in 1910.

3. Albert was as famous for his work in structural engineering as he was for aeronautical developments. Among his many constructions and innovations he was responsible for the internal supporting structure of the Corcovado Christ overlooking Rio de Janeiro.

4. In the 1930s Rex with Barnes Wallis created the Vickers Wellington at Brooklands and 11,462 of these were built to meet the demands of World War II. It was usually called the Wimpy after 'J. Wellington Wimpy', Popeye's friend, and this cartoon character was also responsible for the name of the Wimpy hamburger restaurants, introduced into Britain through J. Lyons and Co.

Chapter 11

1. William Heath Robinson was an English cartoonist and illustrator. Critical of the machine age, he was known for inventing absurdly complicated 'Heath Robinson contraptions' to perform simple actions.

2. Frank Goodden was a Royal Aircraft Factory Test Pilot. He was killed on 28th January 1917 when his S.E.5 suffered a structural failure and crashed. He had been one of the designers and this particular aircraft was due to be flown out to France on completion of the test flight. Subsequently, the S.E.5 and S.E.5a's design was changed to correct the fault.

Chapter 12

1. In his patent Fleming refers to his new device as an 'electric valve', blocking current flowing in one direction but allowing it to flow in the other. Hence, from 1904 the electronics era began with a prolonged period of technology based upon the 'Valve' (or in the USA, the vacuum 'Tube') before the semi-conductor (transistor) period began in the late 1940s.

Chapter 16

1. The French officer Alfred Dreyfus, accused of spying in 1894, spent years in the penal colony of French Guiana, the institution made famous in Henri Charrière's novel *Papillon*. The Dreyfus affair was world famous and long running. An item in a Boston review of 18th February 1899 quoted the French humorist, Alfred Capus: 'The current formula of speech in parliament and in parlor, in the street, and in the newspaper, is "We long to see the end of the Dreyfus affair!" Everything tends to prolong the agony … each trial begets inquiry …. But the truth is that no mortal in France could live without it. It is an element of social life …. Certain individuals, suffering from boredom, are advised by their physicians to talk about it one hour a day. Oh, we should all be deadly dull without it …. France has decided that the Dreyfus affair shall go on forever … while Mr. Henry Norman remarks that when France suppresses the free utterance of her highest court of justice, she has ceased to exist as a civilized country.'

    Another officer, of a more 'acceptable' background, Ferdinand Walsin Esterhazy was eventually uncovered as the culprit. However, Esterhazy was released and, exiled in London, using the assumed name Fitzgerald, and then switched to style himself Count Jean Marie de Voilement. Many years later Sir Henry recalled 'The last time I saw him (Esterhazy), he was fashionably attired and looking ten years younger. He assured me he was overwhelmed with all sorts of offers for his future services and with letters from women admirers desirous of his acquaintance.'

    Dreyfus was pardoned in 1906. In 1985 the French army refused to place a statue of Dreyfus at the Ecole Militaire, in defiance of President François Maurice Adrien Marie Mitterrand, who had commissioned it.

2. Re-marriage for the divorced was a 'sensitive' issue in Edwardian Britain, as it was for Sir Henry and Fay. At this time the clergy were able to exercise an amount of discretion on marriage for divorcees following the Matrimonial Clauses Act of 1857 that had moved the legal basis of the marriage contract from the ecclesiastical to the civil courts. It was to become more difficult again following the Convocation Resolutions of 1938 that were provoked in part by the attention to such matters following Edward VIII's abdication.

3. John Henry 'Jack' Squire was destined to become even more famous, selling over 2 million gramophone records and becoming a significant celebrity on the new medium of the wireless in the 1920s and 30s.

4. The concert had been held in aid of Lady Henderson's Fund for Wounded RFC Men. Just over a year later, on 21st June 1918 the human cost of the war was to hit the Henderson family when two more fatalities in a military flying accident in the U.K. added to the countless prangs over the previous years. Sir David and Lady Henderson's only son, Captain Ian Henry David Henderson M.C. and Lieut. Harold Bolton Redler M.C. from South Africa were both killed when their Airco DH9 crashed. They were only in their early 20s. This accident occurred at Turnberry in Ayrshire, Scotland which was then 'The School of Aerial Gunnery and Fighting'. The ace, Captain Ian Henderson was credited with seven aerial victories during his RFC service in France and he is buried at Doune Cemetery, Girvan, Ayrshire.

Chapter 17

1.   Morgan cited The Conference of the International Law Association at Madrid in 1913.

     (1) It is the right of every state to enact such prohibitions, restrictions, and regulations as it may think proper in regard to the passage of aircraft through the air space above its territories and territorial waters.

     However, Morgan felt obliged to include notes on the contradiction this produced with the historic right of landowners to the air above their estates 'up to heaven' and the pre-war muted possibility of an internationally recognised 'High Air', analogous to the 'High Seas'. He acknowledged that, 'The legislature has not regarded the air, and such rights over it as exist in law at all with the same tenderness as it has treated the land' and it goes on to confirm that the Air Navigation Acts of 1911 and 1913 take precedence over the rights of the land owners.

2.   'The Legion of Frontiersmen' was created in 1905 with the aim of forming an empire wide paramilitary force as a bolster against threats to the nation and the empire. It did not gain the membership numbers needed to demand formal recognition or a significant role in society.

3.   Eventually, to assuage US criticism of the reporting, five more journalists were given the rank of captain and khaki uniforms with green bands on their right arm as appointed war correspondents. These were Philip Armand Hamilton Gibbs, the American, Percival Phillips, William Beach Thomas, Henry Perry Robinson and Herbert Russell. They were followed over the next three years by other luminaries and journalists such as John Buchan, George Valentine Williams (who enlisted in 1915 and won the Military Cross), Henry Hamilton Fyfe, Keith Arthur Murdoch and Henry Woodd Nevinson.

4.   McClintock received the DSO in 1900 for his services in South Africa. He was a talented surveyor and cartographer and his maps were produced as cyanotype blueprints on cotton cloth for use in the field. In 1912 while serving in the British Indian Army Madras Sappers and Miners unit at Bangalore, he invented his famous torpedo. It was a means of exploding ordnance left over from the Boer and Russo-Japanese Wars. McClintock's unit may well have been the inspiration behind the jam-tin and other improvised grenades used in the first years of the Great War.

Chapter 18

1.   The DCB weapon was not armed with a torpedo and was intended to be packed with the maximum possible charge of explosives and guided onto the target from its controlling mother aircraft. To power and stabilise the DCBs they were fitted with twin propellers and bilge keels.

Chapter 19

1.   Lord Aberdare served on the International Olympic Committee and on the organising committee of the 1948 Summer Olympics in London. Sadly, he drowned on 4th October 1958, aged 72 when his car fell over a precipice in Yugoslavia into three feet of water in a river bed.

Index

Index of Vehicles

General Index